MW01257450

International Relations Theory and European Security

This book engages with key contemporary European security issues from a variety of different theoretical standpoints, in an attempt to uncover the drivers of foreign policy and defence integration in the European Union (EU).

Although European foreign policy has been attracting an ever-increasing number of International Relations (IR) scholars since the end of the cold war, consensus on what drives European foreign policy integration has not yet emerged. This book seeks to encourage debate on this issue by examining a wide range of high-profile security issues which have roused significant interest from policy makers, academics and the public in recent years. The volume discusses, among other issues, the strategic posture of the EU as a security actor, the troubled relationship with Russia, the debate regarding France's relations with the US following France's rapprochement with NATO and the EU's influence in the Israeli–Palestinian conflict. The collective intent of the contributors to highlight the drivers of EU foreign policy and defence integration ties together the wide variety of topics covered in this volume, forming it into a comprehensive overview of this issue. By paying considerable attention not just to the internal drivers of EU cooperation but also to the critical role played by the US as an incentive or obstacle to European security, this book presents a unique contribution to this field of debate.

This book will be of much interest to students of European security, IR theory, Transatlantic Relations, European politics and EU foreign policy.

Lorenzo Cladi is a Lecturer at the University of Birmingham, UK, and has a PhD in International Relations from Loughborough University, UK.

Andrea Locatelli is Assistant Professor at the Catholic University of Milan, Italy. He has a PhD in Political Science from the University of Florence, Italy.

Routledge Global Security Studies
Series Editors: Aaron Karp and Regina Karp

Global Security Studies emphasises broad forces reshaping global security and the dilemmas facing decision-makers the world over. The series stresses issues relevant in many countries and regions, is accessible to broad professional and academic audiences as well as to students, and is enduring because of its explicit theoretical foundations.

Nuclear Proliferation and International Security
Edited by Morten Bremer Maerli and Sverre Lodgaard

Global Insurgency and the Future of Armed Conflict
Debating fourth-generation warfare
Terry Terriff, Aaron Karp and Regina Karp

Terrorism and Weapons of Mass Destruction
Responding to the challenge
Edited by Ian Bellany

Globalization and WMD Proliferation
Terrorism, transnational networks, and international security
Edited by James A. Russell and Jim J. Wirtz

Power Shifts, Strategy, and War
Declining states and international conflict
Dong Sun Lee

Energy Security and Global Politics
The militarization of resource management
Edited by Daniel Moran and James A. Russell

US Nuclear Weapons Policy after the Cold War
Russians, 'rogues' and domestic division
Nick Ritchie

Security and Post-Conflict Reconstruction
Dealing with fighters in the aftermath of war
Edited by Robert Muggah

Network Centric Warfare and Coalition Operations
The new military operating system
Paul T. Mitchell

American Foreign Policy and the Politics of Fear
Threat inflation since 9/11
Edited by A. Trevor Thrall and Jane K. Cramer

International Relations Theory and European Security

We thought we knew

Edited by Lorenzo Cladi and Andrea Locatelli

LONDON AND NEW YORK

First published 2016
by Routledge
2 Park Square, Milton Park, Abingdon, Oxon OX14 4RN

and by Routledge
711 Third Avenue, New York, NY 10017

Routledge is an imprint of the Taylor & Francis Group, an informa business

British Library Cataloguing-in-Publication Data
A catalogue record for this book is available from the British Library

Library of Congress Cataloging-in-Publication Data
International relations theory and European security: we thought we
knew / edited by Lorenzo Cladi and Andrea Locatelli.
  pages cm. – (Routledge global security studies)
  Includes bibliographical references and index.
  1. European Union. 2. Security, International–European Union
countries. 3. European Union countries–Foreign relations.
  4. International relations–Philosophy. I. Cladi, Lorenzo, editor.
  JN30.I555 2015
  355'.03304–dc23   2015010142

ISBN: 978-1-138-84727-9 (hbk)
ISBN: 978-1-315-72573-4 (ebk)

Typeset in Times New Roman
by Wearset Ltd, Boldon, Tyne and Wear

To Emma and Alessandra

Contents

Contributors

Lorenzo Cladi is a Lecturer at the University of Birmingham, UK, and has a PhD in Political Science/International Relations from Loughborough University, UK.

Andrea Locatelli is Assistant Professor at the Catholic University of Milan, Italy. He has a PhD in Political Science from the University of Florence, Italy.

Tom Dyson is Senior Lecturer in International Relations at Royal Holloway College, University of London. He has a PhD in Political Science from the London School of Economics.

Serena Giusti is Assistant Professor at the Sant'Anna School of Advanced Studies in Pisa and Senior Associate Research Fellow at ISPI, Milan. She has a PhD in Political and Social Sciences from the European University Institute in Florence.

David Haglund is a Professor of Political Studies at Queen's University in Canada. He has a PhD in International Relations from the Johns Hopkins School of Advanced International Studies in Washington.

Carla Monteleone is Assistant Professor at the University of Palermo, Italy. She has a PhD in International Relations from the University of Milan, Italy.

Benjamin Pohl is a Senior Project Manager at Adelphi in Berlin. He has a PhD from Leiden University, the Netherlands.

Friederike Richter is a recent graduate. She holds an MA in Contemporary European Studies: Politics, Policy and Society (Euromasters) from the University of Bath, UK, and Sciences Po, Paris, France.

Olivier Schmitt is Associate Professor of International Relations at the University of Southern Denmark, where he is a member of the Center for War Studies. He has a PhD from the Department of War Studies, King's College London (UK).

Luis Simón is Research Professor at the Institute for European Studies at Vrije Universiteit, Brussels, Belgium, and has a PhD in Political Science/International Relations from Royal Holloway, University of London (UK).

Cynthia M. C. van Vonno is a researcher and PhD candidate in the Department of Political Science at Leiden University, the Netherlands.

Niels van Willigen is Assistant Professor of International Relations in the Department of Political Science at Leiden University, the Netherlands. He has a PhD from Leiden University.

Kamil Zwolski is a Lecturer at the University of Southampton, UK, and has a PhD in International Relations/European Studies from the University of Salford, UK.

Foreword

So what do we know?

Aaron and Regina Karp

The years since the crisis of 2007–8 witnessed a transformation of European affairs, but, with the emphasis on the Euro and European economic stagnation, attention naturally focused most on intra-European cooperation and domestic policy. European security policy seemed pushed aside by financial preoccupation. Military intervention in the Mediterranean and Africa showed that the mechanisms of the Common Security and Defence Policy (CSDP), never the equal of the European Union's economic foundations, were not shabby either. But specific accomplishments hardly seem to matter when compared to Europe's seeming irrelevance in the face of the consequences of the Arab Spring or Russian revanchism.

For students of these problems, the result is a deeper and wider empirical puzzle. No theory of European security emerges from the end of the post-Cold War era unscathed. Nor does any major theory come away entirely discredited. We are lucky that Lorenzo Cladi and Andrea Locatelli saw the chaos as an invitation to start digging. It may be the first responsibility of a scholar to question the obvious, but that cliché usually melts away for want of the bravery that most of us lack.

The answers Cladi and Locatelli stress show the diversity of the field, building on the rich theoretical veins that matured in the post-Cold War era. With problems of incommensurability in mind, the contributors to this review stress Realist, Liberal, Institutional and Constructivist schools. All capture important truths, making final winnowing all but impossible. In lieu of picking a single, persuasive tool kit, Cladi and Locatelli conclude that the most meaningful answers require analytical eclecticism. Every approach to European security has a few answers, but no single approach offers enough. The editors and contributors have their own favorites, but share this pluralist conclusion.

It is no small frustration to arrive at this conclusion. During the past twenty years, International Security Studies enjoyed an unprecedented blossoming of theoretical tools and approaches, as theoretical studies emerged as the locus of much of our most engaging and influential work. Security Studies textbooks became numerous and fat with theory. Lost in this growth was the certitude of true believers, their voices increasingly diluted by the variety of possibilities. Maybe we asked too much of International Relations theory. Chastened, scholars have not gone back to the drawing board, not yet at least, but we are more modest. No longer can we carry on like a tribe of Popperians in pursuit of both explanation and prediction. Explanation alone is problem enough.

This awareness makes this book something of a stocktaking exercise. After the excitement of the fat years comes a lean time, when even intellectual progress requires much greater effort. For security studies generally this is an era of retrenchment. For European security this reorientation has profound implications. One of the great pleasures of this book is benefitting from a cadre of scholars ready for the fray, ready to reexamine the shibboleths of security cooperation, willing to ask why hurdles arose, why more was not accomplished and to question the preconditions of renewed conflict resolution.

But above all, the message in *We thought we knew* is about the future of a particular project. As with much else in the European integration project, CSDP represents not the affirmation of linear causal phenomena, but a unique balance of national interests and collective norms. As highlighted here, the relative mix between interests and norms can vary substantially, not least because we continue to ascribe interests to states and norms to institutions. This creates a formidable dichotomy between the promotion of shared values and satisfying state interests. As Cladi and Locatelli show, CSDP remains a contested enterprise, mired in the stresses and strains of pursuing both national and common goals.

Cladi and Locatelli are cautious about where this leads. Theirs is a preliminary effort. Even the goals of security policy have become more obscure. Eclecticism is an invitation to opportunism, they warn. Eclectic theory, they point out, is not the stuff of policy doctrine. Theory and phenomena instead need to be kept distinct. The implication is that scholars should not be missionaries, or bloggers for that matter.

That the post-Cold War era has come to a close is getting harder to deny. And the waiter has just arrived with a bill for the party. The blossoming of theories and approaches that made for an intoxication of possibilities during that period no longer is sustainable. But just because studies of European security cannot continue as they did does not mean they must be reinvented. The greatest danger after the close of an era is to think we know less than we actually do. As the contributors to *We Thought We Knew* make clear, there is much we still know. Separating the pearls from the ash is a messy task, both for advocates of the European project and for long-time skeptics. With familiar remnants all around, it is tempting to think the job easily done. By refusing to take sides, Cladi, Locatelli and their authors chose the more difficult path, but far and away the bravest and most important. Any effort to engage in the future of European security policy can find no better place to start.

Aaron and Regina Karp
Norfolk, Virginia

Acknowledgements

Like all collective endeavours, this book involved a good deal of coordination and *fine tuning* among the contributors to this volume. The editors would like to thank all the colleagues and friends who participated in this project for their dedication, enthusiasm and diligence. Their warm acceptance of our (sometimes disturbing) requests, the uncommon commitment to deadlines and willingness to engage in an inter-paradigmatic debate – all this greatly eased our work as editors. At Routledge, Andrew Humphrys and Hannah Ferguson provided timely and helpful guidance from the inception to the final stages of publication. We would also like to thank the two anonymous reviewers for their helpful and constructive comments on our proposal. Aaron and Regina Karp have provided an endless source of support and encouragement for this project. We can safely admit that without them we would scarcely have embarked on this publication. Finally, we dedicate this book to our wives, Emma and Alessandra, for they have shared with us the role of editing this book in too many ways to count.

Abbreviations

AA	Association Agreements
ACT	Allied Command Transformation
ASEAN	Association of South-East Asian Nations
AU	African Union
CBRN	Chemical, Biological, Radiological and Nuclear
CFSP	Common Foreign and Security Policy
CoE/CBRN CoE	CBRN Risk Mitigation Centres of Excellence
CPCC	Civilian Planning and Conduct Capability
CSDP	Common Security and Defence Policy
DCFTA	Deep and Comprehensive Free Trade Agreement
EaP	Eastern Partnership
EC	European Community
EDA	European Defence Agency
EDC	European Defence Community
EEAS	European External Action Service
EEC	European Economic Community
EMP	European Mediterranean Policy
ENP	European Neighbourhood Policy
EPC	European Political Cooperation
ERRF	European Rapid Reaction Force
ESDP	European Security and Defence Policy
ESS	European Security Strategy
EU	European Union
EUMC	European Union Military Committee
EUMS	EU Military Staff
HR	High Representative of the Union for Foreign Affairs and Security Policy
IAEA	International Atomic Energy Agency
IfS	Instrument for Stability
IO	International Organisation
I–P	Israeli–Palestinian
IR	International Relations
IS	Islamic State

LFB	Leading from behind
LI	Liberal Intergovernmentalism
MAP	NATO Membership Action Plan
NI	Neoliberal Institutionalism
NRC	NATO–Russia Council
NRF	NATO Response Force
PA	Palestinian Authority
PCA	Partnership and Cooperation Agreement
PCC	Prague Capabilities Commitment
PfM	Partnership for Modernisation
PLO	Palestine Liberation Organisation
PSC	Political and Security Committee
QMV	Qualified majority voting
REDWG	Regional Economic Development Working Group
TACIS	Technical Aid to the Commonwealth of Independent States
UK	United Kingdom
UN	United Nations
UNICRI	United Nations Interregional Crime and Justice Research Institute
UNGA	UN General Assembly
UNSC	UN Security Council
US	United States
USSR	Soviet Union
WMDs	Weapons of Mass Destruction

Introduction

On theories, paradigms and CSDP

Lorenzo Cladi and Andrea Locatelli

IR theory and CSDP: let the debate restart

It is widely recognised that the European Union's (EU) integration in the foreign and security policy domain constitutes an empirical puzzle for International Relations (IR) scholars (Andreatta, 2011). Several features of the Common Security and Defence Policy (CSDP)[1] defy any serious theoretical account of this phenomenon. From a Realist perspective, for instance, the EU and its foreign policy machinery represent an exceptional case of cooperation. In fact, as Realists love to remind us, examples of military cooperation in the absence of a direct threat, apart from that of the EU, are virtually non-existent (see Chapter 1). On the other hand, while other theories are well equipped to account for the complexity of the CSDP process (see for instance Chapters 3 to 5), they are sometimes in difficulty when it comes to explaining the poor output of this process. In other words, they fail to grasp the non-linear evolution of CSDP, where progress and retreat proceed side by side. Finally, considering the multi-faceted nature of security – now transcending the mere military dimension (see, among others, Buzan and Hansen, 2009) – the very same definition of what the EU security policy is (and what it is not), remains debatable. So, disagreement on the range of empirical referents that may or may not be included within CSDP makes dialogue among scholars even more difficult.

As a result, it should not come as a surprise that the CSDP is still an object of contention among IR scholars. The literature on the topic is abundant and apparently on the rise once again (recent valuable overviews of the field include Merlingen and Ostrauskaitė, 2007; Kurowska and Breuer, 2012; Larivé, 2014). As many authors seem to admit, the debate is still open, and no single account is likely to prevail (Bickerton *et al.*, 2011). However, in their search for theoretical validation, most authors took greater care in confirming their favourite paradigm at the expense of the substantial relevance of their studies. In other words, except for a few fortunate exceptions (Merlingen and Ostrauskaitė, 2007), they contributed to deepening the gap between theory- and policy-oriented analysis.

This volume is intended to contribute to the ongoing debate with a pragmatic approach. Bringing together scholars with diverging theoretical orientations, the book aims to fulfil two interrelated goals: first and foremost, to present the reader with state-of-the-art contributions from different research traditions; second, to describe a number of important issues of European security (such as the relationship between CSDP and NATO, France's rapprochement with NATO, the EU's relations with Russia, to name but a few) through the lens of mainstream IR theories. The *fil rouge* that ties the chapters together is the contributors' collective attempt to highlight the drivers of foreign policy and defence integration in the realm of CSDP. The collective aim of the editors is to stimulate inter-paradigmatic dialogue as well as to offer the chance to reflect on some of the challenges of CSDP, both from a theoretical and an empirical point of view.

The promise of analytic eclecticism

In order to make inter-paradigmatic dialogue fruitful, the whole volume is inspired by analytic eclecticism, as put forward by Sil and Katzenstein (2010; 2010a). So, differently from other works, the attempt here is not to perform a 'two-' or 'three-cornered' fight à la Lakatos (1970, p. 115), but rather to extrapolate which mechanisms are at play in the making of EU foreign and defence policy integration.

Being a relatively recent epistemological approach, analytic eclecticism has spurred a lively meta-theoretical debate (Lake, 2011, 2013; Sil and Katzenstein, 2011; Checkel, 2012; Bennett, 2013) but it has not inspired many studies so far (a few exceptions are Acharya, 2014; Checkel, 2013; Hayes and James, 2014). However, as Andrew Moravcsik (2003, p. 132, quoted in Sil and Katzenstein, 2010, p. 412) acknowledges, events such as 'the evolution of the European Union ... are surely important enough events to merit comprehensive explanation' along the lines suggested by analytic eclecticism. It is then reasonable to apply this approach to the CSDP, as it meets the three criteria set out by Sil and Katzenstein:

> open-ended problem formulation encompassing complexity of phenomena, not intended to advance or fill gaps in paradigm-bound scholarship;

> middle-range causal account incorporating complex interactions among multiple mechanisms and logics drawn from more than one paradigm;

> findings and arguments that pragmatically engage both academic debates and the practical dilemmas of policymakers/practitioners.
>
> (2010a, p. 19)

In more detail, as concerns the first point, the complexity of the issue at stake will be reflected throughout the book in the open-ended formulation of how to operationalise the CSDP – or, more broadly, its empirical referents. For instance, while Neorealism would opt for a rather narrow vision of the phenomenon (see Chapter 1), focussing almost exclusively on EU states' behaviour, other paradigms will relax and complement this vision by including both sub-state and supranational actors (see Chapters 2, 4, 6). As for the second point, multiple mechanisms of causation will be discussed. In this sense, again following Sil and Katzenstein (2010a, p. 21), the cleavage between second- and third-level explanations, as well as between material and ideational factors, will be a crucial element of the inter-paradigmatic dialogue. Finally, the CSDP represents a substantive problem as distinct from an analytical problem (Sil and Katzenstein, 2010, pp. 418–19). Almost paradoxically, for our purposes, CSDP is empirically relevant not just because of its exceptionality (a feature that qualifies it as an analytical problem) but also for its mixed record in terms of actual achievements. In line with analytic eclecticism, therefore, the aim of the volume is to generate insights that could be of direct utility for IR scholars and practitioners alike.

With these aims in mind, the volume discusses four main research traditions: Realism (in its two ramifications: Neorealism and Neoclassical Realism), Liberalism (also in two overlapping camps: Neoliberal Institutionalism and Liberal Intergovernmentalism), Social Constructivism and Sociology of Bureaucracy. There are obviously other paradigms that have been deliberately left out – most notably Critical Theory, Post Modernism and Historical Materialism. This body of literature has successfully engaged in the debate with other paradigms, producing high-quality works (see for instance Merlingen, 2011, 2012; Oikonomou, 2012). Yet, there is at least one good reason to focus on just the four above-mentioned traditions: due to an ontological and epistemological chasm, with the partial exception represented by Social Constructivism, mainstream approaches are set apart from their Critical and Post Modern counterparts. In other words, including these latter approaches would have raised the so-called 'incommensurability problem' (Sil and Katzenstein, 2010, pp. 414–15; 2010a, pp. 13–16). In contrast, albeit with some significant differences, Realism, Liberalism, Constructivism and Sociology of Bureaucracy share a similar (or at least compatible) view of the world and of the purpose of scientific enquiry. In other words, as noted by Hayes and James (2014, p. 405) with respect to the three main research traditions in IR, they 'tend to be toward the middle range in the continuum of critical versus positive IR. Their potential for eclectic combination is therefore at a maximum'.

Contents of the volume

The analytic eclecticism that shapes this volume is reflected in the contributions that follow, which are divided into two parts. The first part presents the following IR approaches as they have sought to shed light on the drivers of CSDP: Structural Realism, Neoclassical Realism, Liberalism, Social Constructivism and Transnational Security Governance. The second part questions the validity of theories by focussing on empirical observations. These concern the purported lack of strategy in the CSDP, the relationship between CSDP and NATO, the effects of France's rapprochement with NATO in 2009, the EU's relationship with Russia and, finally, the EU's foreign policy towards the Israeli–Palestinian conflict.

Lorenzo Cladi and Andrea Locatelli open the inter-paradigmatic debate by focussing on Structural Realism. Being conscious of the difficulty of the task of explaining CSDP from a Structural Realist standpoint, Cladi and Locatelli argue that the concept of _bandwagoning_, understood as _intra-alliance behaviour_, is a helpful tool to allow us to understand the CSDP. In doing so, they seek to depart from at least two Structural Realist arguments which have been advanced to make sense of CSDP. First, that because European states have not faced a common threat to their security since the end of the Cold War, there is no reason for them to cooperate. This is the Realist standpoint according to which no cohesion is possible in the absence of a common threat (Walt, 1997). Second, that the creation of CSDP can be understood as a balancing device against the US. Cladi and Locatelli argue that, while the above arguments are incorrect, a Structural Realist explanation of CSDP is still possible if we understand it as a tool with which the Europeans enhanced their cooperation with the US under unipolarity.

The Realist literature on CSDP has continued to flourish and, while Cladi and Locatelli focus on the structural version, in Chapter 2 Tom Dyson undertakes an analysis of the CSDP through the lens of Neoclassical Realism. Building on Stephen Walt's (1985) balance of threat theory, Dyson argues that there are material factors such as US power at play, which drive the CSDP process. However, the impact of such material factors is mitigated by key domestic variables which affect the convergence among European states in their willingness to use the EU as a means to respond to challenges in its neighbourhood. By focussing on the example of energy supply security since the early 2000s, Dyson shows how a process of _reformed bandwagoning_ has dominated the ways in which the EU's great powers (France, Germany and the UK) have coordinated their foreign policy response as a result of the intervention of domestic variables.

As we depart from the Realist paradigm, Chapters 3 and 4 analyse the extent to which Liberalism can explain the emergence of the CSDP. Much like Realism, Liberalism is a broad church, and a multitude of Liberal approaches have therefore developed in an effort to contribute to this fascinating debate.

In Chapter 3, Friederike Richter shows that European states embarked upon the CSDP project as a result of their increased level of interdependence, which positively affected, in turn, their ability and willingness to create institutions which equipped the EU as a fully fledged security actor. Richter argues that this was the case in 1998, when the St. Malo Declaration by British Prime Minister Tony Blair and French President Jacques Chirac took place and gave rise to the European Security and Defence Policy (ESDP). Yet, institutions remain as powerful as states allow them to be, and the outbreak of the Great Recession in 2008, Richter shows, seems to have had a negative impact on CSDP. The extent to which inter-governmental bargaining among EU states is going to contribute to revamping the debate on CSDP remains to be seen.

Benjamin Pohl, Niels van Willigen and Cynthia van Vonno, in Chapter 4, further delineate the Liberal approach by focussing more on domestic variables. A more comprehensive analysis of CSDP can be gained, according to Pohl, van Willigen and van Vonno, by distinguishing between different types of government, such as single party or coalition ones. The authors focus on Andrew

Moravcsik's New Liberalism and show how CSDP is the result of some overlapping and some diverging national preferences. Such divergences are not the consequence of states' relative power in the international system, but rather the result of cross-national differences in societal expectations.

In Chapter 5, Carla Monteleone analyses the process of EU integration in the area of foreign and security policy through a Social Constructivist approach. As Monteleone focusses on Social Constructivism, a consideration of material factors such as the military and economic distribution of power necessarily loses explanatory power. In fact, the concept of identity is very important in order to understand the *we* feeling that EU states have developed by being part of a security community. Evidence of this is found in the adoption of the European Security Strategy (ESS) in 2003 and the practices of coordination among EU Member States when they vote at the United Nations General Assembly (UNGA). Monteleone argues that, since the 1990s, EU Member States have increasingly coordinated their foreign policy positions; this is remarkable, as it alters the EU's Member States' identities and strategic culture.

The theoretical part is completed with Kamil Zwolski's Chapter 6. Here the author argues that the changes in the governance of international security allow us to make a link between IR theory and European Studies. The author proceeds to apply the Governance approach to the case study of the EU's policy on Chemical, Biological, Radiological and Nuclear (CBRN) matters. Differently from previous chapters, this one does not engage in conventional IR theory, but the point here is that the peculiar nature of the EU as an international bureaucracy is worth investigating, as this has an impact upon the ways in which patterns of governance at the international level are currently being shaped. This can have, in turn, interesting repercussions on the ways in which IR theory interacts with the process of European security cooperation, a key theme of this volume.

In Chapter 7, Olivier Schmitt recognises that theoretical approaches tend to focus on the reasons why CSDP has emerged. Indeed, the first part offers plenty of explanations focussing on material factors (Chapter 1), the interplay between material and domestic factors (Chapter 2), governmental preferences (Chapter 3), societal expectations (Chapter 4), common identity (Chapter 5) and patterns of governance (Chapter 6). In a provocative but fair fashion, Schmitt argues that the *what for* question has not been addressed so much by IR theory, yet this has some important repercussions for the ways in which we understand CSDP. The absence of a European political project goes hand in hand with the lack of common European strategic thinking. The policies of the EU as an international actor, including the European Security Strategy, as well as the growing institutionalisation of the EU, do not sufficiently qualify it as a strategic actor. In the absence of a clear strategic purpose, Schmitt concludes, IR theories should give way to other approaches, such as Public Policy Analysis.

Going back to the *why* question, in Chapter 8 Luis Simón scrutinises the Realist perspective and departs from both Structural Realism (Chapter 1) and Neoclassical Realism (Chapter 2) for his Classical Realist analysis of the complex relationship between CSDP and NATO. According to Simón, a pattern of cooperation between CSDP and NATO has developed since the end of the Cold War and particularly over the past decade. Such cooperation is neither linear nor automatic. Rather, it is the complex result of the interplay between power maximisation and an intra-EU relative gains problem. This argument is advanced through an analysis of the ways in which the Big Three have sought to project their security preferences at both EU and NATO levels. Simón notes that there are differences in the ways in which the Big Three carry out this process, this in turn influencing the conflicting priorities over the direction of the EU and NATO.

The debate on the complex CSDP–NATO relationship has therefore not waned in light of France's reintegration with NATO in 2009. Reading Simón's chapter, one might be inclined to believe that this move did not necessarily make the relationship between the CSDP and NATO much easier than before, as France expressed its concerns over European 'vassalisation' to US power (Holm, 2008, p. 485). Subsequently, Chapter 9, written by David Haglund, allows us to further reflect on the issues surrounding France's reintegration with NATO. Haglund helpfully distinguishes between two cycles at play when analysing France's relations with the US since the end of the Cold War: the first is the optimistic one, according to which we live in the *best of times* for Atlantic relations, whereas the second is slightly more problematic, having to do with the recurrent issue of American hard power. So, the argument goes, for all the European (particularly French in this case) attempts to cooperate more closely with each other, the main variable affecting both the Transatlantic and intra-European partnerships is Washington. In particular, Haglund argues that regardless of the relatively optimistic state of the alliance, this is likely to change as a result of the doctrinal change in the US administration from Wilsonianism to Jeffersonianism.

Haglund's chapter is a very important opener for the last two contributions to this volume, namely the EU's relationship with Russia (Chapter 10 by Serena Giusti) and the EU's foreign policy towards the Israeli–Palestinian conflict (Chapter 11 by Lorenzo Cladi). Given the metamorphosing nature of the transatlantic link, as evidenced by Simón and Haglund, we are left to wonder about the potential for Europe to deal with security issues on its doorstep (a resurgent Russia) and in its neighbourhood (the long-standing Israeli–Palestinian dispute).

Giusti argues that the EU's approach to Russia in the post-Cold War period is the result of the inter-governmental nature of the institution. Every time the national interests of the EU's Member States are at stake when dealing with Russia, the normative value of CSDP falls short. The EU's relationship with Russia remains puzzling from a theoretical point of view, and an eclectic approach might prove more suitable to explain the trajectory of the EU's policy towards Russia. The EU has put forward a normative plan to deal with Russia in the post-Cold War period but this has clashed with apparently insurmountable obstacles, such as the lack of proper long-term strategy, Russia's alternative view of a stable neighbourhood, and different Member States' priorities.

As we turn to Cladi's chapter dealing with the European Community (EC)/ EU's foreign policy towards the Israeli–Palestinian conflict, the theme regarding the limits of the EU as a normative power is given similar consideration. The EC/EU, as Cladi shows, has had a normative-based approach to the Israeli– Palestinian conflict since it first got involved with it back in 1973. Only since the formation of the Quartet for Peace, back in 2002, has the EU had the opportunity to exert influence in the peace process by means of its inclusion in the Quartet for Peace alongside the US, Russia and the UN. Yet, with the opportunity to be more influential and to maintain the link to the US, the EU has compromised over its normative approach, thus limiting its credibility in the end.

Finally, in the concluding chapter, the main themes of the book are recapitulated in order to highlight the potential benefits of analytical eclecticism. A concise description of the mechanisms at play in the CSDP is offered and future avenues of research discussed.

Note

1 CSDP is the well-known acronym forged in the Lisbon Treaty. Needless to say, the empirical referent of this volume transcends this term to include earlier integration attempts. As a result, when referring to the integration process, here and in the chapters that follow, we will also include the Common Foreign and Security Policy (CFSP), the European Security and Defence Policy (ESDP) and even European Political Cooperation (EPC). For the sake of simplicity, throughout the volume we will use CSDP as a catch-all label, and refer to CFSP, ESDP and EPC only as time-contingent experiences.

References

Acharya, A. (2014) Power Shift or Paradigm Shift? China's Rise and Asia's Emerging Security Order. *International Studies Quarterly*. 58 (1). pp. 158–73.

Andreatta, F. (2011) The European Union's International Relations: A Theoretical View. In Hill, C. and Smith, M. (eds) *International Relations and the European Union*. 2nd Ed. Oxford: Oxford University Press.

Bennett, A. (2013) The Mother of All Isms: Causal Mechanisms and Structured Pluralism in International Relations Theory. *European Journal of International Relations*. 19 (3). pp. 459–81.

Bickerton, C., Irondelle, B. and Menon, A. (2011) Security Co-Operation beyond the Nation-State: The EU's Common Security and Defence Policy. *Journal of Common Market Studies*. 49 (1). pp. 1–21.

Buzan, B. and Hansen, L. (2009) *The Evolution of International Security Studies*. Cambridge: Cambridge University Press.

Checkel, J. T. (ed.) (2013) *Transnational Dynamics of Civil War*. Cambridge: Cambridge University Press.

Checkel J. (2012) Theoretical Pluralism in IR: Possibilities and Limits. In Carlsnaes, W., Risse, T. and Simmons, B. (eds) *Handbook of International Relations*. London: Sage.

Hayes, J. and James, P. (2014) Theory as Thought: Britain and German Unification. *Security Studies*. 23 (2). pp. 399–429.

Holm, U. (2008) The Old France, the New Europe and a Multipolar World. *Perspectives on European Politics and Society*. 5 (3). pp. 469–91.

Kurowska, X. and Breuer, F. (eds) (2012) *Explaining the EU's Common Security and Defence Policy*. Basingstoke, UK: Palgrave Macmillan.

Lakatos, I. (1970) Falsification and the Methodology of Scientific Research Programmes. In Lakatos, I. and Musgrave, A. (eds) *Criticism and the Growth of Knowledge*. Cambridge: Cambridge University Press.

Lake, D. (2013) Theory Is Dead, Long Live Theory: The End of the Great Debates and the Rise of Eclecticism in International Relations. *European Journal of International Relations*. 19 (3). pp. 567–87.

Lake, D. (2011) Why 'isms' Are Evil: Theory, Epistemology, and Academic Sects as Impediments to Understanding and Progress. *International Studies Quarterly*. 55 (2), pp. 465–80.

Larivé, M. (2014) *Debating European Security and Defense Policy: Understanding the Complexity*. London: Ashgate.

Merlingen, M. (2012) Applying Foucault's Toolkit to CSDP. In Kurowska, X. and Breuer, F. (eds) *Explaining the EU's Common Security and Defence Policy*. Basingstoke, UK: Palgrave Macmillan.

Merlingen, M. (2011) From Governance to Governmentality in CSDP: Towards a Foucauldian Research Agenda. *Journal of Common Market Studies*. 49 (1). pp. 149–69.

Merlingen, M. and Ostrauskaitė, R. (2007) Introduction. The European Union in International Security Affairs. In Merlingen, M. and Ostrauskaitė, R. (eds) *European Security and Defence Policy. An implementation perspective*. Abingdon, UK: Routledge.

Oikonomou, I. (2012) A Historical Materialist Approach to CSDP. In Kurowska, X. and Breuer, F. (eds) *Explaining the EU's Common Security and Defence Policy*. Basingstoke, UK: Palgrave Macmillan.

Sil, R. and Katzenstein, P. J. (2010) Analytic Eclecticism in the Study of World Politics: Reconfiguring Problems and Mechanisms across Research Traditions. *Perspectives on Politics*. 8 (2). pp. 411–31.

Sil, R. and Katzenstein, P. J. (2010a) *Beyond Paradigms: Analytic Eclecticism in the Study of World Politics*. Basingstoke, UK: Palgrave Macmillan.

Sil. R. and Katzenstein, P. J. (2011) De-Centering, Not Discarding, the 'Isms': Some Friendly Amendments. *International Studies Quarterly*. 55 (2). pp. 481–85.

Walt, S. M. (1997) The Ties That Fray: Why Europe and America are Drifting Apart. *The National Interest*, No. 54, Winter.

Walt, S. (1985) Alliance Formation and the Balance of Power. *International Security*. 9 (4). pp. 3–43.

Part I

Do IR theories have something to say about CSDP?

1 Structural Realism

Balancing, bandwagoning or what?

Lorenzo Cladi and Andrea Locatelli

Introduction

Realism has traditionally been left out of the debate regarding European foreign policy, especially with reference to the EU's international outlook towards the US in the post-Cold War period. For instance, Realist scholars have mistakenly labelled European attempts to create a common defence policy as evidence of the EU balancing the US. Based on this assumption, in our article 'Bandwagoning, Not Balancing: Why Europe Confounds Realism', we advanced two key arguments: first, that Realism can still shed light on the dynamics of European defence policy and, second, that Realists ought to refine their balancing concept in favour of bandwagoning. With our key assertion that European security and defence policy represents an instance of bandwagoning with US power, we rejected the alternative Realist soft balancing and balancing for autonomy explanations but we still placed ourselves within the Realist camp. A more articulate explanation of bandwagoning aimed at intra-alliance behaviour rather than alliance-formation is therefore in order here, because we believe that it offers a powerful tool to explain European security policy in the post-Cold War era.

This chapter proceeds as follows. The first section reviews Realist explanations that have sought to move beyond Waltz's balance of power theory to account for European security policy. We identify three different explanations here. The explanations all use different case studies and methodologies. What they have in common, however, is the insistence on the concept of balancing to explain European security policy. First, we tackle Sebastian Rosato's explanation of the creation of the European Community (EC). Then we move on to review the soft balancing and balancing for autonomy explanations. The second section is about the concept of bandwagoning. We find that there is consensus among scholars on what bandwagoning entails – i.e. siding with the stronger. However, on the issue of why and with whom states tend to bandwagon, scholars are split. In particular, we isolate the explanation of Randall Schweller, who theorised bandwagoning as a strategy states employ for *profit* rather than survival, and we use it as a foundation for our understanding of bandwagoning as intra-alliance behaviour. In the third section, we illustrate how bandwagoning as intra-alliance behaviour can be applied to European security policy and reply to our early critics. The final section summarises our main findings and suggests future avenues of research.

Balancing, again

While Realist thinkers have developed different explanations to account for the European cooperation in foreign and defence issues, scholars who have employed the structural approach have usually focussed on the distribution of power at the systemic level as a main source of integration.[1] Put simply, in this view European integration is seen as the result of external pressures – a system-induced behaviour. Relying on Kenneth Waltz's (1979) theory, integration as experienced in Europe has been considered either as an exception (Grieco, 1988; Mearsheimer, 1994), or as a form of balancing vis-à-vis an external power (Andreatta, 2011, pp. 28–9). In the first case, the utility of Realism is admittedly limited. Thus, it is not surprising that leading scholars – Waltz (2000) included – turned to the second option.

Balance of power theory is at the heart of Structural Realism – and of course it is also embedded in the Realist tradition (Little, 2007; Paul *et al.*, 2004). It should also be stressed that, contrary to other strands of Realism, the systemic approach does not see it as a voluntary behaviour as was the case with early Realists such as Morgenthau (1948; 1959). On the contrary, it makes of it an automatic, system-level, response to power imbalances. Put differently, no matter what states actually want, they will either opt for balancing, or pay a price for failing to do so (Feaver *et al.*, 2000). Moreover, balancing would regularly take place independently from the configuration of the system (multipolar or bipolar). The only difference would be the mechanism at play: while the bipolar system would rely on only two competing alliances (each run by a superpower), the multipolar configuration would promote a web of multiple, flexible, alliances. As a result, cooperation in foreign and security policy would find a very simple explanation – namely, the need to aggregate capabilities to oppose an external enemy.

This view has been recently articulated by Sebastian Rosato (2011, 2011a). In his work on the origins of the EC, he argues that the main driver of integration was represented by the superior power of the Soviet Union (USSR). In particular, he finds that, since the mid-1940s, the power imbalance on the continent was so remarkable that a simple coalition of European states would not suffice to balance Moscow. In order to be effective, European states had to go beyond simple power aggregation, as an alliance or coalition would allow. In Rosato's own words,

> This relative weakness leads groups of minor powers confronting a great power to place a premium on organizing their coalitions as efficiently as possible. Because they are inferior to their adversary, even in combination, they understand that even a slight increase in its power could leave them at its mercy.... So they turn to improving their organization, fearing that poor organization could be the difference between life and death.
>
> (Rosato, 2011a, p. 51)

In the European experience, then, the exceptional form of cooperation that resulted in economic integration and limited handing over of sovereignty came as a consequence of an external and threatening power. Following this argument, it goes without saying that with the demise of the USSR and the lack of a direct threat to Europe, no real motive for further integration has been in place since the early 1990s. Borrowing again Rosato's words (2011a, p. 68), 'since the end of the Cold War, they [the Europeans] have made no real effort to construct a political or military community, and their economic community has slowly started to fray'.

Rosato's argument sparked a lively debate. Some scholars took issue with his methodology (Moravcsik 2013; Parsons, 2013), challenging both his geopolitical mono-causal explanation and his empirical analysis. Others took issue with his (allegedly narrow) Realist approach (Krotz *et al.*, 2012, pp. 182–5), and even more the marginal attention devoted to the US (Krotz *et al.*, 2012, pp. 186–7, 189–90). Since most of these charges have been addressed (Rosato 2013; Krotz *et al.*, 2012, pp. 192–9), we will not discuss them at greater length. However, for our purposes, two points need to be stressed. The first one concerns Rosato's characterisation of the European military initiatives of the past fifteen years (on similar lines, see also Krotz *et al.*, 2012, pp. 180–1). He may even be right in claiming that these initiatives were far from successful, but at least some of them are examples of cooperation, and to some extent even integration, as they give EU institutions (admittedly small) prerogatives. This is the case with the European Defence Agency (EDA), but the twenty-five or so missions that have been launched under the framework nation principle are also witnesses to it. Therefore, empirical evidence shows that, even after the demise of the USSR, integration has been moving on. Or, following Seth Jones's argument (2007), it has even increased, as witnessed not only by the expansion of EU institutions, but also by the growing use of economic sanctions, cooperation in the arms industry and the establishment of military forces.

Second, Rosato's view of power raises another problem. If one had to focus on military might and power projection as a source of integration, he/she could note that the Soviet threat varied over time, even during the Cold War. Consequently, we should also witness a variation in the incentive to integrate – something that Rosato finds only once in history, with the fall of the USSR. Or, by the same token, following his definition of power, we could infer that the US in the past twenty years represented a superior power, one that the European states could well decide to balance. So, it is up to Rosato to explain why balancing did not take place on this occasion. It is one of the two: either balancing the USSR is an ad-hoc explanation, or other variables should be added to explain why the US is not a source of balancing.

Departing from these considerations, a different strand of Realist thinkers tried to amend the balancing hypothesis. Contrary to Rosato, they turned their back on Moscow and looked toward Washington: for a number of reasons, they saw the US as the real target of European balancing. In particular, as we discussed elsewhere (Cladi and Locatelli, 2012), authors as varied as Christopher

Layne, Robert Pape, Barry Posen and T. V. Paul can be grouped around two main versions of balancing: the soft balancing and balancing for autonomy hypotheses. Apart from the focus on the US, they all agree that an exclusive concern for power alone is not sufficient to develop a sound explanation of EU cooperation in security and defence issues. Where they seem to differ the most is on how to conceive of power as an explanatory variable.

As concerns proponents of soft balancing, they all agree that what ignites balancing is not the sheer power of the US, but its policies. Put simply, the more assertive US foreign policy becomes, the stronger the European need to water down the American influence (Oswald, 2006). Not surprisingly, this body of literature emerged mostly in the wake of the controversial unilateral turn in US foreign policy under the first Bush administration (see in particular Pape, 2005; Paul, 2005).

In Stephen Walt's wording, soft balancing can be termed as 'conscious coordination of diplomatic friction in order to obtain outcomes contrary to American preferences – outcomes that could not be gained if the balancers did not give each other some degree of mutual support' (Walt, 2005, p. 126). In the case of European states, as Robert Art (2004) argues, this is precisely the rationale driving their efforts to forge a common security and defence policy – namely, to pursue interests that may be otherwise frustrated by the US. More generally, in its simplest form, soft balancing is the rational response of second-tier states willing to limit the actual capacity of the dominant state to fully grasp its potential. Contrary to the classical version, then, this new form of balancing does not require a shift in alignments, but just the concerted use by a group of states of their own diplomatic instruments. This is admittedly a defensive and moderate policy, as its goal is just to curb US influence, not to alter the power asymmetry (in traditional jargon, it could not be considered as a revisionist policy). Likewise, its means are also limited, as the use of military capabilities is explicitly ruled out (not least, for its patent ineffectiveness).

Following Paul's analysis, for soft balancing to occur, three conditions need to be met (Paul, 2005, p. 59): first, power asymmetry must be perceived as a concern, but not up to the point of representing a real threat to 'the sovereignty of second tier powers'; second, smaller powers must enjoy the benefits of public goods that only the superior power can produce and cannot simply replace them; finally, this form of balancing prevents the hegemon's retaliation 'either because the balancing efforts ... are not overt or because they do not directly challenge its power position with military means'. It is therefore evident that, compared to classical balance of power theory, this hypothesis is closer to Walt's balance of threat (Walt, 1987), as it relegates power asymmetry to the role of antecedent condition rather than independent variable.

Not surprisingly, soft balancing received widespread attention and generated a lively debate. However, especially as concerns the European experience, one can easily highlight logical inconsistencies and lack of sound empirical evidence. Starting from the former, the main weakness results from the secondary role played by power asymmetry, as we discussed above. The ultimate cause of balancing is a purportedly unilateral US foreign policy. Evidently, this is in stark contrast with the structural approach that informs balance of power theory, since the main explanatory variable for that is located at the domestic level (Cladi and Locatelli, 2012, p. 271). Moreover, soft balancers fail to provide adequate operationalisation of this variable: as we have seen, according to Paul, the dominant power must be perceived by second-tier states as a challenge to their interest, *but not* as an existential threat. At the same time, the dominant power must be benevolent enough to provide public goods. This is intuitive: benign hegemony does not spur balancing, while predatory hegemony triggers hard balancing. Between the two extremes, we could find countless intermediate positions. What foreign policy course is assertive enough to prompt balancing, but still avoid its hard form? As far as we know, the answer to this question is still wanting.

Second, as concerns empirical evidence, proponents of soft balancing rely almost exclusively on the European (mostly French) reactions to George W. Bush's foreign policy. Not surprisingly, they find that the 2003 war in Iraq or other unilateral initiatives actually led most (but not all) European capitals to voice their dissent. But is diplomatic complaint enough to qualify as balancing (albeit in its soft version)? And, equally important, how can they account for the European efforts in the 1990s – i.e. before the Bush administration? Admittedly, the Transatlantic partnership had been occasionally put under stress even under the Clinton administration (Walt, 1998/99), but this hardly qualifies as soft balancing.

The limits of soft balancing lead us to turn to the balancing for autonomy hypothesis. In Barry Posen's analysis, for example, systemic pressures provide the European states with a simple alternative: either balancing or bandwagoning. Unfortunately for Europe, according to this logic, the second option is not really feasible, as it is too risky (Posen, 2006, p. 157). As echoed by Christopher Layne (2006), bandwagoning is appealing only for smaller states, since they know that even aggregating power it would not be possible to effectively balance the US. They also rule out the possibility for bigger states to bandwagon with the US on the ground that such a policy would be detrimental to their own security. This is not to say, as Waltz (1979) once claimed, that siding with the stronger would eventually lead to subjugation; however, they argue that bandwagoning would lead to dependence on the US and this would subsequently entail the risk of entrapment or abandonment.

So, the hypothesis that follows is that, in order to maximise their own security, European states would try to maximise their own autonomy (Jones, 2007, p. 186). As a result, this form of balancing is not really an attempt to counterbalance the US, since Washington is not perceived as a threat. But still, it is motivated by the American role as a security provider. Thus, we might find that the logic of balancing is similar to the defection strategy in a prisoner's dilemma. It is worth recalling that for players in a prisoner's dilemma, defection is the dominant strategy because they are driven by positive and negative incentives: the first one is to maximise their payoff, the second is to avoid the risk of the worst outcome. Similarly for the EU, building an autonomous capacity follows a two-fold rationale: it provides the EU with security assets, and lowers the risk of being dependent on American preferences.

Like the other strands of balancing before, the balancing for autonomy hypothesis also shows methodological and epistemological flaws. As we have discussed elsewhere (Cladi and Locatelli, 2012, p. 270), we find that this explanation ascribes a disproportionate weight to intentions. Actually, intentions are key to test the validity of the argument. Since balancing, in this view, is motivated by the effort to gain autonomy, empirical evidence of balancing is not enough to confirm the theory. Borrowing Andrew Moravcsik's words, 'Demonstration of causality requires direct evidence of real-world "causal mechanisms" linking concrete causes and mechanisms to outcomes [...] working in ways that support one theory above others' (Moravcsik, 2013, p. 777).[2] For this to happen one should prove that: (1) the power asymmetry creates dependence on the US; (2) such a dependence is perceived as a problem by European policymakers; and (3) building autonomous capabilities is held to be the best option to address this unpleasant situation. From a methodological point of view the problem is how to assess these points. In the absence of clear empirical indicators, 'the balancing-for-autonomy proposition is doomed to remain unverifiable' (Cladi and Locatelli, 2012, p. 270).

Bandwagoning: rule or exception?

In addressing the issue of European security cooperation, scholars have tended to amend the concept of balancing but they have paid less attention to the concept of bandwagoning. Key IR scholars have used it as the polar opposite of balancing. The father of Neorealism, Kenneth Waltz, arguably made a sharp distinction between balancing and bandwagoning and critically dismissed the occurrence of the latter in the international system. As Waltz (1979, p. 126) put it, 'if states wished to maximize power, they would join the stronger side, and we would not see balances form but a world hegemony forged. This does not happen because balancing, not bandwagoning, is the behaviour induced by the system'. Given the fact that Waltz is still regarded, rightly one may add, as the key reference for Realist scholars, it is not surprising that bandwagoning remains understood by many as the opposite of balancing.

Waltz's balance of power theory seemed to suit the bipolar standoff between the US and the USSR rather well. During those long decades, bandwagoning within the Western bloc was academically accepted and pursued politically. For instance, during the Cold War, President Kennedy once declared that 'If the United States were to falter, the whole world would inevitably move towards the Communist bloc' (cited in Jablonsky 1995, p. 54). With reference to European foreign policy, Western European states sided with the US in order to counter the Soviet threat, this meaning that they relied on the military arm provided by NATO. However, in the eyes of balance of power theory the decision of Western European states to ally with the US was problematic while arguably accepted for the following reasons. First, the Europeans were able to *free ride* the US horse

(Olson and Zeckhauser, 1966; Oneal, 1990). European military initiatives were rare during the Cold War and did not cause any significant tension across the Atlantic. Second, containing a threat coming from the USSR was key to the Euro-American partnership because of the overriding concern with the Soviet threat (Forster and Wallace, 2001). Third, Waltz's theory aimed at explaining great power balancing rather than small states bandwagoning. The dissolution of the Soviet threat opened up space for the Europeans to become more autonomous in the defence sphere.

If Waltz ruled out the possibility of bandwagoning as a rational and structurally induced foreign policy behaviour, other scholars got to grips with this concept. The literature on bandwagoning has flourished accordingly, and, while we cannot cover it all here, we can set the scene to understand how the concept can be applied to European defence initiatives in the post-Cold War era. Stephen Walt (1987) studied the diplomatic history of the Middle East between 1955 and 1979 and refined Waltz's argument with his key finding that states tend to balance against threats, not power. While Walt agreed with Waltz that states tend to balance rather than bandwagon, he also argued that in some cases weak states may bandwagon, such as when a threatening state is much stronger, when no other allies are available or when an armed conflict is in progress. As Walt (1987, p. 17) put it, 'Balancing is defined as allying with others against the prevailing threat; bandwagoning refers to alignment with the source of danger'.

Hence, Walt's theoretical findings were important as they re-opened up space for a discussion of the behaviour of weak states and their supposed tendency to bandwagon in order to counter a threat (Rothstein, 1968; Handel, 1981). Jack Levy accepted the fact that weak states tend to bandwagon, as he argued that

> hypotheses regarding balancing behaviour refer to the great powers more than to other states. Great Powers balance against potential hegemons, whereas weaker states in the proximity of stronger states do what is necessary to survive, which often involves bandwagoning with the strong instead of balancing against them.
>
> (1989, p. 231)

The question was then the following: whether or not weak states bandwagon with a great power to counter a threat.

Here, scholars tended to split between those who considered bandwagoning as the rule and those that considered bandwagoning as the exception. For instance, Eric Labs (1992) showed how even weak states tend to balance and not bandwagon against an aggressor in his study of German unification between 1860 and 1866. Stephen Van Evera (1990/91, p. 36) similarly dismissed bandwagoning as a 'rare event'. Robert Kaufman (1992) instead argued that weaker states can also use the strategy of *buckpassing* in order to balance against a threat as he investigated European states' responses to the Nazi threat in the 1930s. Paul Schroeder (1994), in considering European history between 1648 and 1945, demonstrated that instead of balancing states have a propensity to engage in alternative strategies such as *hiding, transcending* and *bandwagoning*. In particular, for Schroeder (1994, p. 117) bandwagoning was 'historically more common than balancing, particularly by smaller powers'.

Despite the fact that scholars started to pay more and more attention to the concept of bandwagoning, its definition and applicability remained confined to weak states preferring to free ride, remain neutral or counter threats. An exception is represented by Deborah Larson (1991), who advanced the argument that great powers may actually bandwagon and weak states may balance instead. In general, however, bandwagoning was a behaviour dictated by the necessity of giving in to threats, not as a behaviour dictated by systemic incentives. Put differently, bandwagoning was understood in the realm of alliance formation, so its duration would be limited and its choice risky. This overall conclusion did not significantly depart from the findings of Kenneth Waltz (1979), who also considered bandwagoning as irrational.

The important step forward in this debate was arguably made by Randall Schweller, who aptly captured the point that bandwagoning could not just be the opposite of balancing (i.e. giving in to threats instead of countering them). Furthermore, bandwagoning is not just another plausible strategy for states to achieve greater security. As Schweller (1994, p. 74) put it, 'balancing is driven by the desire to avoid losses; bandwagoning by the opportunity for gain'. The important contribution to the debate made by Schweller was that, in order for states to decide to bandwagon, no threat necessarily needs to be in place, so bandwagoning is not just a behaviour to avoid capitulation, but a strategy that states adopt in order to gain something without having survival at stake. The applicability of the concept of bandwagoning was expanded to include situations in which states that do not face threats to their security bandwagon with other states in order to gain benefits. While useful, Schweller's contribution discussed Walt's theory of alliance formation, and his case studies all pointed towards instances of alliance formation rather than alliance management. Since the Euro-American partnership has survived the end of the Cold War era, it seems plausible to explore the applicability of the concept of bandwagoning as intra-alliance behaviour.

Bandwagoning as intra-alliance behaviour

To our knowledge, the effort of studying European defence with reference to the concept of bandwagoning is new in IR theory scholarship. Bandwagoning as intra-alliance behaviour rests upon the following assumptions. First, the post-Cold War scenario in which European security and defence initiatives took place is different to the scenario in which IR scholars had previously debated the occurrence of balancing vs bandwagoning. In fact, the system may be considered as unipolar (Krauthammer, 1993; Wohlforth, 1999; Mowle and Sacko, 2007; Monteiro, 2014), not bipolar or multipolar. This entails significant implications: under unipolarity, the power asymmetry between the US and its European allies is so considerable that the Europeans were left with little choice as to how to define their foreign policy vis-à-vis the US. To link their preferences to the US may not have seemed altogether captivating for the Europeans, but balancing against them was clearly unfeasible (Wohlforth, 1999, p. 38; for alternative views, see Walt, 2009; Monteiro, 2011).

It was also a situation in which there was no great power confrontation: on the contrary, other possible great powers such as Russia or China (at least in the immediate post-Cold War period) did not try to catch up with the US militarily, nor did they seem willing to pose a direct threat to Europe. The second assumption is that the alliance between the US and the EU was already in place as we entered the post-Cold War period. As embodied more clearly by NATO, such institutional arrangements could mitigate European security concerns (see, among many others, Ikenberry, 2000; Haftendorn *et al.*, 1999). Because of these peculiar conditions, for European states bandwagoning seemed a more rational behaviour. In fact, European bandwagoning on the US was not in response to an American threat, l*et al*one an external challenge. Drawing on the insight of Davide Fiammenghi (2011), in the post-Cold War period the US had crossed the 'absolute security threshold' (Fiammenghi, 2011, pp. 136–243) – i.e. it was too powerful to be balanced and in a position to extend its influence through NATO, so attracting European bandwagoning (Schmidt, 2006/7).

Even if secure, European states still faced a degree of uncertainty. While not under a direct threat, as was the case during the Cold War years, they still had to deal with instability in their own backyard (as witnessed first by the Balkan Wars in the 1990s). They could decide either to pursue an independent foreign policy or to rely on the US in order to keep the Atlantic Alliance for as long as possible. There was not pressure from the US to bandwagon; rather, requests for burden-sharing by the Americans have been continuous in the post-Cold War period along with episodes during which the US committed itself to strengthening NATO with the help of European states (Sloan, 2005). An example of this is when US Secretary of Defense Donald Rumsfeld pronounced the following statement at a NATO Defense Ministerial Meeting in Warsaw: 'If NATO does not have a force that is quick and agile, which can deploy in days or weeks instead of months or years, then it will not have much to offer in the world of the twenty-first century' (quoted in Ringsmose, 2009, p. 288).

From a Neorealist perspective, then, the European attempt at integration in foreign and defence policy can be explained as a rational response to systemic pressures. Borrowing Glenn Snyder's (1996) apt discussion of *relationships* as systemic but not structural variables, we can come to a better understanding of the situational context in which European states embarked on the CSDP process. On one hand, the sheer power distribution within the system (a structural-level variable) made the US–European partnership deeply unbalanced, so creating the alliance power dilemma – i.e. the risk of becoming too weak to be accommodating partners in the US's eyes (Cladi and Locatelli, 2012, p. 281). On the other hand, relationships, and alignments in particular (Snyder also includes as other elements conflicting/diverging interests and capabilities), contributed to shape European states' strategic calculation: by virtue of their entanglement in the

Atlantic Alliance, they did not have to worry as much about the risk of being dominated (even less about their survival), and even the relative gains problem was less acute (a point already raised by Keohane, 1993, p. 279). The intrinsic value gained by NATO over the years ruled out the strategic value of balancing *sensu stricto* and called for bandwagoning as the only alternative. In other words, bandwagoning represents the European attempt to have it both ways: to maintain their privileged relationship with the US and, by fostering integration, to make power asymmetry within the alliance less acute.

As we have introduced this point elsewhere (Cladi and Locatelli, 2012, 2013), it is worth recapitulating some of the critiques we have received. Some of them concern the theoretical coherence, others the empirical soundness of our account. Although just a few share our ontology, we will address them in the attempt to strengthen our point. To begin with, from a Liberal perspective, Benjamin Pohl (2013) argued that America and Europe have moved beyond the age of power politics and into an era characterised by democracy, interdependence and institutionalisation (see also Mandelbaum, 2001). We acknowledged that Liberalism is a very important alternative approach, and its tenets account for a good deal of EU policies, but the ontological assumptions of Realism remain different and incompatible with this Liberal account. As a result, while acknowledging the exceptional level of cooperation between the US and Europe, we still maintain that competition is an inescapable part of the Atlantic Alliance (Cladi and Locatelli, 2013). Put differently, for all the common interests uniting the two shores of the Atlantic, a number of diverging interests exist that justify Realism's ontological basis.

It is also true that different EU states approach such competition in different ways, with the result that there is no single EU stance towards the US, but rather a set of complex and individual European states' outlooks towards Washington (Ringsmose, 2013). Yet, these differences across Europe are a matter of quality, not quantity. In other words, it is certainly true that Eastern European countries have different motivations than, say, the United Kingdom (UK), but this does not challenge our argument: systemic pressures (power imbalances in particular) make bandwagoning with the US a rational behaviour. Actually, as witnessed by as diverse states as France and Italy (Cladi and Webber, 2011; Cladi and Locatelli, 2012; Ratti, 2012), alignment with the US has always been the preferred choice for European states. Bandwagoning, understood as maintaining the alliance with the more powerful, is therefore a behaviour induced by the system. As other contributors to this volume suggest (see in particular Chapters 2 and 4), domestic variables may and actually do intervene to shape European states' foreign policy, but their role results in an intervening variable (i.e. one that amplifies or downgrades the systemic incentive), not an independent variable.

The type of bandwagoning we identified is not understood in terms of non-alignment or 'contributing nothing to the cause like Austria and Ireland did in post world war II Europe by aligning with NATO' (Labs, 1992, p. 389). It is also not understood as free riding such as Western European states did during the Cold War under the security assurance of NATO. This form of bandwagoning is not cost-free: the Europeans have indeed undertaken a number of defence initiatives in the post-Cold War period, albeit with a view to deploying military force in low intensity security scenarios (Cladi and Locatelli, 2012; Locatelli and Testoni, 2009). Although most of them were far from successful, they implied economic and political costs.

Another controversy has been raised about the (lack of) strategic thinking behind ESDP-CSDP (Schmitt, 2013; see also Zielonka, 1998; see also Chapter 7 and, for a different view, Chapter 5). If the policies we consider are not driven by rational calculation, the argument goes, then we cannot use bandwagoning as an explanation. For sure, the strategic posture of the EU as such cannot be compared to a US *grand strategy*. Whether the EU can develop a grand strategy in response to the recent US rebalance to Asia remains uncertain (Stokes and Whitman, 2013). Yet, the strategy of bandwagoning and the EU's choice to rely on the US to carry out high-intensity operations appears like a rational and strategic, albeit limited, response to unipolarity.

The Petersberg tasks were defined in 1992, and outlined the three purposes for which military units could be deployed: humanitarian and rescue tasks, peacekeeping tasks and tasks of combat forces in crisis management, including peacemaking (Western European Union, 2014). In June 2001, the EU has revised the Petersberg tasks with the so-called 'Gothenburg Programme' for the prevention of 'violent conflict, human suffering and social and economic dislocation' (European Council, 2011). The Petersberg tasks were later revised with the Lisbon Treaty in 2009. While the tasks have been expanded and now include 'humanitarian and rescue tasks, conflict prevention and peace-keeping tasks, tasks of combat forces in crisis management, including peacemaking, joint disarmament operations, military advice and assistance tasks, post conflict stabilization tasks', there is no significant reason to assume that the EU will be able to undertake high-intensity operations (European Union External Action, 2014).

The issue revolves around what the EU can contribute to the Atlantic Alliance through the strategy of bandwagoning. As we originally argued,

> Due to the American superiority, for Washington the problem is how to make sure that Europe will not try to compete with the United States, but will still remain of some utility. For the European allies, on the other hand, the point is to keep the American involvement whilst keeping some bargaining power at the same time.
>
> (Cladi and Locatelli, 2012, p. 18)

The EU's current and most discussed military initiative is the Battlegroup Concept. The Battlegroup was declared operational in January 2007 but is the result of three previous arrangements of European Security policy, namely the initial Helsinki Headline Goal Process in 1999, the ESS in 2003 and the deployment of Operation Artemis in Congo in 2003 (Kaitera and Ben Ari, 2008). With reference to the Helsinki Headline Goal in particular, the EU Member States agreed to create by 2003 the European Rapid Reaction Force (ERRF) consisting of 60,000 troops available at sixty days' notice to be sustainable for up to a year (Howorth, 2007). At Helsinki, the EU laid down important principles for EU–NATO cooperation by stating that

> The European Union should have the autonomous capacity to take decisions and, where NATO as a whole is not engaged, to launch and then to conduct EU-led military operations in response to international crises in support of the Common Foreign and Security Policy.
>
> (European Council, 1999)

The Battlegroup was therefore placed in the context of the ERRF to create smaller, more agile rapid response forces where NATO was not involved, unlike with Operation Concordia in Macedonia in 2003. The EU then updated the Headline Goal in 2004 promising a readiness to deploy the Battlegroup in responding rapidly to possible UN requests (European Council, 2004). The need for rapid mechanism defence initiatives was however endorsed by NATO in 2002 (Ringsmose, 2009). While similar in scope, there are key differences between the two initiatives. First, the NATO Response Force (NRF) would be 25,000 men strong, the EU battlegroup only 1,500 men strong. Second, the focus of the NRF is global, whereas the EU battlegroup is regional, with a strong focus on Africa (Balossi-Restelli, 2011). A recent example of this is the military campaign in Libya. As Menon (2011, p. 75) reminds us, CSDP was not taken seriously when the war in Libya escalated and 'such inactivity in the face of a crisis with obvious security implications for the Union's Member States, at a time when the US administration was desperate for its European partners to take the lead, has led to anguished soul-searching'.

Finally, Trine Flockhart (2013) has argued that bandwagoning hides an intention of the Europeans to seek gains through an alliance of convenience. In this context, 'intentions, motives, concerns and preferences are sentiments that require reflection and analysis well beyond the assumption of agents as simple benefit maximisers' (Flockhart 2013, p. 394). We agree that bandwagoning is aimed at the convenience of keeping the alliance with the US for as long as possible, but we understand bandwagoning as a result of structural incentives under unipolarity which pointed the Europeans towards the direction of keeping the US involved. Put differently, our understanding of bandwagoning is as outcome rather than process.[3] As mentioned in relation to balancing for autonomy, this is a systemic explanation and it does not require consideration of motivations.

Conclusion

Realist scholars who sought to explain the drivers of European defence policy in the post-Cold War period have advanced the balancing proposition. As we argued in the first part of this chapter, the balancing proposition is deterministic in the sense that the logic of balancing always prevails. In the literature, it is now possible to find several examples of scholars who adopted the Realist framework to make sense of European foreign policy. In this chapter, we have tackled some of the most notable and contemporary Realist frameworks that include soft balancing, balancing for autonomy and, more recently, the theory outlined by Sebastian Rosato.

The latter was especially significant because it arguably brought Structural Realism back into the debate regarding European foreign policy. With the earlier soft balancing and balancing for autonomy explanations, the attention of scholars who wished to explain balancing shifted to intentions. Therefore it would be possible to think that Waltz's (1993, 2000) Structural Realist explanation of balancing as a system-induced behaviour could be considered history. As Andrew Moravcsik (2013, p. 773) has recently asserted, 'With much realist writing having degenerated (in the "philosophy of science" sense) into a neoclassical form often undistinguishable from Liberal theory, Rosato remains a real realist'.

The fact that even *real Realism* remains alive in this debate testifies to the fact that the inter-paradigmatic debate will most likely continue in the future. In this chapter, we have done two things: first, we have addressed the continuing insistence on the concept of balancing by Realist scholars. In fact, the concept of balancing in Rosato's analysis is quintessential to understanding why European states have decided to cooperate. Rosato's answer is that they have done so to balance against the USSR. We have dealt with this argument in the chapter but, to recapitulate, we share Rosato's assumption that the balance of power is very important in order to understand how states behave in the international system. Second, we have carried out an analysis of the concept of bandwagoning and its possible application to European defence initiatives in the post-Cold War period. Here, our analysis departs from Rosato's in that we argue that European states had an important reason to cooperate in the post-Cold War period, namely to foster their relationship with the US under unipolarity. We believe this behaviour can be captured with the concept of bandwagoning, a concept which belongs to the Realist toolbox but which has not been used in the context of Euro-American relations in the post-Cold War period.

Notes

1 Another strand is represented by authors like Joseph Grieco and Adrian Hyde-Price. In different ways, these scholars still focus on power and its distribution. However, they find as a mainspring for cooperation the European internal distribution of power, finding the main cause for cooperation in German superiority (Grieco, 1995, 1996), or in the regional distribution of power (balanced multipolarity, as Hyde-Price (2007) put it). In this view, they can aptly be considered as Systemic Realists, as they consider the relational level of interaction among states (Snyder, 1996, 1997). However, we find these works to be of little utility here. As concerns Grieco's analysis, this is better suited to explain the European integration process per se, rather than mere cooperation in the security sector. In fact, if the EU is to be seen as a *binding* strategy to contain Germany, binding is better achieved through diplomatic and economic agreements, rather than defence and foreign policy initiatives. On the other hand, Hyde-Price's balanced multipolarity thesis rests on an ambiguous claim, as he argues that the rise of

then ESDP was made possible by the concomitant presence of global unipolarity and regional *balanced* multipolarity (Hyde-Price 2007, p. 112). Here we find that a systemic account of the ESDP/CSDP process should be focused on unipolarity alone.
2 It is worth noting that this remark came as a critique to Rosato's book, that, as we have previously discussed, remains purely systemic in its approach. We believe the charge is even more penetrating for the balancing for autonomy theory.
3 In a similar vein, Fiammenghi discusses the balancing proposition as an outcome rather than a behaviour (Fiammenghi, 2011, pp. 130–1).

References

Andreatta, F. (2011) The European Union's International Relations: A Theoretical View. In Hill, C. and Smith, M. (eds) *International Relations and the European Union*. Oxford: Oxford University Press. 2nd edn.

Art, R. (2004) Europe Hedges Its Security Bets. In Paul, T. V., Wirtz, J. L. and Fortmann, M. (eds) *Balance of Power: Theory and Practice in the 21st Century*. Stanford, CT: Stanford University Press.

Balossi-Restelli, L. (2011) Fit for What? Towards Explaining Battlegroup Inaction. *European Security*. 20 (2). pp. 155–84.

Cladi, L. and Locatelli, A. (2013) Worth a Shot: On the Explanatory Power of Bandwagoning in Transatlantic Relations. *Contemporary Security Policy*. 34 (2). pp. 374–81.

Cladi, L. and Locatelli, A. (2012) Bandwagoning, Not Balancing: Why Europe Confounds Realism. *Contemporary Security Policy*. 33 (2). pp. 264–88.

Cladi, L. and Webber, M. (2011) Italian Foreign Policy in the post-Cold War Period: A Neoclassical Realist Approach. *European Security*. 20 (2). pp. 205–19.

European Council (2011) *Council Conclusions on Conflict Prevention. 3101st Foreign Affairs Council Meeting*. Luxembourg. 20 June. Available from: www.consilium.europa. eu/uedocs/cms_data/docs/pressdata/EN/foraff/122911.pdf [accessed: 16 February 2015].

European Council (2004) *Headline Goal 2010*. Brussels. 17 and 18 June 2004. Available from: www.consilium.europa.eu/uedocs/cmsUpload/2010%20Headline%20Goal.pdf [accessed: 16 February 2015].

European Council (1999) *Presidency Conclusions*. Helsinki European Council. Helsinki. 10 and 11 December. Available from: www.consilium.europa.eu/uedocs/cms_data/docs/pressdata/en/ec/ACFA4C.htm [accessed: 16 February 2015].

European Union External Action (2014) *About CSDP – the Petersberg Tasks*. Available from: http://eeas.europa.eu/csdp/about-csdp/petersberg/index_en.htm [accessed: 16 February 2015].

Feaver, P., Schweller, R., Taliaferro, J., Wohlforth, W., Legro, J. and Moravcsik, A. (2000) Correspondence: Brother, Can You Spare a Paradigm? (Or Was Anybody Ever a Realist?). *International Security*. 25 (1). pp. 165–93.

Fiammenghi, D. (2011) The Security Curve and the Structure of International Politics: A Neorealist Synthesis. *International Security*. 35 (4). pp. 126–54.

Flockart, T. (2013) Why Europe Confounds IR Theory. *Contemporary Security Policy*. 34 (2). pp. 392–96.

Forster, A. and Wallace, W. (2001) What is NATO for?. *Survival*, 43 (4). pp. 107–22.

Grieco, J. (1996) State Interests and Institutional Rule Trajectories. A Neorealist Interpretation of The Maastricht Treaty and European Economic and Monetary Union. In Frankel, B. (ed.) *Realism: Restatements and Renewal*, special issue of *Security Studies*. 5 (3). pp. 261–306.

Grieco, J. (1995) The Maastricht Treaty, Economic and Monetary Union and the Neo-Realist Research Programme. *Review of International Studies*. 21 (1). pp. 21–40.

Grieco, J. (1988) Anarchy and the Limits of Cooperation: A Realist Critique of the Newest Liberal Institutionalism. *International Organization*. 42 (4). pp. 485–507.

Handel, M. (1981) *Weak States in the International System*. London: Frank Class.

Hyde-Price, A. (2007) *European Security in the 21st Century: The Challenge of Multi-polarity*. Abingdon, UK: Routledge.

Haftendorn, H., Keohane, R. O. and Wallander, C. A. (eds) (1999) *Imperfect Unions. Security Institutions over Time and Space*. Oxford: Oxford University Press.

Howorth, J. (2007) *Security and Defence Policy in the European Union*. Basingstoke, UK: Palgrave Macmillan.

Ikenberry, J. (2000) *After Victory, Institutions, Strategic Restraint, and the Rebuilding of Order after Major Wars*. Princeton, NJ: Princeton University Press.

Jablonsky, D. (1995) *Paradigm Lost? Transition and the Search for a New World Order*, Westport, CT, Praeger.

Jones, S. G. (2007) *The Rise of European Security Cooperation*, Cambridge: University Press.

Kaitera, J. and Ben-Ari, G. (2008) *EU Battlegroups and the NATO Response Force: A Marriage of Convenience?* Center for Strategic and International Studies, April. Available from: http://csis.org/files/media/csis/pubs/eurofocus_v14n01.pdf [accessed: 16 February 2015].

Kaufman, R. G. (1992) To Balance or to Bandwagon? Alignment Decisions in 1930s Europe. *Security Studies*. 1 (3). pp. 417–47.

Keohane, R. (1993) Institutional Theory and the Realist Challenge after the Cold War. In Baldwin, D. (ed.) *Neorealism and Neoliberalism. The Contemporary Debate*. New York: Columbia University Press.

Krauthammer, C. (1990–91) The Unipolar Moment. *Foreign Affairs*. 70 (1). pp. 23–33.

Krotz, U., Maher, R., McCourt, D., Glencross, A., Ripsman, N., Sheetz, M., Haine, J.-Y. and Rosato, S. (2012) Debating the Sources and Prospects of European Integration. *International Security*. 37 (1). pp. 178–99.

Labs, E. (1992) Do Weak States Bandwagon? *Security Studies*. 1 (3). pp. 383–416.

Larson, D. W. (1991) Bandwagon Images in American Foreign Policy: Myth or Reality? In Jervis, R. and Snyder, J. (eds) *Dominoes and Bandwagons: Strategic Beliefs and Great Power Competition in the Eurasian Rimland*. Oxford: Oxford University Press.

Layne, C. (2006) The Unipolar Illusion Revisited: The Coming End of the United States Unipolar Moment. *International Security*. 31 (2). pp. 7–41.

Levy, J. (1989) The Causes of War: A Review of Theories and Evidence. In Tetlock, P., Jervis, R., Stern, P., Husbands, J. and Tilly, C. (eds) *Behavior, Society and Nuclear War*. New York: Oxford University Press.

Little, R. (2007) *The Balance of Power in International Relations: Metaphors, Myths and Models*. Cambridge: Cambridge University Press.

Locatelli, A. and Testoni, M. (2009) Intra-allied Cooperation and Alliance Durability: The Case for Promoting a Division of Labour among NATO Allies. *European Security*. 18 (3). pp. 345–62.

Mandelbaum, M. (2001) Bad Statesman, Good Prophet: Woodrow Wilson and the post-Cold War Order. *The National Interest*. 64. Summer. pp. 31–41.

Mearsheimer J. (1994) The False Promise of International Institutions. *International Security*. 19 (3). pp. 5–49.

Menon, A. (2011) European Defence Policy from Lisbon to Lybia. *Survival*. 53 (3). pp. 75–90.

Monteiro, N. (2014) *Theory of Unipolar Politics*. Cambridge: Cambridge University Press.

Monteiro, N. (2011) Unrest Assured. Why Unipolarity Is Not Peaceful. *International Security*. 36 (3). pp. 9–40.

Moravcsik, A. (2013) Did Power Politics Cause European Integration? Realist Theory Meets Qualitative Methods. *Security Studies*. 22 (4). pp. 773–90.

Morgenthau, H. (1959) Alliances in Theory and Practice. In A. Wolfers (ed.) *Alliance Policy in the Cold War*. Baltimore, MA: Johns Hopkins University Press.

Morgenthau, H. (1948) *Politics among Nations. The Struggle for Power and Peace*. New York: Knopf.

Mowle, T. and Sacko, D. (2007) Global NATO. Bandwagoning in a Unipolar World. *Contemporary Security Policy*. 28 (3). pp. 597–618.

Olson, M. and Zeckhauser, R. (1966) An Economic Theory of Alliances. *Review of Economics and Statistics*, 48 (3). pp. 266–79.

Oneal, J. (1990) Testing the Theory of Collective Action: NATO Defense Burdens, 1950–1984. *Journal of Conflict Resolution*. 34 (3). pp. 426–48.

Oswald, F. (2006) *Europe and the United States: The Emerging Security Partnership*. London: Praeger Security International.

Pape, R. A. (2005) Soft Balancing against the United States. *International Security*. 30 (1). pp. 7–45.

Parsons, C. (2013) Power, Patterns, and Process in European Union History. *Security Studies*. 22 (4). pp. 791–801.

Paul, T. V. (2005) Soft Balancing in the Age of US Primacy. *International Security*. 30 (1). pp. 46–71.

Paul, T. V., Wirtz, J. J. and Fortmann, M. (eds) (2004) *Balance of Power: Theory and Practice in the 21st Century*. Stanford, CA: Stanford University Press.

Pohl, B. (2013) Neither Bandwagoning nor Balancing: Explaining Europe's Security Policy. *Contemporary Security Policy*. 34 (2). pp. 353–73.

Posen, B. (2006) European Union Security and Defence Policy: Response to Unipolarity? *Security Studies*. 15 (2). pp. 149–86.

Ratti, L. (2012) All Aboard the Bandwagon? Structural Realism and Italy's International Role, *Diplomacy and Statecraft*. 23 (1). pp. 87–109.

Ringsmose, J. (2013) Balancing or Bandwagon? Europe's Many Relations with the United States. *Contemporary Security Policy*. 34 (2). pp. 409–12.

Ringsmose, J. (2009) NATO's Response Force: Finally Getting it Right? *European Security*. 18 (3). pp. 287–304.

Rosato, S. (2013) Theory and Evidence in Europe United: A Response to My Critics. *Security Studies*. 22 (4). pp. 802–20.

Rosato, S. (2011) *Europe United: Power Politics and the Making of the European Community*. Ithaca, NY: Cornell University Press.

Rosato, S. (2011a) Europe's Troubles: Power Politics and the State of the European Project. *International Security*. 35 (4). pp. 45–86.

Rothstein, R. L. (1968) *Alliances and Small Powers*. New York: Columbia University Press.

Schroeder, P. (1994) Historical Reality Vs Neo-Realist Theory. *International Security*. 19 (1). pp. 108–48.

Schmidt, J. R. (2006–7) Last Alliance Standing? NATO after 9/11. *The Washington Quarterly*. 30 (1). pp. 93–106.

Schmitt, O. (2013) A Tragic Lack of Ambition: Why EU Security Policy is no Strategy. *Contemporary Security Policy*. 34 (2). pp. 413–16.

Schweller, R. (1994) Bandwagoning for Profit: Bringing the Revisionist State Back In. *International Security*. 19 (1). pp. 72–107.

Sloan, S. (2005) *NATO, the European Union, and the Atlantic Community: The Transatlantic Bargain Challenged*. Oxford: Rowman & Littlefield Publishers.

Snyder, G. (1997) *Alliance Politics*. Ithaca, NY: Cornell University Press.

Snyder, G. (1996) Process Variables in Neorealist Theory. In Frankel, B. (ed.) *Realism. Restatements and Renewal*. London: Cass.

Stokes, D. and Whitman, R. G. (2013) Transatlantic Triage? European and UK 'grand strategy' after the US rebalance to Asia. *International Affairs*. 89 (5). pp. 1087–1107.

Van Evera, S. (1990–1991) Primed for Peace: Europe after the Cold War. *International Security*. 15 (3). pp. 7–57.

Walt, S. M. (2009) Alliances in a Unipolar World. *World Politics*. 61 (1). pp. 1–27.

Walt, S. M. (2005) *Taming American Power*. New York: W. W. Norton and Company.

Walt, S. M. (1998/99), The Ties that Fray: Why Europe and America are Drifting Apart. *The National Interest*. 54. Winter. pp. 3–11.

Walt, S. M. (1987) *The Origins of Alliances*. Ithaca, NY: Cornell University Press.

Waltz, K. (1993) The Emerging Structure of International Politics. *International Security*. 18 (2). pp. 44–79.

Waltz, K. (1979) *Theory of International Politics*. New York: McGraw Hill.

Western European Union (2014) *Petersberg Declaration*. Western European Union Council of Ministers, Bonn, 19 June 1992. Available from: www.weu.int/documents/920619peten.pdf [accessed: 11 February 2015].

Wohlforth, W. (1999) The Stability of a Unipolar World, *International Security*. 24 (1). pp. 5–41.

Zielonka, I. (1998) *Explaining Euro-paralysis: Why Europe is Unable to Act in International Politics*. Basingstoke, UK: Palgrave Macmillan.

2 Neoclassical Realism

Clarifying the nature and role of systemic- and domestic-level variables in CSDP

Tom Dyson

Introduction: theorising CSDP's patterns of progress and stasis

Since its launch in 1999, the Common Security and Defence Policy (CSDP) has been characterised by both progress and stasis. On the one hand, in the Political and Security Committee (PSC), EU Military Committee (EUMC) and EU Military Staff (EUMS), the EU has developed a significant institutional architecture that bolsters the capacity of European states to launch military operations within their geopolitical neighbourhood. European states have also undertaken a number of cross-national capability procurement programmes, which will enhance the ability of the EU to deploy military force autonomously from the US. These programmes include the A400M military transport aircraft and Galileo satellite navigation system that will provide a European alternative to the US Global Positioning System. Furthermore, the EDA, established in 2004, provides an institutional forum for the pooling and sharing of military capabilities and for measures to enhance Europe's Defence Technological and Industrial Base (EDTIB). In addition, European states have begun to pool military forces to bolster their rapid reaction capabilities. Such initiatives include the 2004 Battlegroup Concept that has, to date, established 19 battalions of 1,500–2,500 troops capable of humanitarian, peace-making and peacekeeping tasks, two of which remain on permanent readiness. These developments are important steps in facilitating European states to meet key strategic challenges, most notably, the need for European states to enhance their capacity to pick up the security burden in their geopolitical neighbourhood in the context of the shift in US strategic priorities to the Asia–Pacific region and the implications of austerity measures for national defence budgets.

On the other hand, CSDP suffers from a number of deficits which limit the extent to which Europe can decouple itself from the US security guarantee. First, despite the above capability procurement projects and pooling/sharing initiatives under CSDP, the EU remains heavily dependent on NATO assets and lacks its own independent operational headquarters (Koops, 2010). Second, the EDA has failed to act as a means for European states to pool and share military capabilities, particularly 'enablers'. The 2010 EU Foreign Affairs Council initiated eleven projects which were designed to fill gaps in a number of enablers. Areas such as air-to-air refuelling, helicopter training, a medical field hospital and satellite procurement have witnessed progress (Biscop, 2013, p. 2). Yet Europe lags behind in areas such as drones, smart munitions and military satellites. In addition, even in areas where projects have been established, such as air-to-air refuelling, an expansion in the depth and scope of EU Member State involvement is necessary (Biscop, 2013).

Third, while some progress has been made in consolidating the EDTIB, through mergers such as the European Aeronautic Defence and Space Company (EADS, now Airbus) in 2000, and joint ventures such as the Eurofighter, NHIndustries' multi-role helicopter, Telespazio and Thales Alenia Space, Europe's defence industry remains highly fragmented (Caruso and Locatelli, 2013, pp. 89–104). This is particularly evident when Europe is compared with the US, whose defence technological and industrial base is dominated by three key players (Boeing, Lockheed Martin and Northrop Grumman). Attempts to consolidate Europe's defence industry, most notably the merger between BAE and EADS in 2012, have faltered due to opposition in national capitals (in this case from Germany's Chancellor Angela Merkel) (Milmo *et al.*, 2012). This duplication in infrastructure and research and development expenditure and lack of an economy of scale is a significant hindrance to Europe's attempts to get more 'bang for the buck' from defence expenditure (Briani, 2013).

Finally, CSDP remains under-utilised, as NATO remains the institution of choice for major European military operations. While the EU has launched thirty-four operations under CSDP, these have largely involved small-scale missions at the lower end of the spectrum of conflict intensity (Engberg, 2013). Where security challenges have emerged which necessitate the use of higher-intensity force, such as the 2011 Libya crisis, divisions between EU Member States about key security challenges – as well as the role of the US in European security – have undermined the credibility of CSDP by making it redundant as a forum for coordinating military action.

A substantial theoretical literature has emerged during the post-Cold War era that provides a variety of different perspectives on the drivers of these patterns of progress and stasis in CSDP, including Liberal Intergovernmentalist (LI) accounts (Dover, 2007); Two-Level Games Theory (Matlary, 2009); Institutionalist Theory (Menon, 2011), Liberal accounts (Pohl, 2013) and Classical Realism (Rynning, 2011). However, Constructivism forms the dominant approach. United by a belief in the importance of norms and identity as the foundation of interests, Constructivist scholars point to the emergence of a 'European strategic culture' driven, in particular, by 'elite socialisation' emerging from common military operations through CSDP and by interaction between officials and military personnel within the PSC, EUMS and EUMC (Biava *et al.* 2011; Meyer, 2005). Stasis in CSDP is viewed as a consequence of the stickiness of national strategic cultures which are resistant to the 'top down' processes of normative convergence consequent upon elite socialisation (see also Chapter 5).

This chapter undertakes a neoclassical Realist account of CSDP that is distinct from the above approaches in two main ways. First, in contrast to Constructivist and Liberal accounts the chapter demonstrates the important impact of material factors in driving CSDP. Second, the chapter offers a novel approach to the appropriate level of analysis in studies of CSDP by demonstrating the independent role played by the balance of threat, while accounting for the important intervening role played by domestic-level variables. A number of scholars have analysed the utility of Neorealist thought in explaining the rise – and failures – of CSDP. However, they suffer from two main problems. First, they tend to focus on the insights of Kenneth Waltz's (1979) balance of power theory, which leads them to view CSDP as an instance of soft balancing US power. This chapter argues that CSDP is, instead, an instance of 'reformed bandwagoning' on US power. West European states bandwagoned heavily on the US security guarantee during the Cold War to counter the threat posed by the Soviet Union and Warsaw Pact states to their territorial integrity. In the post-Cold War era, this process of bandwagoning has undergone reform whereby European states are seeking to simultaneously retain influence over the US and sustain US engagement in European security, while preparing to 'go it alone' in instances when the US is not willing to support European military operations (Cladi and Locatelli, 2013; Dyson, 2010, pp. 102–6; 2010a; 2013). It argues that, rather than Waltz's balance of power, Neorealist analyses of European defence cooperation can gain greater analytical traction by focusing on the utility of Stephen Walt's (1985) balance of threat theory (Wivel, 2008).

The second problem faced by Neorealist analyses is that, in their focus on the (albeit centrally important) role of systemic-level variables, they fail to fully account for the role played by domestic-level variables in CSDP. As Rathbun (2008) notes, Neoclassical Realist thought is the 'logical and necessary' extension of Structural Realism and provides a very important theoretical mechanism to account for stasis in CSDP. Neoclassical Realism is, however, a theory that is characterised by a strong measure of disagreement over the nature of domestic-level variables (Dyson, 2010, pp. 120–2; Lobell *et al.*, 2009). The approach has been criticised for its departure from the materialist core of Realist thought due to its 'ad hoc' integration of material and ideational variables (Legro and Moravcsik, 1999). This chapter argues that these criticisms of Neoclassical Realism are unfounded. Instead, this ability to integrate the insights of non-material variables is, in fact, a very significant strength as it enables the theory to reconcile the insights of key strands of Constructivist thought on CSDP. The chapter posits that Neoclassical Realism forms a valuable analytical framework for dialogue between what have been viewed as competing theoretical frameworks and has the potential to enhance our understanding of the factors which are restricting Europe from meeting the key strategic challenge of developing greater military autonomy from the US.

The chapter begins by examining the state of play in Neorealist analyses of CSDP and proceeds by developing a 'balance of threat' account of the forces of convergence and differentiation in European defence. The chapter then builds upon this examination of the nature and role of systemic-level variables in European defence by examining the nature and role of domestic-level variables in hindering the ability of European states to launch common military operations and move toward closer pooling and sharing of military forces and capabilities.

Neorealism and CSDP: balancing or bandwagoning?

Waltzian Neorealism argues that the behaviour of states in the international system is dependent upon the distribution of material capabilities – economic, and, in particular, military power (Waltz, 1979). Several power distributions are possible within the international system, which has implications for the level of conflict or cooperation that is present within the international system at any one time. These include unipolarity (an international system dominated by a single state with the ability to strive for regional or global hegemony);[1] bipolarity (a system dominated by two powers of equal capability) and, finally, multipolarity (a system characterised by more than two powers of relatively equal capability).

According to the key indicator of relative power – military power – the current international system remains unipolar. While Chinese defence expenditure has grown significantly in recent years, it has done so from a very low base. At $188 billion in 2013, the Chinese defence budget is still dwarfed by the 2013 US defence budget of $640 billion (Perlo-Freeman and Solmirano, 2014). China's naval and satellite capabilities have witnessed significant development in recent years and it is certainly developing the ability to challenge US naval dominance in the western Pacific. However, China remains a long way from being capable of mounting a challenge to the US dominance of the global commons (*The Economist*, 2014).

According to Waltzian Neorealism, states of common size, geographical position and material capabilities, such as the West European Great Powers (Britain, France and Germany), will exhibit isomorphic responses to a unipolar international system. However, their response can take a number of different forms. First, states can pass on responsibility for balancing to other powers in the international system (Schweller, 2006, p. 166). Such 'buckpassing' is not, however, a rational response for European states to the present international system. Free-riding on the efforts of states such as China and Russia to balance US power would unnecessarily sour EU relations with the US, which, as this chapter will demonstrate, remains an important partner for European states.

Second, European states may seek to take advantage of the opportunities provided by international institutions to 'bind' the behaviour of the US and avoid entrapment in its policies (Press-Barnathan, 2006, p. 285). Binding is a logical response for Defensive Realists, who argue that the nature of security as a finite good provides an incentive for a unipolar leader to work through international institutions, a premise that is also shared by Institutionalist approaches to international cooperation (Ikenberry, 2001). However, binding sits less comfortably with Offensive Realism, a theory that would appear to provide stronger analytical leverage than Defensive Realism in explaining US defence and security policy over the post-Cold War era (Hyde-Price, 2007, pp. 83–6; Mearsheimer, 2001). Due to the inevitability of power maximisation within Offensive Realism, there is little incentive for the dominant state in a unipolar international system to work through international organisations. In short, a focus on CSDP as a means to bind the US by enhancing the EU's ability to wield influence within

NATO (Press-Barnathan, 2006) overestimates the impact that international institutions can exert on the behaviour of a hegemon.

Waltz's balance of power theory argues that states prioritise balancing behaviour when they face a rising hegemonic power (Waltz, 1979, pp. 126–7). European states do not enjoy the material capabilities to undertake significant internal balancing. However, external balancing – the formation of alliances with weaker states – is a more plausible response (Walt, 1985, p. 5). External balancing can be manifested in two ways: 'hard' and 'soft' balancing. Hard balancing involves the establishment of a military alliance explicitly aimed at undermining a rising power. Hard balancing is, of course, not evidenced by European and Transatlantic security dynamics and would be an irrational approach due to the nature of the US and other European states as nuclear powers, as well as the large military power gap between the US and Europe. However, the notion that CSDP represents a form of soft balancing – 'tacit balancing, short of formal alliances' – has received greater attention in the scholarly literature (Paul, 2004, p. 3). A number of US-based scholars, including Art (2004), Layne (2006, pp. 34–6), Pape (2005), Posen (2006) and Walt (2002) view CSDP as a means to disrupt unilateral action by the US and a basis for a more formal military alliance in the future. However, this thesis is not confirmed by the empirical evidence. There is no evidence that the US displays aggressive intentions to the EU and a soft balancing strategy by the EU would risk incurring the wrath of the US at a time when the US constitutes a better partner than an enemy in dealing with more imminent dangers.

Indeed, a focus on threat rather than capabilities provides greater insights into the dynamics underpinning CSDP. While Waltz (1979, p. 126) posited that states make their strategic calculations on the basis of aggregate capabilities, Walt (1985, pp. 8–13) argued that states are concerned not only with capabilities, but also with threat. An enemy who is less powerful than the unipolar leader, but one who is more geographically proximate, and has offensive capabilities and offensive intentions will pose a greater threat than the dominant state in the international system (Walt, 1985, pp. 8–13). Walt's balance of threat theory has received criticism from scholars such as Vasquez (1997), Legro and Moravcsik (1999, pp. 36–8) and Rynning (2011, p. 28) for its focus on non-structural and non-material variables. These criticisms are in part justified, as the emphasis of Walt's balance of threat approach on the importance of perceptions creates a focus on the impact of cognitive variables which sits uncomfortably with Neorealist theory.

However, this does not invalidate Walt's focus on the importance of variables such as the impact of variance in the aggressive intentions of the unipolar leader to different parts of the globe. While not explicitly acknowledged in Walt's work, Walt's framework also provides us with an opportunity to accommodate variance in states' external resource dependencies – which have a very important impact on economic and relative power – within Neorealist theory. In so doing, Walt's balance of threat approach creates an important supplement to balance of power theory. For some states such as Iran or Russia, the offensive capabilities, strategic interests and consequent aggressive intentions of the US incentivise internal and external balancing against it. For other states, the US is an ally against other more immediately threatening local challenges. As a consequence, it is bandwagoning that dovetails most closely with the way that European states are responding to the unipolar international system.

Yet bandwagoning does not sit very comfortably with Walt's balance of threat theory. Waltz views bandwagoning simply as joining the strongest state in the international system, yet Walt (1985) sees it as giving in to threat and a form of appeasement that draws the attention of the most threatening state away from its allies. Bandwagoning can, however, be incentivised by the opportunity to profit as well as the desire to protect oneself from threat. As Schweller (1994, p. 83) notes: 'Walt identifies this motive but then overlooks it because the logic of his theory forces him to conflate the various forms of bandwagoning into one category: giving in to threat'.

However, as Schweller (1997, p. 928) goes on to highlight: 'It [bandwagoning] is no longer the opposite of balancing (i.e. siding with the actor who poses the greatest threat or has the most power), but simply any attempt to side with the stronger, especially for opportunistic gain'. Indeed, European states share a number of common security concerns with the US where cooperation can lead to common gains. Such security challenges include failed states, the proliferation of nuclear, biological and chemical weapons, international terrorism and managing the rise of powers such as Brazil, China, India and, in particular, Russia (Rees, 2011, pp. 6–11). Other threats including environmental security, demographic change and migration, global pandemics, international crime and cyberterrorism/warfare have also increased in salience over the post-Cold War era and form areas where US–EU collaboration can also be beneficial. This is not to say that the EU and US see eye to eye on these challenges. Significant contestation exists about their priority and how they should be tackled (Rees, 2011). The US has, for example, adopted a more coercive, militarised and, at times, unilateral approach to many of the above issues than Europe. One area of notable disagreement is the US policy of targeted assassinations and the kidnapping of suspected terrorists, notably in Pakistan, Somalia, Sudan and Yemen (Aaronson *et al.*, 2014). These activities have received a high level of criticism from European states such as France and Germany, which profess to prefer a broader holistic approach that tackles the root causes of terrorism and failed states. However, the overall picture of EU–US relations on key security issues is one of cooperation, rather than contestation.

Hence European states are sensitive, not so much to relative gains vis-à-vis the US, but to more imminently threatening states and challenges within their geopolitical neighbourhood. Bandwagoning offers the opportunity to profit and share in the spoils of victory against such immediate common opponents, outweighing the risk of exacerbating the power of the dominant state. European states are allied to the US to maximise their power, influence and security (Hyde-Price, 2007, p. 50). This process of bandwagoning on the US is, of course, not a new phenomenon. European states bandwagoned heavily on the US during the

Cold War to meet the challenge posed by Communism. CSDP represents the 'reform' of this process of Cold War bandwagoning. On the one hand, CSDP permits European states to gain greater influence over the US by developing capabilities which will also be of use to NATO, while on the other hand CSDP is simultaneously creating instruments which will allow European states to go it alone in the event that the US is unable or unwilling to assist.

However, as highlighted in the introduction, European states remain divided, not only in terms of the gravity of key security challenges, but also in relation to the role that the US should play in European defence. As a consequence, European states vary in their willingness to use the EU as a means to respond to security challenges within Europe's geopolitical neighbourhood. The following section explores the systemic-level variables which foster this differentiation.

Systemic factors and differentiation in European defence: variance in energy supply security

This variation is rooted, first of all, in divergence in the balance of threat. While the relatively similar geographical position of European states leads to a measure of convergence around common security challenges and reformed bandwagoning, European states are also characterised by differentiation in key policy areas which are central for the generation of economic, and therefore relative, power. One such area is the security of energy supplies.

The energy supply security of the West European Great Powers varies dramatically, with important implications for CSDP. Since the early 2000s Britain, France and Germany have been preparing for a significant reduction in supplies of North Sea Oil and Gas. Although the international oil market sets the oil price, states have the freedom to select their preferred trading partners to secure their supply (Clayton and Levi, 2012). Germany has looked toward Russia and Soviet successor states as suppliers of oil and gas, importing 39 per cent of its oil and 36 per cent of its gas from Russia (Fuchs, 2014). Germany's focus on this 'strategic ellipse' stretching from the Caucasus to the Arabian Peninsula was elucidated in a document published by the Defence Ministry's think-tank, the Bundeswehr Transformation Centre, examining the security policy implications of Germany's energy dependencies (Peak Oil, 2010, pp. 65–72). Originally classified and intended for internal use only, the document was leaked to the press following its release (Interview 1). The study is candid in its assessment of the implications of Germany's increasing dependence on Russia for oil and gas, which appears especially prescient given recent events in Crimea:

> Given Russia's significance for German and Europe's supply security, maintaining reliable relations with Moscow is a central task for German and European politics.... Unless mutual and thus stable dependencies can be formed, the danger of political exploitation by focusing on a few main suppliers and Russia in particular will fundamentally increase.
>
> (Peak Oil, 2010, pp. 68–9)

Britain, on the other hand, is dependent on Russia for only 7 per cent of its oil supply and around 8 per cent of its gas supply (EIA, 2014; Clingendael, 2014). The UK is looking to shale gas as a means to ensure that it can avoid gas dependency on Russia in the context of falling North Sea gas production (Vincent, 2014). While France imports 15.6 per cent of its gas from Russia, the urgency of decline in North Sea gas is less acute for France whose electricity production is dependent largely upon nuclear power (Chazan and Crooks, 2014; EIA, 2014a).

However, both the UK and France have looked, among other states, to Libya – which has around 3.6 per cent of remaining global oil supplies – as a supplier that will be capable of replacing their dependence on North Sea oil over the medium term (Macalister, 2009; Borger and Macalister, 2011 Goetz, 2007, p. 18). This willingness to attain secure oil supplies fostered a very powerful incentive to assist in the overthrow of the regime of Colonel Gaddafi at the point that Libya seemed to descending into a drawn-out conflict. Unfortunately, due to their reticence to deploy ground troops, the UK, France and the US have not undertaken sufficient measures to secure the post-war settlement, leading to the state of chaos that is plaguing Libya. However, despite these shortcomings, the incentive for British and French intervention lay in their desire to stabilise a country that could be a reliable supplier of oil. As the *Financial Times* notes of the current crisis in Libya: 'Whatever happens now, the west should not ignore Libya. It ought once again to become a leading oil supplier to the west, something essential given the growing uncertainty over the reliability of Russia as a source' (FT, 2014).

While the UK and France had a clear material incentive for intervention in 2011, these incentives were not as pronounced for Germany, which had more to lose than to gain from participating in NATO's Operation Unified Protector. Germany's burden-sharing within NATO and willingness to contribute to US military adventures in the post-Cold War era has been much weaker than that, for example, of the UK. Since the end of the Second World War – and particularly the Suez crisis – the UK has been critically aware of the need for close coordination with the US to attain influence in strategically important areas of the globe, such as the Middle East, which between 1950 and 1980 supplied the UK with between 59 and 81 per cent of its oil (UK Oil Imports, 2007, p. 27). The UK has also become heavily reliant on the US for technology transfer, particularly in relation to its nuclear programme (Trident). These, largely systemic, dynamics fostered a heavy Atlanticism in UK defence and security policy.

Germany, on the other hand, has been less reliant on the US, incentivising slightly looser bandwagoning on US power. The balance of threat creates a strong imperative for Germany to be a reliable alliance partner to the US in order to ensure its commitment to its territorial integrity and to stabilise the European balance of power; a dependency that is particularly pronounced for Germany given its status as a non-nuclear power. However, the Federal Republic is aware that the US has a strong level of self-interest in guaranteeing European security and that committing valuable resources to US military operations will have little impact on US policy towards its article 5 commitment to the collective defence of NATO. As a consequence, Germany has been less willing to commit valuable resources to defence and is able to under 'burden-share' within NATO. If Germany had strong material interests in Libya, those would have provided a stronger incentive for action. As an official in the German Foreign Office noted: 'the lack of material interests in North Africa made it much easier for [foreign minister] Westerwelle to adopt an anti-war position' (Interview 2). Hence, although Constructivist scholars point to the role of Germany's culturally embedded resistance to using force as a tool of foreign policy as a core variable in Germany's non-participation in Operation Unified Protector, Germany's patterns of energy dependency were also very important (Brockmeier, 2013, pp. 63–90; Miskimmon, 2012, p. 395).

Germany's dependence on Russian oil and gas also has an impact on other foreign and security policy issues, incentivising, for example, Germany's more restrained approach to sanctions against Russia in the Ukraine–Russia crisis than that of Britain, France and the US (Waterfield and Freeman, 2014; Interview 5). The willingness of Russia to shut off gas and oil supplies to its major European consumers would be strongly circumscribed by the fact that oil and gas exports form 41 per cent of Russian GDP (Forbes, 2014).[2] Furthermore, Germany would be able to source oil elsewhere on the international oil markets. Nevertheless, the short- to medium-term impact on the German economy of cuts in Russian supplies would be very significant. Evidence of the potentially serious impact of cuts in Russian oil to Germany is provided by the closure of the Druzhba pipeline in January 2007 during a price dispute with Belarus. The pipeline supplies around 20 per cent of German oil, and the shortfalls could not be met through tanker deliveries (*Der Spiegel*, 2014). The negative repercussions of a loss of Russian gas for the German economy would be even more serious. Germany could diversify its supply by importing Liquefied Natural Gas (LNG); however, this come at a very high price – around twice the cost of Russian gas (Fuchs, 2014). Hence as Germany's Vice-Chancellor and Economics Minister Sigmar Gabriel recently noted, Germany has little alternative to Russian gas supplies over the medium to long term (Fuchs, 2014; Interview 5).

In summary, while common security challenges have led to a measure of convergence around a process of reformed bandwagoning on US power, this convergence is only partial. As this section has demonstrated, variance in the balance of threat has circumscribed the capacity of the West European Great Powers to undertake coordinated action in foreign and security policy. Walt (1985, pp. 8–14) argues that variables such as geographical proximity, offensive capabilities and aggressive intentions are key drivers of differentiation in threat assessment. However, energy supply security – which has important implications for the relative power of a state – also plays a vital role. This differentiation in energy supply security has sharpened the alliance security dilemma in CSDP by enhancing the fear, in particular of abandonment by alliance partners, who may not be willing to commit troops and military capabilities to EU operations (Snyder, 1984, p. 466). As a consequence, pooling and sharing within CSDP is limited in its scope and depth. Instead bilateral cooperation has flourished between individual nations with more convergent energy supply security interests, such as the UK and France, who instigated far-reaching defence collaboration at the 2010 Lancaster House Treaties and 2014 Brize Norton Summit. Although bilateral efforts to enhance Europe's military cooperation are a positive step toward greater efficiency in defence spending, more far-reaching multilateral cooperation is necessary to stem Europe's military decline in the context of austerity and the 'Asia Pivot' in US foreign and security policy (Biscop, 2012).

The utility of Neoclassical Realism: domestic-level variables and CSDP

As the last section has established, differentiation in systemic-level variables plays a vital role in limiting the level of convergence of European states around the process of reformed bandwagoning on US power. However, a range of domestic-level variables also plays an important role in reducing the capacity of European states to strengthen CSDP. Neorealists recognise that, although systemic variables play the independent role in driving defence and security policy outcomes, a complete explanation cannot ignore the intervening role of unit-level factors, making Neoclassical Realism a 'logical and necessary extension of structural realism' (Rathbun, 2008). As Rathbun (2008, p. 296) notes, 'Neoclassical Realism explains why states cannot properly adapt to systemic constraints and points out the serious consequences that result'.

Neorealist thought posits that cognitive variables such as culture, nationalism and ideology are resources for policy makers, who are able to deploy them to assist in conforming to the imperative of the dictates of the international system (Posen, 1993, p. 81). However, the empirical evidence from contemporary European defence would appear to contradict this assertion and, at face value, confirm the arguments of Constructivists about the central role played by national strategic cultures in driving defence policy outcomes (see Chapter 5). In the UK, an ideologically embedded commitment to Atlanticism underpins British defence policy, while France remains committed to a (albeit hollowed-out) form of Gaullism (Dunne, 2004; Watanabe, 2013). Germany's societally and institutionally embedded reticence to use force as a tool of foreign policy is viewed by many commentators as an important variable in reducing its willingness to develop CSDP as a tool capable of deploying higher-intensity force within Europe's geopolitical neighbourhood (Berenskoetter and Giegerich, 2010; Brockmeier, 2013; Miskimmon, 2012).

However, while the national 'strategic cultures' of the West European Great Powers retain some traction in guiding defence and security policy, the ideological frameworks underpinning British, French and German defence policy have undergone significant change in the light of the imperatives of the international security environment, signalling that systemic imperatives are leading to domestic change. For example, although Britain is highly sceptical of measures which may weaken the role of the US in European security, it has been at the heart of key measures to strengthen the CSDP, including the 1998 St. Malo Declaration that initiated the CSDP and the 2004 Battlegroups Concept (Biscop, 2012, p. 1302).

The UK's Atlanticism was born during the early years of the Cold War and the decline of the British Empire. This was a context that provided a powerful incentive for close cooperation with the US in defence and security policy in order to maintain influence in areas of the globe, such as the Middle East, which were essential for British interests. The UK was also able to gain privileged access to technology transfer in conventional and nuclear weapons systems (Keylor, 2006, p. 306). These imperatives necessitated the creation of an ideological framework that could legitimate to the UK general public the high-level of British dependence upon the US. Nevertheless, following NATO's 1999 Operation Allied Force, the need to prepare for US disengagement from European security became increasingly apparent to the UK and as a consequence it has begun to move inexorably to a stronger level of Europeanisation in its defence and security policies (Dover, 2007). However, the approach of the UK Conservative–Liberal Democrat coalition government that came into office in 2010 appears to contradict this logic of convergence with systemic imperatives. The UK has been a difficult partner within CSDP under the Conservative–Liberal Democrat coalition and has failed to take advantage of the opportunities provided by the EDA to bolster the EDTIB and launch multinational pooling and sharing initiatives (O'Donnell, 2011).

While Liberal and Constructivist analyses emphasise the important role played by domestic political culture, the recent reticence of the UK to engage with the CSDP cannot simply be reduced to the strength of Atlanticist ideology within the Conservative Party (Pohl, 2013). It is also a product of the low level of autonomy enjoyed by the core executive to make radical changes to the ideological frameworks underpinning UK defence. The large parliamentary majorities that are usually delivered by the UK's unitary political system offers the governing party a significant time frame within which to make radical change to defence policy – be it to push through politically unpopular base closures consequent upon force downsizing, or to make changes to the ideological frameworks of defence policy (Dyson, 2008, pp. 765–71). However, under the 2010–15 conservative/liberal-democrat coalition government, the Conservative Party – which held both the Defence Ministry and the Foreign Office – was acutely sensitive to the Eurosceptics on its backbenches, as well as the potential electoral challenge posed by the UK Independence Party. As a consequence, Prime Minister David Cameron was wary of any initiatives which might expose him to criticism of displaying pro-European sympathies, thereby curtailing British involvement in the CSDP.

Low executive autonomy is also an important factor in the persistence of Germany's 'culture of restraint', which has undermined its willingness to participate in operations at the higher end of the conflict spectrum and has slowed the overall pace of German military reform. The German federal political system is characterised by frequent regional elections, which have important implications for the ability of the Federal Government to deliver on their political agenda. As a consequence, German Defence Ministers – particularly those with the ambition of attaining higher office – have been highly reticent to tread on the toes of powerful political figures within their political party by proposing far-reaching base closures (Dyson, 2010, pp. 163–97). These restrictions of low executive autonomy also enhance the political risk associated with bold leadership to redefine the ideological frameworks of German defence and security policy, incentivising a 'salami-slicing' approach to change to Germany's 'culture of restraint'. It must, however, also be acknowledged that the culture of restraint provides an important means with which to excuse Germany's 'under burden-sharing' within CSDP and the Atlantic Alliance to its alliance partners. For example, the constraints of German public opinion were used effectively by Chancellor Merkel as a means of legitimising to alliance partners Germany's non-participation in NATO's Operation Unified Protector in 2011 (Interview 1; Interview 2).

Where radical change has taken place to the ideological frameworks underpinning European defence, it has been under circumstances of high executive autonomy. This was the case, for example, in France in 2009, where Sarkozy enjoyed a long window of opportunity until the next Presidential election and was able to undertake bold policy leadership in favour of radical change to French defence policy by reintegrating France into NATO's command structures. France's heavy dependence on African minerals, which were vital to its economy and defence, incentivised its attempt to hold onto its colonial possessions in Africa during the early to mid-Cold War and station pre-positioned forces on the African continent (Dyson, 2013a, pp. 428–30; Martin, 1989, p. 625). These divergent interests drew France into a high level of contestation with the US, which was opposed to overt imperialism, and contributed to France's withdrawal from NATO's integrated command structures under President Charles de Gaulle in 1966 (Utley, 2002, p. 30). Hence, while France remained committed to the defence of Europe through the Ailleret–Lemnitzer Accord of 1967 in the event of Soviet attack, it bandwagoned much more loosely on the US security guarantee than the rest of Western Europe and carved out a significant freedom of manoeuvre within NATO.

Gaullist ideology was used to provide an ideological framework that legitimised a French alliance policy that emphasised the importance of French 'grandeur' and 'rank' on the global stage, a scepticism of the Anglo-Saxon security guarantee and national strategic autonomy (Gordon, 1992). However, post-cold war security challenges have incentivised a stronger level of coordination with the US through NATO. As a consequence, in 2007 President Sarkozy proposed the reintegration of France into NATO's command structures. This policy shift was framed within a 'hollowed out' form of Gaullism that prioritised the maintenance of French influence at a global level at the expense of other features of Gaullism such as national strategic autonomy and suspicion of US-dominated security arrangements (Dyson, 2010, pp. 159–63).

A second important intervening variable determining the willingness of European states to pool and share military capabilities is the negative implications for national defence industries. While the alliance security dilemma creates an incentive for states to maintain a strong national defence technological and industrial base (DTIB), the fear of job losses and the negative political ramifications of greater efficiency in defence procurement also plays an important role. For example, Germany's ability to take advantage of the EDA is circumscribed by its powerful armaments industry that is fearful of the loss of revenue that would be consequent upon greater competition over the Europe-wide tendering of contracts and the consolidation of the EDTIB. The capacity of the federal government to override these domestic interests is compounded by the German federal political system that magnifies the influence of the armaments industry. Hence attempts by the German Defence Ministry to route procurement projects through the EDA have often been blocked by the Bundestag's Budgetary Committee (Interview 3). The Budgetary Committee has the responsibility to approve procurement programmes over €25 million and contains highly influential members from Bavaria and Germany's north coast who act in the interests of the German defence industry (Interview 3). The fear of job losses also underpinned the opposition of Chancellor Merkel to the BAE/EADS merger in 2012. She was worried about the uncertainties that the lack of German influence within the new company's proposed corporate governance structure would bring for the 50,000 employees of EADS in Germany (Milmo *et al.*, 2012).

Neoclassical Realism posits that the influence of domestic variables on defence and security policy decision-making is, in most cases, of an intervening nature and should ultimately give way to the imperatives of the international security environment. Hence we should expect that, as the urgency of European military autonomy becomes more apparent, European states will focus on establishing greater defence cooperation with their European partners, albeit within the constraints of the alliance security dilemma and the variance in interests wrought by differentiation in the balance of threat. However, it is not a foregone conclusion that states will converge with the imperatives of the international security environment. As Rathbun (2008) notes, history is replete with examples of states that have chosen to ignore the imperatives of the international system and have allowed domestic imperatives such as culture, nationalism, ideology or vested interests to dictate foreign, defence and security policy.

The empirical and theoretical future of CSDP – digging deeper and broadening out

This chapter has attempted to provide an account of the role and nature of systemic and domestic level variables in CSDP. It has argued that the empirical dynamics of CSDP dovetail well with the insights of Stephen Walt's balance of threat theory. Walt's theory highlights the key factors driving European isomorphism around a process of reformed bandwagoning on US power. However, it also provides a framework that accommodates the important role of energy supply security in fostering centrifugal effects in CSDP by sharpening the intensity of the alliance security dilemma. At the same time, the chapter has attempted to account for the role played by domestic-level variables in CSDP. It has demonstrated, in particular, the impact of the path dependency of culture, ideology and nationalism. While these ideas – of Atlanticism, Gaullism and anti-militarism – emerged as resources in the hands of policy makers during the Cold War, they have, over time, become a constraint in the light of contemporary systemic imperatives and have played an important role in slowing the pace at which European states have been able to converge around reformed bandwagoning.

As noted above, Neoclassical Realism posits that such domestic level variables are intervening. However, there is also the possibility that they may, on rare occasions, have a longer-term effect on defence and security policy. Neoclassical Realists would, however, expect a state to suffer a loss of relative power as a result of following the dictates of culture, ideology and nationalism (Rathbun, 2008). Such 'system punishment' may soon be the fate that awaits the West European Great Powers if they are unable to stem Europe's demilitarisation through pooling and sharing initiatives (Witney, 2011, p. 7). Patterns of executive autonomy will be central in determining the extent to which policy makers are able to overcome the path dependency of culture, nationalism and ideology.

Whether the UK core executive is able to liberate itself from the shackles of low executive autonomy and resume its leadership role in the CSDP is likely to have a determining impact on the future of the CSDP. The Conservative Party was re-elected with a majority of 12 seats in the May 2015 general election. However, this relatively narrow majority will continue to make Prime Minister Cameron sensitive to the large number of Eurosceptic backbenchers in the Party. Britain's difficult relationship with the CSDP is likely to persist until after the planned 2017 in/out referendum on EU membership. Should this referendum deliver a solid majority in favour of staying in the EU, a window of opportunity for decisive British leadership on the CSDP may emerge. This leadership would find support in France and, crucially, would also attract support within Germany, not least given the recent advocacy of the German Social Democratic Party on behalf of strengthening the CSDP (Interview 4). Furthermore, there are encouraging signs that systemic pressures are beginning to lead to changes which will ameliorate the persistent low executive autonomy suffered by the German core executive in defence policy. Merkel's Christian Democratic Party recently initiated an examination, through an expert Commission led by former Defence Minister Volker Ruehe, of how to enhance the formal powers of the core executive in defence by altering the role of Parliament in providing mandates for Bundeswehr deployment under the CSDP (RP, 2014). This will have the effect of insulating defence and security policy from public opinion and will enhance the confidence of Germany's alliance partners in the reliability of its burden-sharing.

This chapter also has implications for future theoretical work on the CSDP. Recent scholarship has attempted to reconcile the role of material and ideational variables in the CSDP. As Meyer and Strickmann (2011) have noted, Neoclassical Realism provides a framework for dialogue between modernist Constructivism and Realist thought. It is an arena where a more precise understanding of the inter-play between structure and agency in defence policy can be developed. For example, one area in need of further scholarship is the impact of policy leadership on the reorientation of national strategy. As argued above, executive autonomy and path dependency play a role in hindering states from convergence with systemic imperatives; however, as Byman and Pollack note, the agency of key individuals is also vital:

> Just because a particular event occurred does not mean it was fated to do so. Scholars often fail to acknowledge that common international behaviour – balancing against a threat, choosing a grand strategy, or marching off to war – results from decisions made by individuals.
>
> (2001, p. 145)

The capacity of figures within the core executive to overcome domestic struc-tural constraints such as executive autonomy is, to a great extent, dependent on personal leadership traits and skills (Dyson, 2007). Further in-depth scholarship on different forms of policy leadership and 'discursive' or 'normative' entrepre-neurship in various European countries would add greater substance to our understanding of the transmission belt through which systemic pressures are translated into policy response.

At the same time, theoretical debates on sources of defence cooperation would benefit from broader scholarship that helps test the utility of theoretical frameworks like Neoclassical Realism in other regional contexts. Over the post-Cold War period, defence cooperation has become increasingly institutionalised across a number of regions and sub-regions, including South America (UNASUR), West Africa (ECOWAS), Africa (the AU) and Asia (ASEAN). While there has been some comparative work analysing the broader security activities of such regional and sub-regional organisations (Kirchner and Dominguez, 2011; Tavares, 2009), their emerging defence components remain under-examined and would provide an increasingly fertile testing ground, not only for Neoclassical Realism, but also for a number of other theoretical models used to conceptualise the CSDP.

Notes

1 On the implications of unipolarity for conflict and cooperation in the international system, see, for example, Waltz, (1997, p. 915) and Wohlforth (1999).
2 Russia is, however, attempting to reduce the dependence of its economy on the Euro-pean energy market. For example, in May 2014 Russia signed a $400 billion gas supply deal with China to export up to thirty-eight billion cubic metres of gas to China over a thirty year period, starting in 2018. Over time, Russian gas exports to Asia are expected to rise to around 130 billion cubic metres per year, equalling exports to Europe (Hornby *et al.*, 2014).

References

Aaronson, M., Aslam, W., Dyson, T. and Rauxloh, R. (eds) (2014) *Precision-strike Warfare and International Intervention: Strategic, Ethico-legal and Decisional Implications*. Abingdon, UK: Routledge.

Art, R. (2004) Europe Hedges its Security Bets. In Paul, T. V. (ed.) *Balance of Power: Theory and Practice in the 21st Century*. Stanford, CA: Stanford University Press, pp. 179–204.

Berenskoetter, F. and Giegerich, B. (2010) From NATO to ESDP: A Social Constructivist Anlaysis of German Strategic Adjustment after the end of the Cold War. *Security Studies*. 19 (3). pp. 407–52.

Biava, A., Drent, M. and Herd, G. (2011) Characterising the EU's Strategic Culture: An Analytical Framework. *Journal of Common Market Studies*. 49 (6). pp. 1227–48.

Biscop, S. (2013) Pool It, Share It, Use It: The European Council on Defence. *Egmont, Royal Institute for International Affairs, Security Policy Brief*, 44, March 2013.

Biscop, S. (2012) The UK and European Defence: Leaving or Leading? *International Affairs*. 88 (6). pp. 1297–313.

Borger, J. and Macalister, T. (2011) The Race is On For Libya's Oil with Britain and France Both Staking a Claim. *The Guardian* [Online] 1 September 2011. Available from: www.theguardian.com/world/2011/sep/01/libya-oil [accessed: 23 October 2013].

Briani, V. (2013) Armaments Duplication in Europe: A Quantitative Assessment. *CEPS Policy Brief*, No. 297, 16 July 2013. Available from: www.ceps.eu/book/armaments-duplication-europe-quantitative-assessment [accessed: 21 May 2014].

Brockmeier, S. (2013) Germany and the Intervention in Libya. *Survival*. 55 (6). pp. 63–90.

Byman, D. and Pollack, K. (2001) Now Let Us Praise Great Men: Bringing the Statesman Back In. *International Security*. 25 (4). pp. 107–46.

Caruso, R. and Locatelli, A. (2013) Company Survey Series II: Finmeccanica amid International Market and State Control: A Survey of Italian Defence Industry. *Defence and Peace Economics*. 24 (1). pp. 89–104.

Chazan, G. and Crooks, E. (2014) Europe's Dangerous Addition to Russian Gas Needs Radical Cure. *Financial Times* [Online] 3 April 2014. Available from: www.ft.com/intl/cms/s/0/dacfda08-ba64-11e3-8b15-00144feabdc0.html#slide0 [accessed: 8 September 2014].

Cladi, L. and Locatelli, A. (2013) Worth a Shot: On the Explanatory Power of Bandwagoning in Transatlantic Relations, *Contemporary Security Policy*. 34 (2). pp. 374–81.

Clayton, B. and Levi, M. (2012) The Surprising Sources of Oil's Influence. *Survival*. 54 (6). pp. 107–22.

Clingendael (2014) Fact Sheet: Russia Imports to Europe and Security of Supply. Clingendael International Energy Programme.

Dover, R. (2007) *The Europeanisation of British Defence Policy 1997–2005*. Aldershot, UK: Ashgate.

Dunne, T. (2004) When the Shooting Starts: Atlanticism in British Security Strategy. *International Affairs*. 50 (1). pp. 893–909.

Dyson, T. (2013a) The Material Roots of European Strategy: Beyond Culture and Values. *Contemporary Security Policy*. 34 (3). pp. 419–45.

Dyson, T. (2013) Balancing Threat, Not Capabilities: European Defence Cooperation as Reformed Bandwagoning. *Contemporary Security Policy*. 34 (2). pp. 387–91.

Dyson, T. (2010a) Defence Policy: Spatial and Temporal Differentiation within Reformed Bandwagoning. In Dyson, K. and Sepos, A. (eds) *Whose Europe? The Politics of Differentiated Integration* (Basingstoke, UK: Palgrave), pp. 322–43.

Dyson, T. (2010) *Neoclassical Realism and Defence Reform in post-Cold War Europe.* Basingstoke, UK: Palgrave Macmillan.

Dyson, T. (2008) Between International Structure and Executive Autonomy: Convergence and Divergence in British, French and German Military Reforms. *Security Studies.* 17 (4). pp. 725–74.

Dyson, T. (2007) *The Politics of German Defence and Security: Policy Leadership and Military Reform in the post-Cold War Era.* New York: Berghahn.

The Economist (2014), China's Military Spending: At the Double, 15 March 2014. Available from: www.economist.com/news/china/21599046-chinas-fast-growing-defence-budget-worries-its-neighbours-not-every-trend-its-favour [accessed: 21 May 2014].

EIA (2014) *UK Country Report 2014.* US Energy Information Administration. Available from: www.eia.gov/countries/analysisbriefs/United_Kingdom/uk.pdf [accessed: 08 September 2014].

EIA (2014a) *Country Overview, France.* US Energy Information Administration. Available from: www.eia.gov/countries/country-data.cfm?fips=fr [accessed: 08 September 2014].

Engberg, K. (2013) Ten Years of EU Military Operations. *European Institute for Security Studies Brief Issue.* No. 41. Available from: www.iss.europa.eu/uploads/media/Brief_41_EU_military_operations.pdf [accessed: 21 May 2014].

Forbes (2014) *It's Time to Drive Russia Bankrupt – Again*, 30 March 2014. Available from: www.forbes.com/sites/louiswoodhill/2014/03/03/its-time-to-drive-russia-bankrupt-again/ [accessed: 20 May 2014].

FT (2014) The Deepening Chaos in Libya: Tripoli Remains a Battlefield Years after Gaddafi's Fall. *Financial Times* 20 May 2014. p. 10.

Fuchs, R. (2014) Germany's Russian Energy Dilemma. *Deutsche Welle.* 29 March 2014. Available from: www.dw.de/germanys-russian-energy-dilemma/a-17529685 [accessed: 20 May 2014].

Goetz, R. (2007) Germany and Russia: Strategic Partners? *Geopolitical Affairs.* No. 4.

Gordon, P. (1992) *A Certain Idea of France.* Princeton, NJ: Princeton University Press.

Hornby, L., Anderlini, J. and Chazan, G. (2014) China and Russia Sign $400 bn Gas Deal, *Financial Times* [online] 21 May 2014. Available from: www.ft.com/cms/s/0/d9a8b800-e09a-11e3-9534-00144feabdc0.html#axzz32SFiQKhE [accessed: 22 May 2014].

Hyde-Price, A. (2007) *European Security in the 21st Century: The Challenge of Multipolarity.* Abingdon, UK: Routledge.

Ikenberry, J. (2001) *After Victory: Institutions, Strategic Restraint and the Rebuilding of Order after Major Wars.* Princeton, NJ: Princeton University Press.

Interview 1, Interview, Division for Foreign, Security and Development Policy, Chancellor's Office, Berlin, 1 August 2012.

Interview 2, Interview, Defence and Security Policy Division, German Foreign Office, Berlin, 9 March 2012.

Interview 3, Interview, Division for International Armaments, Political Department, German Defence Ministry, Berlin, 29 May 2013.

Interview 4, Interview, Herr Rainer Arnold, MdB, SPD, Defence Policy Spokesperson, Bundestagsfraktion, 3 July 2013.

Interview 5, Interview, Section A2, Cooperation in the IEA and Bilateral Energy Cooperation with non-OCED States, Ministry for Economic Affairs and Energy, Berlin, 13 August 2014.

Keylor, W. (2006) *The 20th Century World and Beyond.* Oxford: Oxford University Press.

Kirchner, E. and Dominguez, R. (eds) (2011) *The Security Governance of Regional Organisations.* Abingdon, UK: Routledge.

Koops, J. (2010) Unstrategic Partners: NATO's Relationship with the European Union. In Kremp, W. and Meyer B. (eds) *Entangling Alliance: 60 Jahre NATO – Geschichte – Gegenwart – Zukunft.* Trier: Wissenschaftsverlag, pp. 41–77.

Layne, C. (2006) The Unipolar Illusion Revisited: The Coming End of the United States' Unipolar Moment. *International Security.* 31 (2). pp. 7–41.

Legro, J. and Moravcsik, A. (1999) Is Anybody Still a Realist? *International Security.* 42 (2). pp. 5–55.

Lobell, S., Ripsman, N. and Taliaferro, J. (eds) (2009) *Neoclassical Realism, The State and Foreign Policy.* Cambridge: Cambridge University Press.

Macalister, T. (2009) Secret Documents Uncover UK's Interest in Libyan Oil. *Guardian* [online] 30 August 2009. Available from: www.guardian.co.uk/world/2009/aug/30/libya-oil-shell-megrahi [accessed: 23 August 2013].

Martin, G. (1989) Uranium: A Case Study in Franco-African Relations. *The Journal of Modern African Studies.* 27 (4). pp. 625–40.

Matlary, J. H. (2009) *European Union Security Dynamics: In the New National Interest.* Basingstoke, UK: Palgrave.

Menon, A. (2011) Power, Institutions and the CSDP: The Promise of Institutionalist Theory. *Journal of Common Market Studies.* 49 (1). pp. 83–100.

Mearsheimer, J. (2001) *The Tragedy of Great Power Politics.* New York: Norton.

Meyer, C. (2005) Convergence towards a European Strategic Culture. *European Journal of International Relations.* 11 (4). pp. 523–49.

Meyer, C. and Strickmann, E. (2011) Solidifying Constructivism: How Material and Ideational Factors Interact in European Defence. *Journal of Common Market Studies.* 49 (1). pp. 61–81.

Milmo, D., Connelly, K. and Willshire, K. (2012) Angela Merkel Blocks BAE/EADS Merger over Small German Share. *Guardian* [online] 10 October 2012. Available from: www.theguardian.com/business/2012/oct/10/angela-merkel-bae-eads-merger-german [accessed: 21 May 2014].

Miskimmon, A. (2012) German Foreign Policy and the Libya Crisis. *German Politics.* 21 (4). pp. 392–410.

O'Donnell, C. M. (2011) Britain's Coalition Agreement and EU Defence Cooperation: Undermining British Interests. *International Affairs.* 87 (2). pp. 419–33.

Pape, R. (2005) Soft Balancing Against the United States. *International Security.* 20 (1). pp. 7–45.

Paul, T. V. (2004) The Enduring Axioms of Balance of Power Theory and Their Contemporary Relevance. In Paul, T. V. (ed.) *Balance of Power: Theory and Practice in the 21st Century.* Stanford, CA: Stanford University Press. pp. 1–28.

Peak Oil (2010) Armed Forces, Capabilities and Technologies in the 21st Century. Environmental Dimensions of Security: Sub Study 1: Peak Oil, Security Policy Implications of Scarce Resource. Strausberg: Bundeswehr Transformation Centre.

Perlo-Freeman, S. and Solmirano, C. (2014) Trends in World Military Expenditure 2013. *SIPRI Factsheet,* April 2014. Available from: http://books.sipri.org/files/FS/SIPRIFS1404.pdf [accessed: 21 May 2014].

Pohl, B. (2013) Neither Bandwagoning, Nor Balancing: Explaining Europe's Security Policy. *Contemporary Security Policy.* 34 (2). pp. 353–73.

Posen, B. (2006) The European Security and Defence Policy: Response to Uni-Polarity. *Security Studies.* 15 (2). pp. 149–86.

Posen, B. (1993) Nationalism, The Mass Army and Military Power. *International Security*. 18 (2). pp. 80–124.

Press-Barnathan, G. (2006) Managing the Hegemon: NATO Under Unipolarity. *Security Studies*. 15 (2). pp. 271–309.

Rathbun, B. (2008) A Rose by Any Other Name? Neoclassical Realism as the Logical and Necessary Extension of Structural Realism. *Security Studies*. 17 (2). pp. 294–321.

Rees, W. (2011) *The US–EU Security Relationship: The Tensions between a European and a Global Agenda*. Basingstoke, UK: Palgrave.

RP (2014) Kritik an geplanter Rühe-Kommission zur Parlamentsbeteiligung an Ausland-seinsätzen, *Rheinische Post* [online] 7 March 2014. Available from: www.presseportal. de/pm/30621/2681435/rheinische-post-kritik-an-geplanter-ruehe-kommission-zur-parlamentsbeteiligung-an-auslandseinsaetzen [accessed: 9 April 2014].

Rynning, S. (2011) Realism and the Common European Security and Defence Policy. *Journal of Common Market Studies*. 49 (1). pp. 23–42.

Schweller, R. (2006) Unanswered Threats: A Neoclassical Realist Theory of Underbalancing. *International Security*. 29 (2). pp. 159–201.

Schweller, R. (1997) New Realist Research on Alliances: Refining not Refuting Waltz's Balancing Proposition. *The American Political Science Review*. 91 (4). pp. 927–30.

Schweller, R. (1994) Bandwagoning for Profit: Bringing the Revisionist State Back In. *International Security*. 19 (1). pp. 72–107.

Snyder, G. (1984) The Security Dilemma in Alliance Politics. *World Politics*. 36 (4). pp. 461–95.

Der Spiegel (2014) Energy Wars: Russia Halts Oil Deliveries to Germany, 8 January 2007. Available from: www.spiegel.de/international/energy-wars-russia-halts-oil-deliveries-to-germany-a-458401.html [accessed: 3 March 2014].

Tavares, R. (2009) *Regional Security: The Capacity of Regional Organisations*. Abingdon, UK: Routledge.

UK Oil Imports (2007) *UK Oil Imports since 1920*. UK Department for Business, Innovation and Skills, June 2007.

Utley, R. (2002) Not to do Less…. But to do Better: French Military Policy in Africa. *International Affairs*. 78 (1). pp. 129–46.

Vasquez, J. (1997) The Realist Paradigm and Degenerative Versus Progressive Research Programmes: An Appraisal of Neo-traditional Research on Waltz's Balancing Proposition. *The American Political Science Review*. 91 (4). pp. 904–5.

Vincent, J. (2014) Fossil Fuels: UK to Run Out of Oil, Gas and Oil in Five Years, *Independent* [online] 16 May 2014. Available from: www.independent.co.uk/news/uk/uk-to-run-out-of-fossil-fuels-in-five-years-9385415.html [accessed: 20 May 2014].

Walt, S. (2002) Keeping the World Off-Balance: Self Restraint and US Foreign Policy. In Ikenberry, J. (ed.), *America Unrivalled: The Failure of the Balance of Power*. Ithaca, NY: Cornell University Press. pp. 121–54.

Walt, S. (1985) Alliance Formation and the Balance of Power. *International Security*. 9 (4). pp. 3–43.

Waltz, K. (1997) Evaluating Theories. *American Political Science Review*. 91 (4). pp. 913–17.

Waltz, K. (1979) *Theory of International Politics*. Reading, MA: Addison Wesley.

Watanabe, L. (2013) France's New Strategy: The 2013 White Paper. *CSS Analyses in Security*. No. 139. Zurich: Centre for Security Studies.

Waterfield, B. and Freeman, C. (2014) EU Leaders Divided over New Sanctions to Punish Russia for Annexing Crimea. *Daily Telegraph* [online] 20 March 2014. Available from:

www.telegraph.co.uk/news/worldnews/europe/ukraine/10710268/EU-leaders-divided-over-new-sanctions-to-punish-Russia-for-annexing-Crimea.html [accessed: 20 May 2014].

Witney, N. (2011) How to Stop the Demilitarisation of Europe. *European Council on Foreign Relations Policy Brief.* No. 40. November 2011.

Wivel, A. (2008) Balancing Against Threats or Bandwagoning with Power? *Cambridge Review of International Affairs.* 21 (3). pp. 298–305.

Wohlforth, W. (1999) The Stability of a Unipolar World. *International Security.* 21 (1). pp. 5–41.

3 The emergence and evolution of CSDP

A Liberal approach

Friederike Richter

Introduction

For over fifty years, Europe mainly focussed on the establishment of a common market and, hence, the integration of *low politics*. While the EU thus emerged as a *civilian power* (Duchêne, 1972, 1973), common military ambitions have virtually been absent during this time. This was mainly due to the fact that security and defence have been considered to be the 'ultimate guardian of state sovereignty' (Sjursen, 2011, p. 1092) for quite a long time, which, in turn, made it difficult for Member States to reach agreement on the level and the scope of security and defence cooperation. Most EU integration and IR theories, therefore, came to the conclusion that integrative pressures were rather unlikely, if not even impossible, to occur in *high politics*. While integration theorists thus assumed that the EU would remain a civilian power, the post-Cold War period showed a significant increase in security and defence cooperation, with security going beyond traditional territorial defence. This broadening and deepening of security and defence (Buzan, 1991) suggested that Europe was not merely a civilian power, but had the ambition to project power abroad, thereby contributing to the resolution of reappearing ethnic conflicts and border disputes in its periphery and beyond.

Empirical evidence shows that EU Member States strongly increased their cooperation on security and defence in the 1990s, with the CFSP and the ESDP emerging as the key policies of the EU's external action in 1992 and 1998 respectively (Fraser, 1999; Howorth, 2000; Gnesotto, 2004; Smith, 2004). This militarisation of the EU contributed to the creation of several institutions, agencies and services, including, for example, the PSC, the EDA and the European External Action Service (EEAS), all of which have gained considerable autonomy from the governments of the Member States (Tonra, 2003; Meyer, 2006; Vanhoonacker *et al.*, 2010). This development is not only remarkable for the process of European integration itself (Forsberg, 2010), but also represents an anomaly for most integration theories (Howorth, 2007). For this very reason, it is particularly interesting to analyse why and under which conditions governments decided to launch the ESDP, renamed the CSDP with the coming into effect of the Lisbon Treaty in 2009. This chapter now explains the emergence and evolution of the CSDP through a Liberal lens, contrasting the explanatory power of Liberal IR theory with Realist and Constructivist perspectives on security and defence cooperation at the EU level.

Liberal IR theory has frequently been used to grasp the exceptional features of EU integration in low politics, but was often left out of the debate on the CSDP. Nevertheless, Liberalism may be a powerful tool for explaining both the institutional innovations and the dynamics in security and defence cooperation since the Franco-British summit in St. Malo in 1998. This chapter, therefore, analyses the CSDP through a Liberal lens, and places Liberal IR theory in the debate on EU security and defence cooperation. The aim is not only to comprehend the reasons behind the emergence of the CSDP, but also to understand the twists and turns in its evolution. The first section of this chapter provides a theoretical overview of Liberalism, focussing in particular on Neoliberal Institutionalism (NI), and LI. Although NI and LI work with the same premises, the first stresses the role of institutions while the latter marries NI and Bargaining theory, thus concentrating to a greater extent on domestic politics. Together, they promise to elucidate particularly well why the EU embarked on a project of closer security and defence cooperation. Based on this theoretical framework, section two subsequently explains the reasons behind the emergence of the CSDP, and explicates why cooperation has been ebbing and flowing over time. Finally, the last section of this chapter outlines the limits of Liberal IR theory in accounting for CSDP, contrasting its explanatory power with Realist and Constructivist studies of European security and defence cooperation.

Theoretical framework: Liberalism as an IR theory

Generally speaking, Liberalism has a long tradition, dating back *inter alia* to Immanuel Kant's essay, *Perpetual Peace: A Philosophical Sketch* (1795). Initially guided by the work of Adam Smith, Jeremy Bentham, David Ricardo, and John Stuart Mill, for instance, Liberalism as an IR theory really only emerged in the 1970s, mainly in response to Neorealism with its focus on power and conflict. Instead of concentrating on anarchy and state sovereignty, Liberal IR scholars analysed the growth of transnational processes, the reasons for increased economic interdependence, and, consequently, the incentives for states to cooperate and integrate at the regional level (Kaufman, 2013, p. 53). Since the emergence of Liberalism as an IR theory in the 1970s, there have been many innovations and offshoots of Liberal theory, including, for instance, Interdependence theory, LI, Liberal Internationalism, Liberal peace theory, NI, Pluralism, Transnationalism, and World Society approaches more generally (see, for example, the work of Bruce Russett, Robert Putnam, Peter J. Katzenstein and Michael Doyle).

Although there is no canonical definition of Liberalism that captures the particularities of each of the aforementioned strands of thought, they have certain assumptions and principles in common, and share – at least to a certain extent – a set of economic, philosophical and political ideas. Contrary to the position of

Realists who often argue that 'states want to maintain their sovereignty' (Mearsheimer, 1994/1995, p. 10), Liberal IR scholars generally believe that states may decide to (partly) give up their sovereignty in order to coordinate their policies at the regional and international level. For Liberals, such a decision is rooted in rationality, i.e. states first calculate the outcome of alternative courses of actions – in this case *coordination* versus *no coordination* – and then choose the action that is most likely to maximise the utility for them. There is, consequently, room for choice and progress which, in turn, may lead to collective action, cooperation and, if required, also reform. As Kaufman (2013, p. 42) underlines, 'liberal thinking focuses less on power and more on other components of nation-state relationships, including … the structures that can hold them together'.

Structures holding states together are increasingly indispensable to tackling the complex nature of today's threats and challenges. Climate change, organised crime and international terrorism are only a few examples of security threats and challenges which cannot be addressed at the domestic level alone, and, therefore, create incentives for states to overcome anarchy. Due to these increased levels of interdependence, states are more inclined to coordinate their policies at the regional level, and may even decide to cooperate at the international level, e.g. by adapting institutions to guide and channel their behaviour. In order to better understand why states embark on such projects of closer cooperation, and why this cooperation may then ebb and flow over time, it is crucial to comprehend the different stages – including the role of different actors – in the process of institutionalisation. Shedding light on these issues is necessary for grasping the reasons behind the emergence of the CSDP as well as the twists and turns in its evolution; the next two sub-sections, therefore, deal with NI and LI, and the prominence they give to institutions and domestic politics in international cooperation.

Neoliberal Institutionalism

Debates about the emergence of institutions are often centred on Robert Keohane's seminal work (1984), *After Hegemony: Cooperation and Discord in the World Political Economy*, in which he studied the relationship between states and international non-state actors. Generally speaking, Neoliberal Institutionalists acknowledge the existence of an anarchic society of states in which states act in their own interest, but have a much more optimistic view on cooperation. Indeed, they believe that states may 'adjust their behaviour to the actual or anticipated preferences of others, through a process of policy coordination' (Keohane, 1984, p. 51), if it is in their best interest to do so. Pursuant to NI, this process of policy coordination may subsequently lead to an institutionalised arrangement, containing rules and principles that further promote cooperation between states (Keohane, 1984, p. 66). Institutions can, hence, result from both policy coordination and increased levels of cooperation. They are arbitrary bodies which provide states with information, and potentially also prevent them from cheating on each other. Reaching such an institutionalised arrangement is, however, not always easy, and may lead to tensions and discords between states (Keohane, 1984).

Tensions and discords may, for example, arise when states try to set up an institution. State behaviour is, indeed, not 'a set of discrete, isolated acts', but depends on the 'pattern of cooperation' (Keohane, 1984, p. 56). Duncan Snidal (1985), therefore, argued that institutions may also result from coordination problems. These coordination problems are due to a prisoner's dilemma in which states – although willing to coordinate their policies in order to ease regional cooperation – nonetheless aim for maximising their individual, final pay-offs. Once this dilemma is overcome, institutions offer a platform for states to consult each other and pursue common causes, potentially benefitting all participating states. Since institutions are based on common rules and principles, they are also a rather credible commitment to cooperation. Nevertheless, if states feel that the institution advances policies that are not in line with their national interests, they may refuse to adhere to its rules, thereby weakening the institution. Institutions are, hence, only as powerful as their members allow them to be which, in turn, implies that the strength of any institution may vary over time (Keohane, 1989, p. 2).

From a Neoliberal Institutionalist perspective, the EU is mainly the result of shared economic interests: it is a forum in which Member States share information and negotiate over issue areas in which they aim for reducing transaction costs (Steans *et al.*, 2010). The end of the Cold War, however, significantly transformed the international system and led to new security threats and challenges, which increasingly require collective action, including in fields other than economics (Haugsdal, 2005; Rieker, 2006). Increased levels of interdependence thus significantly contributed to a rising number of agreements and treaties in the 1990s and 2000s, not only in monetary and fiscal policy, but also in foreign, security and defence policy, for instance – a development which Neoliberal Institutionalists did not expect to see. According to Hofmann and Mérand (2012), such integrative pressures are mainly the result of negotiations between the most interdependent states, pushing for agreements and common institutional bodies (Haftendorn *et al.*, 1999). NI may, consequently, shed light on the circumstances that led to the Franco-British summit in St. Malo in 1998 and, hence, the launch of the ESDP.

Liberal Intergovernmentalism

Particular credit for reformulating Liberal IR theory in a non-ideological and non-utopian way must be given to Andrew Moravcsik. His framework of international cooperation – laid out in a series of articles during the 1990s (Moravcsik, 1991, 1993, 1994, 1995, 1998) – marries NI and Bargaining theory to provide a more complex account of institutional formation. LI is 'a set of assumptions that permit us to disaggregate a phenomenon we seek to explain – in this case, successive rounds of international negotiations – into elements each of which can be treated separately' (Moravcsik, 1998, pp. 19–20). In Moravcsik's three-stage framework, states first define their preferences, then bargain to reach a common agreement, and eventually create (or reform) institutions to secure the negotiation result. Each of the three stages relies on a more focussed theory, 'consistent with the assumption of the overall rationalist framework' (Moravcsik, 1998, pp. 19–20). LI thus promises to explain why and under which conditions security and defence cooperation was put on the European agenda, and why some Member States, like Denmark, decided to opt out of this particular integration process.

Stage 1: Liberal theory of national preference formation

During the first stage of LI, the heads of governments aggregate the societal interests of their constituencies, including interests groups and civil society. Combined with the state's economic, political and institutional setting (Pollack, 2012, p. 10), governments then translate these societal interests into national preferences towards European integration (Moravcsik, 1997, pp. 518–20; Moravcsik, 2008, pp. 237–9). Governments thus have a gate-keeping role. While domestic preferences mostly represent coherent national strategies, they are not fixed (Moravcsik, 2003, p. 20). On the contrary, preferences may vary across issue and time, in particular in response to exogenous shocks (Moravcsik, 2003, p. 23). This, in turn, suggests that societal interests and domestic pressures – and, hence, national preferences towards European integration – are closely linked to the EU's economic and political situation.

Stage 2: Intergovernmental theory of bargaining

During the second stage of LI, the heads of governments bring their state's preferences to the intergovernmental bargaining table. Since the interests of Member States do not completely coincide (as each state has its own economic, political and institutional setting), their domestic preferences are likely to be in conflict with each other (Moravcsik and Schimmelfennig, 2009, p. 70). Nevertheless, if mutually beneficial cooperation is in sight, bargaining may lead to the convergence of national interests (Moravcsik, 2003, p. 51). The central negotiations are then conducted by the most powerful Member States so that the final outcome of the bargaining is likely to reflect their relative domestic preferences (Pollack, 2001, p. 226). During this process, supranational organisations have no (or only little) influence on the final outcome.

Stage 3: Theory of institutional choice

Once Member States have reached an agreement on the level and the scope of their cooperation, they create (or reform already existing) institutions as a credible commitment to their negotiation outcome. The institutional choice either takes the form of pooled sovereignty through qualified majority voting (QMV) or delegated responsibility to a supranational actor. The latter is often chosen for policies in which Member States have a high risk of defection from the agreement (Moravcsik, 1998, p. 9). While states thus restrict their control over certain issue areas, they also guarantee durable and sustained cooperation which, in turn, reduces uncertainty about each other's future preferences and behaviour (Moravcsik, 2003, p. 67).

From a liberal institutionalist perspective, EU integration is mainly the result of a 'multi-stage process of constrained social choice' (Moravcsik, 2008, p. 250). LI marries NI with Bargaining theory and therefore promises to have a particularly strong explanatory power for the various stages in security and defence cooperation, unequally unfolding over time. Like NI, LI assumed that the control over security and defence issues was likely to remain at the national level and hence failed to *anticipate* the emergence of the CSDP in the 1990s (Moravcsik and Schimmelfennig, 2009). Nevertheless, this does not mean that LI is inadequate for accounting for the emergence and evolution of security and defence cooperation at the EU level. On the contrary, under LI 'unforeseen or initially undesired policies may change over time' (Moravcsik and Schimmelfennig, 2009, p. 79), especially if shocks – such as the end of the Cold War – change national preferences in favour of further integration. Thus, with its three-stage framework, LI may well account for the various stages in the CSDP.

LI and NI: the role of domestic politics and institutions in European integration

The theoretical framework of this chapter is based on NI and LI, two related Liberal approaches to the study of European integration. Having a rational choice foundation, both strands of thought consider cooperation to be a deliberate state choice and, therefore, suggest that EU Member States control the nature and the pace of the integration process. This assumption is fully in line with the EU's aim to accommodate the preferences of its Member States. Although NI and LI did not expect to see integration happen in the field of high politics, both theories allow a better understanding of the EU's 'institutional elasticity' in security and defence cooperation (Hofmann and Mérand, 2012, p. 134), including, for instance, the deliberate choice Member States have to participate (or not) in CSDP missions and operations. Shedding light on the role of domestic politics and institutions, respectively, LI and NI promise to elucidate particularly well why and under which conditions the EU embarked on a project of closer security and defence cooperation in the late 1990s, and to explicate why this cooperation has been ebbing and flowing over the past fifteen years.

The emergence and evolution of the CSDP: a test case for the Liberal approach

With the end of the Cold War, both the level and the scope of security and defence cooperation strongly increased, leading to the emergence of the CFSP and the ESDP in 1992 and 1998, respectively. Yet, when trying to understand the reasons behind the emergence of the CSDP, it is of great importance to bear in mind that the project of European integration was initially meant to start with defence (Howorth, 2000; Rosato, 2011, 2011a). Indeed, both the Treaty of Dunkirk (1947) and the Treaty of Brussels (1948) aimed for a security and defence community in Europe, but failed in introducing the latter. Member States, subsequently, scaled down their ambitions, and tried to coordinate their foreign policies instead. Several attempts, including the European Defence Community (EDC), the EPC and the Fouchet Plan, fell through in the 1950s and 1960s because Member States did not agree on the level and scope of cooperation (Smith, 2004, p. 1).

Why was this the case? From a Neoliberal Institutionalist perspective, cooperation in security and defence initially failed because it was not yet in the best interest of Member States to reach an institutionalised agreement on high politics. Liberal Institutionalists would support this explanation: from their point of view, Member States were willing to bring national preferences towards European integration in security and defence to the intergovernmental bargaining table, but could not decide on the purpose of the military (territorial defence versus force projection), the instruments to be used (civilian versus military means), and the arena in which cooperation was to take place (EU level only or Atlanticism) (Giegerich, 2006). Take the case of the EDC, for example. In 1950, the then French Prime Minister René Pleven pled for a European army, based on military capabilities from the Benelux countries, France, Germany and Italy. A treaty was signed, but subsequently not ratified by the French national assembly, which feared that the project entailed an unacceptable loss of national sovereignty. The case of the EDC thus suggests that cooperation in high politics was not mutually beneficial and, consequently, not in the best interest of all Member States at this point in time.

The failure of the EDC, the EPC and the Fouchet Plan is thus fully in line with the Liberal assumption of cooperation being a deliberate state choice: it is the Member States of the EU that control the nature and the pace of the European integration process. Liberal IR theory, consequently, accounts for the multiple stages in security and defence cooperation, unequally unfolding over time. These stages not only include the failed attempts of the 1950s and the 1960s, but also the ongoing negotiations on foreign policy coordination which, for instance, gave rise to the EPC in 1970, the Single European Act in 1986, and the Maastricht Treaty in 1992. While these developments are rooted in domestic politics, they can hardly be explained without referring to the international security environment. When trying to understand the emergence and the evolution of the CSDP in the 1990s and the 2000s, respectively, it is, therefore, indispensable to take into account the impact that the end of the Cold War has had on the international system, and, consequently, Member States' preferences towards European integration in security and defence matters.

The end of the Cold War significantly transformed the international system and led to a new international security environment, being characterised inter alia by a certain disengagement of the US from its role of guarantor of EU security, re-emerging ethnic conflicts and border disputes in Europe's neighbour-hood, and new security threats and challenges, including climate change, organised crime and international terrorism. It is precisely in this context of increased interdependence that the upgrade of foreign and security issues on the EU agenda, including the emergence of the CSFP at Maastricht and the ESDP at St. Malo – has to be understood and analysed. Although Liberal IR theory did not expect to see any form of EU cooperation in high politics, both NI and LI may actually account for the new dimension that the Maastricht Treaty added to the project of European integration. NI and LI do not assume only that states are rational, but also believe that there is always room for choice and progress. With increased levels of interdependence in the post-Cold War period, and security threats that states could not address at the domestic level anymore, Liberal IR theory may thus – at least implicitly – account for Member States' national preferences changing in favour of collective action in foreign and security policy.

Although foreign and security policy was strongly upgraded on the EU agenda in the early 1990s, Member States did not manage to reach an institution-alised arrangement, containing – in line with NI – rules and principles to further promote their cooperation. Since EU Member States did not succeed in implementing common rules and principles to guide and channel their behaviour through a formal institution, there was no credible commitment to the CFSP yet. The risk of defection in security and defence cooperation was, consequently, relatively high, especially in light of exponentially rising costs for military equipment and manpower (Hartley and Sandler, 1995), and decreasing levels of defence spending (Forster, 2011). The *peace dividends* of the post-Cold War period suggested inter alia that Member States were not really willing to mobilise resources for defence, either at the domestic or the European level. This may have been because of several reasons, including a perverted picture of the new international security environment, and hence the lack of a strong feeling of interdependence within the EU which, in turn, would have pushed more Member States towards bilateral and multilateral agreements and institutionalised arrangements in security and defence.

Nonetheless, the political and security environment of the post-Cold War period seems to have had a positive impact on Member States' preferences for cooperation in security and defence. In 1998, the Franco-British summit in St. Malo eventually initiated the development of independent military capabilities at the EU level. Accounting for 50 per cent of the military spending, 50 per cent of the purchase of arms, and 60 per cent of the research in security and defence within the EU (EDA data in Foucault, 2012, p. 50), it was mainly France and the UK – the EU's leading military powers – that conducted the negotiations about security and defence cooperation. Despite initial disagreements as to the nature of such a common European policy, the summit laid the groundwork for the ESDP. While the Cologne European Council subsequently set the institutional framework for the ESDP in June 1999, the Helsinki European Council stipulated the EU's defence capabilities in December 1999 (Howorth, 2007). The ESDP became operational in 2001, suggesting that the political and security environment of the post-Cold War period had triggered the convergence of national preferences in favour of security and defence cooperation and had pushed Member States to quickly reach agreements on issues they had been discussing since the very inception of the EU.

In line with Hofmann and Mérand's (2012) analysis of integration in high politics, the CSDP seems to have resulted from the Franco-British summit in St. Malo, with France and the UK pushing for an agreement in security and defence cooperation, and institutional bodies to support the latter. While the French initiative in advancing a European security and defence policy is less surprising (see the attempt of Prime Minister René Pleven to put forward an EDC in the 1950s) (Schmidt, 2012, p. 184), the decision of the usually rather Eurosceptic UK to bring European defence cooperation to the bargaining table was more unexpected. Tony Blair, the gate-keeper of the British government, however, was willing to negotiate on high politics (Simón, 2014), thus taking a decision against the Conservatives, including his predecessor John Major, who had strongly opposed the ESDP in Amsterdam, and his own party (Gegout, 2002). Although Blair's decision to reopen the discussion on security and defence cooperation seems to be incoherent and, consequently, in contrast to Liberal IR theory, opposing in particular Moravcsik's first stage of national preference formation, Blair wanted to ensure inter alia that British key concerns were on the EU agenda.

In his critical volume on the Europeanisation of British defence policy, Robert Dover (2007) analyses in great detail the reasons behind Blair's decision to embrace the ESDP under the Labour government. He argues that the British government primarily aimed for coordinating national security and defence policies within the EU, in particular across peace-building and peace-keeping issues. According to Dover, Blair also wanted EU governments to restructure their armed forces, following the UK's example and, hence, the Strategic Defence Review of British armed forces in 1998. Such reforms would have allowed the EU to have the capabilities necessary for intervening in humanitarian crises, such as the ethnic conflicts and border disputes which had reappeared in the EU's periphery after the end of the Cold War. Dover underlines that Blair wanted to use these capabilities with or in the absence of US/NATO capabilities which, in turn, would strengthen the transatlantic solution to the new international security environment. From a utilitarian point of view, the ESDP may hence be said to have maximised the British, but also the French, national interests, at least in the late 1990s.

The period between 1999 and 2003 was subsequently characterised by negotiations on the components of the ESDP, and EU–NATO relations. The Treaty of Amsterdam determined the responsibilities of the EU, defining inter alia the humanitarian, rescue, and peacekeeping tasks of EU crisis management, and the tasks combat forces were to carry out under the EU flag. The Council of Santa Maria de Feira then defined EU–NATO relations, obliging France and the UK to find a compromise on the future of Transatlantic relations (Gegout, 2002). While the UK aimed for strong EU–NATO relations (Dover, 2007), France was initially in favour of the ESDP being autonomous vis-à-vis NATO (Gegout, 2002, pp. 72–3). The fact that the French finally accepted relatively close EU–NATO contacts strongly implies that France wanted to reassure its partners that it was not showing complete disregard for Transatlantic relations. In line with NI and LI, it was in France's best interest to adjust its preferences, and credibly commit to the ESDP. During the negotiations for the Treaty of Nice, it was, however, not France but the UK that had to adapt its national preferences, accepting restrictions on EU–NATO relations. In line with NI and LI, the final outcome of the bargaining on the components of ESDP, and in particular on EU–NATO relations, does not only show that security and defence cooperation in Europe seemed to be mutually beneficial for Member States, but also illustrates that French and British preferences towards European integration in high politics had been converging since the early 1990s.

Within only five years, EU Member States thus reached agreement on the level and scope of cooperation in high politics. To guarantee that the ESDP was also operational, the Council created the EDA in 2004, now responsible for fostering European defence cooperation (Giegerich and Nicoll, 2012). The Lisbon Treaty subsequently aimed at increasing the coherence of the EU's external action. It provided a legal basis for the EDA, introduced new institutions such as the EEAS, and further enhanced the role of the High Representative of the Union for Foreign Affairs and Security Policy (HR). Since 2009, Member States have hence had all the instruments and tools that they potentially need for engaging in crisis management at their disposal. However, there is no credible commitment to the CSDP yet, since Lisbon failed to extend the use of QMV to defence matters (Burgess, 2009, p. 311). The institutionalisation of security and defence cooperation has, consequently, not reached the stage where a 'set of rules … prescribe[s] behavioural roles, constrain[s] activity, and shape[s] expectations' (Keohane, 1989, p. 66). On the contrary, the CSDP strongly depends on legitimacy at home, with Member States preserving their armed forces, and military, industrial and technological capabilities. The nature and the pace of EU crisis management – and, hence, the overall success of the CSDP – is, consequently, highly dependent on Member States' political willingness and financial ability to participate in missions and operations under the EU flag.

Generally speaking, the first ten years of the CSDP have shown that Member States consider cooperation in security and defence to be an asset within their national security strategies (Simón, 2014), and therefore only participate in EU missions and operations if such a contribution serves their national interests (Bujun *et al.*, 2014). While cooperation worked out well in Bosnia, Darfur and Kosovo, for example, with Member States taking unified stands, the EU as a whole can do relatively little when states cannot agree on the purpose and conduct of the mission (Kaufman, 2013). This has been the case in Iraq in 2003 and Libya in 2011, for instance. In line with Liberal IR theory, the CSDP is hence only as strong as Member States allow it to be which, in turn, explains why security and defence cooperation has been *flowing* (2003–5) and *ebbing* (since 2007–8) over time, both from an operational and an institutional perspective. From an institutional perspective, most initiatives – including the creation of the EUMC and the EDA – were, indeed, launched before the political crisis in 2005 (Schmitt, 2013). Lisbon subsequently broadened only the level but not the scope of security and defence cooperation, by failing to pool sovereignty through QMV for European defence matters, including CSDP.

The fact that the CSDP is currently *ebbing* is confirmed by the operational perspective. Out of thirty-four missions and operations launched under the CSDP between 2003 and 2015, eighteen were set up over the period 2003–8. In 2008, five operations were launched, followed by a total of ten missions between 2009 and 2014. This said, it is worth underlining that no operation was set up in 2009, i.e. the year following the outbreak of the global financial crisis. The operational development of the CSDP is rather surprising as the shock of the economic and financial crisis was initially assumed to be a catalyst for eventually addressing the institutional shortcomings of security and defence cooperation at the EU level. In line with Moravcsik's three-stage framework, further integration – in the form of pooled sovereignty through QMV – was quite likely to arise since Member States – being rational actors aiming for utility maximisation – had a strong incentive to relieve their budgets through increased cooperation (stage 1) which, in turn, would have led to a new round of intergovernmental negotiations (stage 2) and eventually brought about QMV for defence matters (stage 3).

However, instead of maximising defence spending at the EU level, most Member States significantly reduced their share of national budget devoted to security (Mölling and Brune, 2011; Fägersten, 2012). The three largest CSDP troop providers, France, the UK and Germany, have strongly curtailed their defence policy ambitions since 2008. While France's defence sector was supposed to save €3.5 million by 2013, the UK decided to cut its spending by 7.5 per cent until 2014; Germany, similarly to the UK, aimed at saving around 8 per cent of its expenditure between 2011 and 2015 (Keller, 2011, p. 2; Marrone, 2012, p. 5; Fägersten, 2012, p. 12). Many medium-sized Member States, such as the Czech Republic, have cut their resources for defence by 10 to 15 per cent since 2009 (Mölling, 2011, p. 6). The most drastic reductions can be observed in smaller Member States, such as Latvia and Lithuania, who cut their defence spending by 21 per cent and 36 per cent in 2009 and 2010, respectively (Mölling and Brune, 2011, p. 37). Overall, these cuts are likely to negatively affect Member States' military capabilities, and hence the ability of the EU to assume its crisis management responsibilities in the future, especially as defence spending has already been on a downward trend following the end of the Cold War.

While it is still too early to determine the long-term impact of the political and economic crises on the CSDP, current trends are rather worrying. Although Member States have all the instruments and tools at their disposal that they need for successfully engaging in the CSDP, there is a strong lack of political willingness to effectively do so. Force structures such as the EU Battlegroups, on standby since 2007, have not yet been deployed in any military action under the CSDP. Member States, however, do not only seem to be increasingly reluctant to participate in EU missions and operations, but now also risk being financially unable to support security and defence cooperation at the EU level. Indeed, defence expenditures have been relatively low since the end of the Cold War, with most Member States devoting less than 2 per cent of GDP – NATO's target for military spending – to security and defence matters (Giegerich and Nicoll, 2012). This development is quite alarming, as defence sectors are very specific, i.e. Member States' investments of today are decisive for the capabilities they will have at their disposal in fifteen to twenty years of time. From a purely operational perspective, the current underinvestment in security and defence is, therefore, quite worrying. Consequently, if the EU wants to fulfil its responsibilities in crisis management in the future, Member States need to show more commitment to the EU's external action, e.g. by coming to terms with a reform which – in line with LI – makes the CSDP more efficient and brings about the pooling of sovereignty through QMV for European security and defence matters.

The limits of Liberalism in explaining the emergence of the CSDP

The first two sections of this chapter have shown that the emergence and evolution of the CSDP is a quite complex, empirical puzzle (Hyde-Price, 2013). Although LI and NI shed light on the role of domestic politics in the institutionalisation of the CSDP, including the different stages of cooperation, unequally unfolding over time, this chapter also suggests that Liberal IR theory – with its focus on rationality, national preference formation towards EU integration, bargaining power, credible commitments, and the institutionalisation of negotiations outcomes – may be too narrow to fully capture the reasons behind closer security and defence cooperation at the EU level. Since Liberal approaches such as NI and LI concentrate to a large extent on the domestic level, and the different steps in the process of institutionalisation, they often fail to take into account the regional and the international perspectives as well as the structural environment those two levels create for decision makers at the domestic level. Since understanding the dynamics between the domestic, regional and international level promises to provide a quite complex explanation for security and defence issues making it on the European agenda, any purely Liberal study of CSDP risks being an oversimplification of the *real story* of European security and defence cooperation.

The domestic level

According to Moravcsik (1997, 2008), the heads of governments first aggregate societal interests and then translate these interests into national preferences towards European integration. Although LI takes into account that states have different economic, political and institutional settings, it somehow fails to grasp the complexity of the structural environment in which the heads of government take decisions, including the 'multiple actors interacting across various domains and levels of social totality' (Hyde-Price, 2013, p. 403). Liberal Intergovernmentalists thus omit, for example, the role of strategic culture (see Chapter 5) and key policy makers such as Tony Blair in the process of national preference formation. They also fall short of explaining how structural changes affect the domestic level and hence Member States' preferences towards the process of European integration.

The international level

Indeed, foreign, security and defence policy cannot be treated as a mere function of domestic factors, but should be analysed with reference to the system level (Hyde-Price, 2013). Contrary to Liberal IR theory, which tends to overlook the international perspective (Cladi and Locatelli, 2013), Realists such as Jones (2003, 2007), Posen (2006), and Cladi and Locatelli (2012) explicitly argue that security and defence cooperation may also arise in response to a change in the external environment. From a Realist perspective, Member States primarily launched the CSDP to safeguard and maximise their respective powers in light of the new international security environment, emerging with the end of the Cold War.

The regional/EU level

However, national preference formation towards EU integration does not only depend on domestic and international factors. To a certain extent, Member States can be said to have been *path dependent* (Haugsdal, 2005; Duke and Ojanen, 2006), an aspect Liberal IR theory neglects by focussing on the different stages in the process of institutionalisation. The emergence of the CSDP, however, is at least partly due to the politics carried out by the European Economic Community (EEC), the EC, and the EU (Koutrakos, 2013). Constructivists would thus argue that Member States launched the CSDP inter alia to enlarge the tool box for the EU's external action, thereby facilitating the implementation of the community's normative objectives in crisis management.

Overall, Liberal IR theory is quite a powerful approach to the institutional innovations and dynamics in European security and defence cooperation, and therefore sheds light on the reasons behind the emergence of the CSDP in the late 1990s. Nevertheless, this section has shown that Liberalism fails to capture the complexity of the process which led to closer security and defence cooperation at the EU level. This is mainly due to the fact the Liberal IR theory focusses on one level of analysis only, thereby falling short on analysis of the regional and international factors relevant for the launch of the CSDP. Such factors are more easily addressed in other theoretical frameworks, including, for example, Structural Realism (see Chapter 1), Neoclassical Realism (see Chapter 2) and Constructivism (see Chapter 5). Together, these approaches promise to give a rather clearer indication of the motives Member States had for embarking on a project of closer cooperation in security and defence matters at the St. Malo summit in 1998.

Conclusion

This chapter has analysed the emergence and the evolution of the CSDP through a Liberal lens, and tried to place Liberal IR theory in the debate on EU security and defence cooperation. The aim was not only to understand the reasons behind the launch of the CSDP, but also to comprehend the twists and turns in its evolution. The first section of this chapter provided a theoretical overview of Liberalism, focussing in particular on NI and LI. Although NI and LI are based on the same premises, the first stresses the role of institutions while the latter concentrates to a greater extent on domestic politics, and national preference formation. Since LI marries NI and Bargaining theory to provide a more complex account of institutional formation, both strands of thought promised to elucidate particularly well why and under which conditions the EU embarked on a project of closer security and defence cooperation. Based on this framework, section two illustrated how rationality, national preferences, bargaining and credible institutional arrangements explain the emergence of the CSDP in the late 1990s.

In line with Liberal IR theory, the increased level of interdependence that Member States faced after the end of the Cold War positively affected their national preferences for closer security and defence cooperation at the EU level. The CSDP thus emerged as a political, civilian and military capacity in 1998 and added to the tools and instruments that EU Member States have at their disposal for implementing a coherent foreign, security and defence policy. There is, however, no credible commitment to the CSDP yet, as Lisbon failed in extending QMV to defence matters. Consequently, Member States still control the nature and the pace of security and defence cooperation which, in turn, explains why the CSDP has been ebbing and flowing over time. After an initial phase of enthusiasm in the early 2000s, the appetite of Member States for the CSDP seems to have been decreasing with the political and the economic crises. Although the EU's security and defence policy is fully operational from an institutional perspective, Member States lack the political willingness to deploy armed forces under the EU flag and to invest in their national defence sectors. Defence budgets continue to be on a downward trend, particularly since the outbreak of the economic and financial crisis in 2008. This development not only creates uncertainty as to the capabilities Member States will have at their disposal in 20 years' time, but also questions their ability to participate in future crisis management to be launched under the CSDP.

Finally, the last section of this chapter outlined the limits of Liberal IR theory in accounting for the CSDP, contrasting its explanatory power with Realist and Constructivist studies of European security. As Waltz (1997, p. 193) argued, 'reality is complex, theory is simple'. Neither NI nor LI are thus able to grasp the complexity of CSDP. This is particularly true as Liberal IR theory focusses on the domestic level only. Consequently, LI and NI explain quite well why and under which conditions Member States were able to bring security and defence issues to the intergovernmental bargaining table. Both strands of thought thus shed light on the drawbacks and successes in the different rounds of negotiations on the level and the scope of security and defence cooperation at the EU level. While Liberal IR theory can hence be said to be a powerful tool for explaining the multiple stages, dynamics and institutional innovations in the process of closer cooperation, it falls short of analysing the regional and international factors relevant for fully grasping the complexity of the CSDP. Realist and Constructivist approaches to the study of European security – taken in other chapters of this volume – focus to a great extent on the regional and the international level, and may therefore help to complete the story of the CSDP's emergence in the late 1990s.

References

Bujun, P. D., Mérand, F. and Foucault, M. (2014) Regional Security Governance and Collective Action. In J. Sperling (ed.) *Handbook of Governance and Security.* Northampton, UK: Edward Elgar.

Burgess, J. P. (2009) There Is no European Security, only European Securities. *Cooperation and Conflict.* 44 (3). pp. 309–28.

Buzan, B. (1991) *People, States, and Fear: An Agenda for International Security Studies in the Post-Cold War Era.* Boulder, CO: Lynne Rienner.

Cladi, L. and Locatelli, A. (2013) Worth a Shot: On the Explanatory Power of Bandwagoning in Transatlantic Relations. *Contemporary Security Policy.* 34 (2). pp. 374–81.

Cladi, L. and Locatelli, A. (2012) Bandwagoning, Not Balancing: Why Europe Confounds Realism. *Contemporary Security Policy.* 33 (2). pp. 264–88.

Dover, R. (2007) *Europeanization of British Defence Policy.* Hampshire, Ashgate Publishing Limited.

Duchêne, F. (1973) The European Community and the Uncertainties of Interdependence. In M. Kohnstamm and W. Hager (eds) *A Nation Writ Large? Foreign-Policy Problems before the European Community.* London: Macmillan.

Duchêne, F. (1972) Europe's Role in World Peace. In R. Mayne (ed.) *Europe Tomorrow: Sixteen Europeans Look Ahead.* London: Fontana.

Duke, S. and Ojanen, H. (2006) Bridging Internal and External Security: Lessons from the European Security and Defence Policy. *Journal of European Integration.* 28 (5). pp. 477–94.

Fägersten, B. (2012) *European Foreign Policy and the Eurozone Crisis: A Swedish Perspective*. Stockholm: Swedish Institute of International Affairs.

Forsberg, T. (2010) *Integration Theories, Theory Development and European Security and Defence Policy.* Fifth Pan-European Conference on EU Politics, 23–26 June Oporto.

Forster, A. (2011) The Transformation of European Armed Forces. In F. Mérand, M. Foucault, and B. Irondelle (eds) *European Security since the Fall of the Berlin Wall.* Toronto: University of Toronto Press.

Fraser, C. (1999) *The Foreign and Security Policy of the European Union: Past, Present and Future.* Sheffield: Sheffield Academic Press.

Gegout, C. (2002) The French and British Change in Position in the CESDP: A Security Community and Historical–Institutionalist Perspective. *Politique Européenne.* 4 (8). pp. 62–87.

Giegerich, B. (2006) *European Security and Strategic Culture: National Responses to the EU's Security and Defence Policy.* Baden Baden: Nomos.

Giegerich, B. and Nicoll, A. (2012) The Struggle for Value in European Defence. *Survival: Global Politics and Strategy*. 54 (1). pp. 53–82.

Gnesotto, N. (2004) *EU Security and Defence Policy. The First Five Years (1999–2004).* Paris: European Union Institute for Security Studies.

Hafterndorn, H., Keohane, R. and Wallander, C. (1999) *Imperfect Unions: Security Institutions over Time and Space.* Oxford: Oxford University Press.

Hartley, K. and Sandler, T. (1995) *Handbook of Defense Economics*, Amsterdam: Elsevier

Haugsdal, R. (2005) *What Explains the Change of European Security Policy? An Analysis of European Security and Defence Policy (ESDP) after September 11th 2001.* Oslo: University of Oslo.

Hofman, S. C. and Mérand, F. (2012) Regional Organizations à la Carte: The Effects of Institutional Elasticity. In T. V. Paul (ed.) *International Relations Theory and Regional Transformation.* Cambridge: Cambridge University Press.

Howorth, J. (2007) *Security and Defence Policy in the European Union.* Basingstoke. UK: Palgrave Macmillan.

Howorth, J. (2000) *European Integration and Defence: The Ultimate Challenge?* Paris: Institute for Security Studies.

Hyde-Price, A. (2013) Neither Realism nor Liberalism: New Directions in Theorizing EU Security Policy. *Contemporary Security Policy*. 34 (2). pp. 397–408.

Jones, S. (2007) *The Rise of a European Security Cooperation.* Cambridge: Cambridge University Press.

Jones, S. (2003) The European Union and the Security Dilemma. *Security Studies.* 12 (3). pp. 114–56.

Kaufman, J. P. (2013) *Introduction to International Relations: Theory and Practice.* Plymouth, UK: Rowman & Littlefield Publishers.

Keller, P. (2011) Challenges for European Defence Budgets after the Economic Crisis. *American Enterprise Institute for Public Policy Research*. 1. pp. 1–8.

Keohane, R. O. (1989) Neoliberal Institutionalism: A Perspective on World Politics. In R. O. Keohane (ed.) *International Institutions and State Power.* Boulder, CO: Westview Press.

Keohane, R. O. (1984) *After Hegemony: Cooperation and Discord in the World Political Economy.* Princeton, NJ: Princeton University Press.

Koutrakos, P. (2013) *The EU Common and Security Policy.* Oxford: Oxford University Press.

Marrone, A. (2012) *Defence Spending in Europe in Light of the Economic Crisis.* Rome: Istituto Affari Internazionali.

Mearsheimer, J. J. (1994–95) The False Promise of International Institutions. *International Security*. 19 (3). pp. 5–49.

Meyer. C. O. (2006) *The Quest for a European Strategic Culture: Changing Norms on Security and Defence in the European Union.* Basingstoke, UK: Palgrave Macmillan.

Mölling, C. (2011) *Europe without Defence.* Berlin: Stiftung für Wissenschaft und Politik.

Mölling, C. and Brune, S. C. (2011) *The Impact of the Financial Crisis on European Defence.* Brussels: European Parliament.

Moravcsik, A. (2008) The New Liberalism. In Reus-Smith, C. and Snidal, D. (eds) *The Oxford Handbook of International Relations.* Oxford: Oxford University Press.

Moravcsik, A. (2003) *The Choice for Europe. Social Purpose and State Power from Messina to Maastricht.* London: Routledge.

Moravcsik, A. (1998) *The Choice for Europe: Social Purpose and State Power from Messina to Maastricht.* Ithaca, NY: Cornell University Press.

Moravcsik, A. (1997) Taking Preferences Seriously: A Liberal Theory of International Politics. *International Organization.* 51 (4). pp. 512–53.

Moravcsik, A. (1995) Liberal Intergovernmentalism and Integration: A Rejoinder. *Journal of Common Market Studies.* 33 (4). pp. 611–28.

Moravcsik, A. (1994) *Why the European Community Strengthens the State: Domestic Politics and International Cooperation.* CES Working Paper, no. 52.

Moravcsik, A. (1993) Preferences and Power in the European Community: A Liberal-Intergovernmentalist Approach. *Journal of Common Market Studies.* 31 (4). pp. 473–524.

Moravcsik, A. (1991) Negotiating the Single European Act. In Keohane, R. O. and Hoffmann, S. (eds) *The New European Community.* Boulder, CO: Westview Press.

Moravcsik, A. and Schimmelfennig, F. (2009) Liberal Intergovernmentalism. In Diez, T. and Wiener, A. (eds) *European Integration Theory.* Oxford: Oxford University Press.

Pollack, M. A. (2012) Realist, Intergovernmentalist, and Institutionalist Approaches. In E. Jones, A. Menon and S. Weatherhill (eds) *The Oxford Handbook of the European Union.* Oxford: Oxford University Press.

Pollack, M. A. (2001) International Relations Theory and European Integration. *Journal of Common Market Studies.* 39 (2). pp. 221–44.

Posen, B. (2006) European Union Security and Defence Policy: Response to Unipolarity. *Security Studies.* 15 (2). pp. 149–86.

Rieker, P. (2006) From Common Defence to Comprehensive Security: Towards the Europeanization of French Foreign and Security Policy? *Security Dialogue.* 37 (4). pp. 509–28.

Rosato, S. (2011) Europe's Troubles: Power Politics and the State of the European Project. *International Security.* 35 (4). pp. 45–86.

Rosato, S. (2011a) *Europe United: Power Politics and the Making of the European Community,* Ithaca, NY: Cornell University Press.

Schmidt, V. A. (2012) European Member States Elites' Diverging Visions of the European Union: Diverging Differently since the Economic Crisis and the Libyan Intervention? *Journal of European Integration.* 34 (2). pp. 169–90.

Schmitt. O. (2013) A Tragic Lack of Ambition: Why EU Security Policy is no Strategy. *Contemporary Security Policy.* 34 (2). pp. 413–16.

Simón, L. (2014) *Geopolitical Change, Grand Strategy and European Security. The EU–NATO Conundrum in Perspective.* London: Palgrave Macmillan.

Sjursen, H. (2011) Not so Intergovernmental after All? On Democracy and Integration in European Foreign and Security Policy. *Journal of European Public Policy.* 18 (4). pp. 1078–95.

Smith, M. (2004) *Europe's Foreign and Security Policy: The Institutionalization of Cooperation.* Cambridge: Cambridge University Press.

Snidal, D. (1985) Coordination versus Prisoners' Dilemma: Implications for International Cooperation and Regimes. *The American Political Science Review.* 79 (4). pp. 923–42.

Steans, J., Pettiford, L., Diez, T. and El-Anis, I. (2010) *An Introduction to International Relations Theory: Perspectives and Themes.* Harlow, UK: Pearson Longman.

Tonra, B. (2003) Constructing the Common Foreign and Security Policy: The Utility of a Cognitive Approach. *Journal of Common Market Studies.* 41 (4). pp. 731–56.

Vanhoonacker, S., Dijkstra, H. and Mauer, H. (2010) Understanding the Role of Bureaucracy in the European Security and Defence Policy: The State of the Art. *European Integration Online Papers.* 14 (1). pp. 1–33.

Waltz, K. (1997) Evaluating Theories. *American Political Science Review.* 91 (4). pp. 913–17.

4 Governmental interest, new Liberalism and the CSDP

Benjamin Pohl, Niels van Willigen and Cynthia M. C. van Vonno

Introduction

Liberalism claims that foreign policy is strongly influenced by domestic processes and events, both at the individual and the group level (Moravcsik, 2008). This holds for national foreign policies as well as for the CSDP of the EU. The basic argument of Liberalism is that the CSDP represents an amalgam of partly overlapping and partly diverging national preferences, and that cross-national differences in societal expectations are the primary causes of differences between EU governmental interests. This chapter puts forward a Liberal framework for explaining the EU's engagement in CSDP operations. It builds in particular on Andrew Moravcsik's New Liberalism insofar as it focuses on the nexus between governments and the societies they represent (Moravcsik, 2008). New Liberalism shares Realism's focus on *national interests* as formulated by governments, but treats national interests not as a consequence of states' relative power position in the international system, but of the preferences of the societies governments represent. This Liberal framework is located on the Rationalist side of the debate between Rationalism and Constructivism in IR theory, and thus assumes that governments primarily follow a consequentialist logic rather than a logic of appropriateness. This Liberal framework has significant analytical leverage when it comes to explaining the existence and evolution of the CSDP.

This chapter asserts that foreign policy is a function of governmental interests. We argue that, in the absence of a direct external threat, these interests are primarily a function of domestic political concerns: governments treat foreign policy as instrumental to their objective of staying in power. Since no direct external threat to European security has emerged since the end of the Cold War, EU governments determine their positioning within the CSDP according to (perceived) domestic political exigencies and expediencies. This has consequences for what the EU does and can do, and by extension for what it is and can be. We reflect on these consequences in the concluding part of this chapter.

The objective of this chapter is to provide a theory-driven explanation of the CSDP as defined by domestic politics and following a Liberal, Rationalist approach. While it is usually acknowledged as playing some part in IR and foreign policy-making, domestic politics is arguably the most important omitted explanation for the CSDP (Krotz and Mahler, 2011). What we seek to show is that the EU's missions can be plausibly portrayed as a response to varying domestic expectations (or the lack thereof) about the objectives and limitations of foreign policy. This analytical framework can explain both the substantial cooperation within the CSDP as well as the substantial differences dividing EU Member States.

For this purpose, the chapter proceeds as follows. The next section deals with the main tenets of Liberalism in IR theory and explains why it has strong explanatory power in terms of understanding the CSDP. The core of our argument is that governmental and national interests should be distinguished when trying to understand foreign policy-making in general and the CSDP in particular. Section three will therefore focus on this particular distinction. Subsequently we argue that in order to understand and explain the CSDP from the perspective of governmental interests, Andrew Moravcsik's New Liberalism (2008) is a good starting point. We explain how societal preferences can explain governmental positions on CSDP missions. However, we also contend that the role of domestic institutions is under-theorised in New Liberalism and that these institutions should also be taken into account when analysing the CSDP. In section four, we therefore make the claim that it is crucial to take into account the institutional setting in which governments make foreign policy. For illustrative purposes, we argue that distinguishing between single-party governments and coalition governments, for example, potentially gives new insights in the emergence and evolution of the CSDP. In particular, we take the constitutional chain of delegation and accountability (Strøm, 2000) as a point of departure. In doing so, we approach foreign policy-making from the perspective of representation studies, focussing specifically on an institutional perspective. The subsequent section shows that external power-based explanations such as Neorealism have only limited leverage when it comes to explaining the emergence and development of the CSDP. Balancing and/or bandwagoning cannot explain the CSDP (Pohl, 2013). In the last section, we will then look at the consequences of our findings for the future development of the CSDP, especially in relation to a common European strategy (or the lack thereof).

Liberalism and CSDP

In explaining international politics, for a long time many IR theorists tended to shy away from crediting the domestic level as more than an intervening variable (Walt, 1998, p. 34; Moravcsik, 1997, 2000). This is justified insofar as there is little point in asserting that foreign policy behaviour can be explained without reference to international crises and the interrelationships between various powers. Yet such crises, and the variety of responses that they may trigger, are often (also) a function of domestic politics (Moravcsik, 2008, pp. 239–40).[1] This has also been true for attempts to explain the CSDP: there are only a few studies (such as Smith, 2004; Hoffman, 2013; Pohl, 2014) that adopt a Liberal perspective in the sense of expressly looking at domestic processes (Krotz and

Mahler, 2011, p. 571). Liberalism in IR theory is of course quite diverse and – depending on one's definition of Liberalism – includes Rationalist theories about the role of institutions, states, non-state actors, norms and interests on the international and/or the domestic levels (see Chapter 3). There is a variety of contributions that adopt an Institutionalist angle. Some studies point to the influence of the EU institutions (both formal and informal) (VanHoonacker and Dijkstra, 2010; Menon, 2011) and the impact of institutional learning on CSDP (Smith, 2012). Others emphasise the influence of other international institutions, including the UN, NATO and the Organisation for Security and Cooperation in Europe (OSCE), on the development of CSDP. For example, Hofmann (2011, p. 102) argues that 'the European security institutional environment shaped the creation and development of CSDP'.

The absence of Liberal, domestic-level explanations for the CSDP is part of a broader 'omitted theory bias' in the theoretical analysis of IR (Moravcsik, 1997, pp. 538–41). Such a bias is peculiar given that the importance of domestic politics has been recognised from the beginning of IR as an academic discipline (Schultz, 2013, p. 478). Drawing on nineteenth century Liberal Internationalism, Wilsonian Idealists in the early twentieth century made a theoretical connection between domestic institutions, interests and norms on the one hand and world peace on the other. By emphasising the importance of national power and leadership, classical Realists, including Hans Morgenthau and Edward Hallet Carr, also brought domestic factors into their analysis of IR. It was mainly with the emergence of the debate between Neorealists and Neoliberal Institutionalists that the attention on domestic processes was lost. Since the debate was aimed at understanding cooperation (or the lack thereof) at the system level of analysis, the domestic dimension received little or no attention. The end of the Cold War, which seemed to contradict a lot of Neorealist analysis, and the continuing confluence of international and domestic issues in a globalising world, arguably led to increased attention for domestic sources of IR (Schultz, 2013).

In particular, foreign policy analysis, as a subfield of IR, has adopted the domestic level as the most important factor to explain foreign policy. Theorists of all types bring the domestic level into their explanations, but some attribute more importance to domestic factors than others. For Neoclassical Realists, for example, domestic politics is merely an intervening variable (see Chapter 2). Foreign policy is shaped by systemic pressure in the first place, and further qualified by domestic factors. Social Constructivist and Liberal approaches tend to give primary causal importance to domestic factors. The Social Constructivist notion of a national security culture, for example, is strongly connected to the domestic dimension of foreign policy-making (see for example Chappell, 2009; see also Chapter 5). It differs, however, in the emphasis it puts on cultural explanations (e.g. focussing on what unites rather than divides national foreign policy elites) and on the logic of appropriateness.

Liberalism, in contrast, assumes that actors are motivated by the consequences that their actions are expected to bring about. Liberalism is characterised by the notion that all domestic foreign policy actors, whether politicians, bureaucracies or interest groups, have particularistic interests (Schultz, 2013, p. 480). At the same time, the Liberal family is quite diverse. Some Liberals focus on the individual level and study political leaders, for example, others focus on domestic bureaucracies and organisations. In this chapter we focus on domestic politics in the broadest sense. More specifically, we take the New Liberalism of Andrew Moravcsik (1993, 1997, 2008), which focuses on the nexus between governments and the societies they represent, as a starting point. In this view, foreign policy is the result of the interaction of a variety of societal actors, including governments, within the context of domestic institutions.

Societal preferences and governmental interest

New Liberalism adopts a 'bottom-up view of politics' (Moravcsik, 1997, p. 517) in which societal interests and preferences precede politics and policy. States are representative institutions 'subject to capture and recapture, construction and reconstruction by coalitions of social actors' (Moravcsik, 1997, p. 518). As in many domestic politics approaches, governments are key in New Liberalism. They are constrained by societal actors, but also have some degree of autonomy in the sense that they can be distinguished from other domestic actors. In the end, even in strongly consolidated democracies, governments represent 'some individuals and groups more fully than others' (Moravcsik, 1997, p. 518).

The obvious inference is that governmental interests are not identical to national interests. Nonetheless, there is a strong conflation of *national* interest and *governmental* interest in much of the academic literature on international politics. That is strange, because, if we assume that governments have an interest in securing the survival and welfare of their states, it would be logical to assume that they have a similar interest in securing their own survival and welfare, i.e. in maintaining themselves in office (Bueno de Mesquita *et al.*, 2005). As Schultz (2013, p. 480) points out, even some Realists admit that the relative strength of states not only depends on other states in the system, but also on their publics (for example Christensen, 1996; Evangelista, 1997; Krasner, 1978; Mastanduno *et al.*, 1989; Taliaferro, 2009; Zakaria, 1998). Consequently, we need to allow for the possibility that governments may (attempt to) use foreign policy not only for the first purpose (national survival), but also for the second purpose (governmental survival). This does not imply that national and governmental interests necessarily conflict. We cannot, however, simply assume that a self-interested, rational government will automatically pursue the national interest – unless we embrace some very idealistic assumptions.

Following the logic of New Liberalism, the present chapter puts governmental rather than national interests at the centre of its analysis. It submits that these interests might be driven more by domestic factors than international factors.[2] Support for governments will partly depend on the perceived legitimacy and competence with which they handle foreign affairs. Even if foreign policy is not particularly salient in citizens' electoral choices, (democratic) governments are motivated to seek approval from their domestic constituencies. These include voters, but also organised interest groups. This takes up Moravcsik's New Liberalism, according to which 'the foreign policy goals of national governments are viewed as varying in response to shifting pressure from domestic social groups, whose preferences are aggregated through political institutions' (Moravcsik, 1993, p. 481; 2008). It implies that the fundamental purpose of foreign policy is not predetermined but depends on (the intensity of) preferences of influential groups in society.

What are the national preferences that direct foreign policy? According to Liberal theory, they can derive from both ideational and material interests. On the one hand, Western societies expect that governments seek to shape an international environment that is conducive to the values of domestic order, i.e. liberal democracy (Owen, 2002, p. 402; Schimmelfennig, 2004, p. 4). Some countries, including the Netherlands, even have constitutional clauses that oblige the government to promote the international rule of law. At the EU-level, the *civilian power* and *normative power* theorists submit that the EU is a force for good in the sense that it aims to promote the European liberal order in its external relations (Duchêne, 1972; Manners, 2002; Telò, 2005). The 2003 *European Security Strategy* includes ideational and normative elements, including the goal to promote a 'stronger international society, well-functioning international institutions and a rule-based international order' (European Council, 2003). On the other hand, Western societies also expect that their material interests in terms of security and welfare be taken into account, i.e. that the government shows competence in handling potential threats at the smallest possible price in treasure and/or blood. When it comes to military interventions, Lawrence Freedman has described these two aspects as governments weighing the *CNN effect* against the *bodybags effect* (Freedman, 2000, pp. 337–9). Since both the perception of the necessity of particular foreign policy projects as well as their legitimacy relative to domestic norms varies cross-nationally, the national preferences that governments represent will be likely to differ.

This begs the question of how governments decide on their foreign policy positions. The mechanism which ensures that governments take societal preferences into account is two-pronged (Doyle, 2008, p. 61). First, there is an incentive for governments to *do something* in response to mediatised events (Robinson, 2001). Direct public pressure will drive governments' foreign policy behaviour only in cases that capture headlines although, as Lawrence Freedman pointed out, the *CNN* and *bodybags* effects 'may have come to grow in importance through anticipation' (Freedman, 2000, p. 339). This anticipation effect is partly due to the fact that '[p]oliticians are motivated primarily by the desire to avoid blame' (Weaver, 1986, p. 371). Moreover, even the absence of public pressure for action does not necessarily imply the absence of political opportunity. David Chandler has pointedly argued that '[e]thical foreign policy is ideally suited to buttressing the moral authority of governments ... because policy-makers are less accountable for matching ambitious policy aims with final policy outcomes in the international sphere' (Chandler, 2003, p. 295). In other words, since governments' self-interest relates to approval from domestic constituencies, it lies foremost in being seen to act (ethically).

Critics may object and argue that contemporary foreign policy in Western countries is more than just a public relations exercise. It clearly is, which brings us to the second feature of governmental self-interest. Overt foreign policy populism carries significant risks because government policy is monitored by organised interests in domestic society. As a representative institution the government constitutes a 'transmission belt' which translates the preferences of societal groups into policy (Moravcsik, 1997, p. 518). Moravcsik primarily discusses economic policy, which makes his notion of societal interests not directly applicable for a public good such as security. However, in the case of security policy, foreign policy elites, including the media, non-governmental organisations, bureaucracies and academia, play an important role. They not only influence foreign policy, but they also form an expert community which can be characterised as 'organized public opinion' (Everts, 1996, p. 136). This community can be useful (or otherwise) for the government to *sell* its policy to the larger public. Governments therefore have an incentive to ensure that their foreign policy is judged as competent and legitimate in the eyes of the foreign policy elite.

This dual mechanism – broader public support as well as elite support – implies that governments do not maximise their interests by simply following public opinion. The relationship between governments and public opinion in foreign policy is both circular and deliberate (Power, 2002, p. 509). It is circular insofar as governments often follow public sentiments. However, politicians also need to show (and be somewhat consistent in) what they stand for (Downs, 1957). Because the public is not subject to similar requirements of consistency, this gives governments incentives to demonstrate leadership on some causes. Governments may thus act against public opinion provided they expect their action to provide the best available pay-off in the longer run. As Richard Eichenberg argues with respect to US military interventions, and Ebru Canan-Sokullu confirms for the major EU powers, 'victory has many friends' (Eichenberg, 2005; Canan-Sokullu, 2012; Koga, 2011). The perceived risks of any foreign policy venture, in terms of the likelihood and price of visible success or failure, will therefore shape governments' positioning in foreign policy.

Related to this is the notion that domestic constraints are not just a given to which governments have to adapt. Moravcsik looks at domestic factors primarily in the form of constraints (Moravcsik, 1997, p. 518). Yet governments are not passive victims or transmitters of domestic constraints. Instead, they may actively use foreign policy as just one more instrument for achieving domestic political victory (as for example the earlier Chandler quote on foreign policy-making as a means of buttressing one's moral high ground illustrates).

The focus on societal demands in combination with the recognition that governments can pursue policies that are not necessarily supported by the larger public does not suggest that governments are always able to achieve foreign policy projects in accordance with idiosyncratic national preferences. Governments are, after all, significantly constrained in their behaviour by what Moravcsik calls 'the interdependence of state preferences' (Moravcsik, 1997, p. 523). Interdependence first arises with respect to the object of foreign policy: as multiple attempts throughout history show, it is simply difficult to influence foreigners (Cooper, 2003, pp. 113–27). Yet nowhere is interdependence more palpable than in the case of multilateral foreign policy cooperation such as in the CSDP, where consensus between all members on whether and how to attempt to exert influence is a prerequisite to interaction with target countries. The foreign policy output of such an institution is usually not the *average* of governmental preferences. New Liberalism instead assumes that the relative intensity of national preferences will be decisive in determining collective policy. '[T]he binding constraint is generally "resolve" or "determination" – the *willingness* of governments to mobilise and expend social resources for foreign policy purposes' – rather than the availability of capabilities that Realists emphasise (Moravcsik, 1997, p. 524; emphasis in original). This is not to say that availability of capabilities does not matter – willingness is not of much use if social resources are insufficient for the purposes sought. However, most foreign policy decisions are not about the mobilisation of all resources. *Weaker* actors frequently carry the day because they care more intensely about the outcome.

New Liberal theorists would thus expect Western governments to anticipate and respond to conflicting societal demands regarding the purpose and acceptable costs of any foreign policy objectives. It is in governments' own interests to be seen as both competent in securing societies' material interests and as acting legitimately. There will be occasions in which the two clash. In that case, the expected political consequences of valuating one interest over the other will determine which one prevails, though governments will be likely to try to fudge the trade-off. By contrast, Realist analysis would expect the CSDP to primarily serve the purpose of maximising members states' relative power and security, implying that the EU's actions would plausibly serve to increase the relative (material) power of its members. Alternatively, Constructivist analysts might expect the CSDP to help implement the international community's normative objectives, for instance the *Responsibility to Protect*. This explanation would imply that the CSDP credibly and sustainably attempts to implement such duties. The great advantage of New Liberalism over Realist and Constructivist approaches is that it enables multi-causal explanations (Moravcsik, 1997, 2008, p. 235), not only in the sense of allowing for ideational *and* material explanations of the CSDP, but also in the sense of investigating causal mechanisms at different levels of the policy-making process.

By acknowledging that the government is a transmission belt through which societal preferences are translated into foreign policy, one is able to show how foreign policy is made through societal preferences and institutions. In our view, the preferences of societal groups are not simply *aggregated through political institutions* but the preferences are also changed and adapted during the process. Hence, outcomes in the foreign policy decision-making process are co-determined by domestic institutions and can therefore be expected to differ across EU members. That is why more attention on the implications of domestic institutions on foreign policy-making is needed. We take a shot at this by thinking about the potential differences between coalition governments on the one hand, and single-party governments on the other. Further, we suggest using the constitutional chain of delegation and accountability (Strøm, 2000) as a tool to better understand the relationship between the CSDP and domestic politics.

The institutional context

In spite of the Treaty of Lisbon's (2007) innovations, foreign policy-making remains a prerogative of the individual EU Member States and is a predominantly intergovernmental affair at the EU level. In order to understand the EU's foreign policy-making process, it is therefore crucial to understand the foreign policy-making processes in individual Member States. Most EU members are countries with coalition governments. This confronts students of the CSDP with two inter-related problems. First, there is a general lack of understanding of how foreign policy is made in coalitions. Most foreign policy analyses focus on the *government* without taking into account the dynamics that occur because of the presence of a coalition of multiple political parties. We don't yet know a lot about the foreign policy decision-making processes and foreign policy outputs of coalition govern-ments. Recent work on government coalitions in parliamentary democracies aims to find out how coalition cabinets engage with and impact on foreign policy (Cladi and Webber, 2011; Kaarbo, 2012; Kisangani and Pickering, 2011; Ozkececi-Taner, 2005, 2009; Oppermann and Brummer, 2013). Oppermann and Brummer (2013), for example, argue that the influence of junior coalition partners on foreign policy depends on the type of coalition arrangement. They argue that an arrange-ment in which junior partners hold one or more departments in the foreign policy executive leads to more extreme foreign policy behaviour. Without such a position in the foreign policy executive junior partners have a constraining influence on foreign policy behaviour. Ozkececi-Taner (2005, 2009) looks at 'institutionalized ideas' in coalition foreign policy making and argues that, under certain conditions, these ideas affect foreign policy outputs. One of the conditions is, for example, that the political actor controls a department in the foreign policy executive.

The second problem is that we do not really know yet to what extent coalition cabinets differ from their single-party government counterparts. Nonetheless, some recent literature suggests that there are significant differences between both types of government. Beasley and Kaarbo (2014), for example, find substantial differences in foreign policy behaviour between parliamentary weak coalitions and parliamentary weak single-party cabinets.

The above mentioned literature represents a good first step in the direction of understanding how coalitions decide on and produce foreign policy related to the CSDP. However, most of these studies involve only the level of cabinet govern-ment. As explained earlier, they focus on coalition arrangements and how the coalition members interact. Following the logic of New Liberalism, we propose also to take the constitutional chain of delegation and accountability (Strøm, 2000) into account. In doing so, we approach foreign policy-making within the context of the CSDP from the perspective of representation studies, focussing specifically on an institutional perspective. Involving the constitutional chain of delegation enables a deeper understanding of the relationship between the CSDP (and foreign policy-making in general) and domestic politics.

Strøm (2000) posits that the constitutional chain of delegation in parliamentary systems moves from (1) voters in the electoral arena to representatives in the legislative arena, (2) legislators to the executive branch, specifically the head of government (Prime Minister), (3) the head of government to the cabinet ministers, and (4) the cabinet ministers to the bureaucratic organisation. In presidential systems, the chain is more complicated because the President, who usually has his/her own voter-mandate, is added to the list and creates a situation of competing principals (Carey, 2007) (although the President often replaces the position of the Prime Minister in terms of power and influence). The chain of delegation is accompanied by the chain of accountability, which runs in the opposite direction. Each link in the chain of delegation and accountability is granted certain institutionalised powers with which it can execute its own tasks, and also holds the further links in the chain accountable.

We argue that it is worthwhile to focus on three important factors in the chain of delegation and accountability, specifically (1) the formal status of foreign policy-making, (2) parliamentary mandate fulfilment, and (3) government mandate fulfilment. A first place to start to further our understanding of the influence of domestic politics on the CSDP from a comparative institutional perspective is to survey the formal status of foreign policy-making in both constitutional and practical terms (Baehr, 1974; Cassese, 1980; Knight, 1976; Risse-Kappen, 1991). Do the legislative and executive branches of government have different (institutionalised) powers when it comes to foreign policy-making and specific acts of foreign policy? These foreign policy acts may range from the declaration of war, the control over armed forces, the implementation of sanctions, the joining and participating (e.g. voting) in international institutions, to the signing of international treaties. Do other, non-formalised features of the democratic system influence the actual use of these powers (e.g. public opinion in the electoral arena, party unity in parliament, etc.)? Are there noteworthy differences between parliamentary and (semi)presidential systems? And within parliamentary systems, does the use of these powers differ between single-party and coalition cabinets?

What do these institutional differences mean for the CSDP? In general we posit that the more formal checks and balances in the constitutional chain, the less decisive governments are in embracing (but not necessarily rejecting) specific foreign policy decisions in the realm of the CSDP. Taking the three most studied countries in the development of the CSDP – the UK, France and Germany – the last few years provide some circumstantial evidence for this claim. With its (semi)presidential system, France has the fewest formal checks and balances when it comes to the deployment of troops or other foreign policy decisions. This corresponds with the eagerness of Paris to support interventions both within and outside the context of the CSDP, including Libya and Mali. The UK is also quite keen to support interventions, but faces more constraints. In the case of Syria, for example, the (coalition) government was willing to support military action in the fall of 2012, but was outvoted in the House of Commons. Arguably, Germany is the country with the strongest domestic restrictions, which leads to a general reluctance to support interventions. This is aptly illustrated by Germany's abstention in the United Nations Security Council (UNSC) on Resolution 1973, which called for a military intervention in Libya in 2011.

Second, political parties are key to understanding foreign policy-making. Although there is an abundance of studies on the relationship between public opinion and government foreign policy (Almond, 1950; Rosenau, 1961; Mueller, 1973; Risse-Kappen, 1991; Holsti, 1992; Everts, 2002; Knecht and Weatherford, 2006), this literature tends to skip a number of steps in the process of policy-making that are held central to the study of comparative politics, specifically the field of representation studies. Most representative democracies rely on political parties for the translation or linkage of citizens' preferences to government policy, and thus the constitutional chain is paralleled by a political chain of delegation (Müller, 2000). In parliamentary systems of government, political parties tend to dominate the electoral, legislative and executive links in the chain of representation. Thus, political parties are considered to be the main (often assumed to be unitary) actors in the political process, and competition between parties is a defining feature of modern democracy (Schumpeter, 1976).

In the study of representation, the normative responsible party model (or mandate model) is widely used for the empirical analysis of representation, specifically in parliamentary systems (Thomassen, 1994). It requires that (1) parties offer voters clear and competing policy choices, usually outlined in their party programmes and election manifestos, (2) voters base their electoral choice on these policy issues and (3) parties fulfil their policy mandate, for which party unity is required (APSA, 1950). Scholars often distinguish between the parliamentary mandate (operationalised in terms of agenda setting, debates and voting in parliament) and the government mandate (measured in terms of government policy and spending; see below), and study their congruence with the opinions in the electorate, or what parties pledge to do during their electoral campaign (Louwerse, 2011; Thomson, 2001). A potential avenue for further investigation could be to compare parties' foreign policy pledges (in relation to the CSDP) and their salience in party programmes and election manifestos to their fulfilment in the parliamentary and executive arena specifically. To what extent are they congruent? Also, is there anything distinct about policy pledges and mandate fulfilment when it comes to foreign policy compared to domestic policy? And are there differences between various types of foreign policy and/or aspects of the CSDP? If so, what can explain these differences? Institutional variables again may include the semi-presidential–parliamentarian distinction (Holmberg, 1999), and, within parliamentarian systems, the difference between majoritarian and consensus systems (Huber and Powell, 1994; Blais and Bodet, 2006). At the party level, ideological positioning and extremism, issue salience, party unity, as well as opposition versus government status, may serve as explanatory variables.

So how does studying parliamentary mandate fulfilment lead to a deeper understanding of the relationship between the CSDP (and foreign policy-making in general) and domestic politics? Looking again at France, the UK and Germany, we see that all centre-left and two of three centre-right political parties have supported the CSDP. Partisan divides do not seem to play a (large) role when it comes to support for the CSDP. The exception is the UK, where the Conservative Party has expressed its discontent with the CSDP.[3] Therefore, looking into parliamentary mandate fulfilment would teach us a lot about the relationship between voters, political parties (domestic politics) and the development of the CSDP.

Third, looking more specifically at government mandate fulfilment, we finally move to the topic of cabinet government. The study of cabinet government in terms of policy representation has often focussed on portfolio allocations (Laver and Shepsle, 1996) and government policy output and spending (Warwick, 2001; Budge and Laver, 1993; Baron, 1998), mainly because these are observable. Other studies have also used citizens' and elite policy preferences as a measure of policy congruence. Huber and Powell (1994), for example, do so specifically in order to ascertain the difference between single-party and coalition governments, and find that policy congruence is generally higher in the latter. In the specific case of multiparty government and competition, coalition agreements (Strøm and Müller, 1999; Timmermans, 2006) and the appointment of (junior) ministerial posts (Bäck *et al.*, 2011) can be added to this list of potential sources to study government mandate fulfilment in general, and the influence of coalition politics on mandate fulfilment in particular. Questions that need to be addressed here in terms of foreign policy-making and more particularly in relation to the CSDP are the relative importance parties ascribe to foreign policy issues when it comes to coalition agreements, government policy output and government spending, but also the portfolio allocation and status of (junior) ministerial posts of foreign affairs (Oppermann and Brummer, 2013).

As rightly pointed out by Kaarbo (2008), the study of coalition cabinet politics is severely lacking when it comes to the actual decision-making process that takes place within the cabinet. In addition to the added element of *national security* that is accredited to issues of foreign policy, this black box results from the double Two-Level Game (Putnam, 1988) played by the political parties in the cabinet. Parties in coalition cabinets play a Two-Level Game in terms of international politics and domestic politics, but also within their party in terms of the party-in-the-executive and the party-in-the-legislature (one could also add the distinction between the party-in-office and the party-on-the-ground as a third, intraparty, Two-Level Game). Although democracy in general can be characterised by conflict and disagreement, coalition politics is *in essence* characterised by conflict and disagreement, both between as well as within political parties (Kaarbo, 2012). Improving our knowledge of the process of policy decision-making in coalition cabinets would improve our understanding of the CSDP. For example, if we take again the UK, France and Germany, we cannot distinguish different national preferences only, but also different institutional settings. Germany is characterised by coalition governments, whereas the UK is (usually) governed by single-party governments. French governments are typically coalition governments, but within a presidential system which makes it different from the German case. So government mandate fulfilment in relation to the CSDP (and other foreign policy domains) takes place in three very different institutional contexts. Studying these differences would increase our knowledge of the development of the CSDP in terms of a better understanding of governmental interests.

The limits of the Neorealist explanation

Above, we presented a Liberal view of the emergence and development of the CSDP. Doing so, we emphasised the importance of domestic sources of the CSDP. However, that does not preclude the possibility that external pressures influenced the development of the CSDP. Societal interest, including the interests of the foreign policy elite, can surely be influenced by the relative position of a state (or in this case the EU) in the international system. However, it would be wrong to conclude that international pressures fully explain the emergence and evolution of the CSDP. The problem of a Neorealist explanation is twofold. First, at the theoretical level there is no convincing argument that the CSDP is the result of systemic pressures. Balancing is the most often found argument that Neorealists put forward to explain the CSDP. From a balancing perspective, the EU devised the CSDP in order to form a counterweight against the US. As Cladi and Locatelli (2013) explain in this volume and elsewhere, balancing can be interpreted in different ways; balancing against a superior (threatening) power, soft balancing and balancing for autonomy. In all three interpretations, the US is the target of the balancing effort. However, even in the case of balancing for autonomy (which, according to our reading, is not balancing at all) one would *theoretically* expect a much stronger CSDP than actually exists. Also, one would expect a European security strategy that includes at least a strong political position against the US. Second, the lack of a strong theoretical argument is matched by weak empirical evidence of balancing. In general, most EU Member States seem to be quite content with the benign hegemony of the US (Pohl, 2014). This is evident both from the political statements and concrete behaviour of EU Member States. On a more detailed level, balancing cannot explain the variation in responses by different EU governments in crises that led to CSDP missions. Moreover, most CSDP missions are civilian rather than military. Even soft balancing (constraining US policy) or balancing for autonomy (making the EU more independent of the US) would logically have to lead to more military operations than there actually are, because the military domain is where US dominance is omnipresent. And second, the cases in which international factors were of influence are not the missions where geopolitical interests were at play. There is evidence that the French and British decisions to support the EU police mission in Afghanistan (EUPOL) were (very differently) influenced by US pressure, but Afghanistan can hardly be considered as a geopolitical battlefield between the US and the EU (Pohl and Van Willigen, 2015).

Given the lack of empirical evidence for balancing, Cladi and Locatelli (2013) argue that the EU does not balance, but bandwagon. EU Member States aim to 'foster their relationship' with the US through bandwagoning with the superpower. Cladi and Locatelli's understanding of bandwagoning departs from earlier interpretations in the sense that in their understanding bandwagoning is not cost-free. In order to link European security to US security, the EU has to contribute. That is where the CSDP comes in. However, the concept of bandwagoning seems ill chosen given the connotations of the concept of bandwagoning – a powerful threat or the prospect of bounty (see also Pohl, 2013a). Bandwagoning connotes great power games that the EU is neither willing nor well equipped to play. Moreover, if the EU did feel threatened (as some Member States probably do, given Russia's recent antics), the case for bandwagoning would rest with NATO. Yet the CSDP came about in contradiction to Washington's wishes, precisely because Washington felt that the CSDP might weaken the Transatlantic link embodied in NATO.

Moreover, the modest military profile of the CSDP does – again – not match very well with the theoretical expectations of bandwagoning. In the last two decades, Washington has repeatedly called for better *burden sharing*. This has perhaps led to concrete initiatives such as the EU Battlegroup, but if bandwagoning were the primary objective of EU Member States, one would expect a different result. It would have led to a much more robust CSDP than exists today, going well beyond European contributions in low intensity security scenarios and taking away US concerns about *burden-sharing*. Also, it would have led to an unambiguous prioritisation of the relationship with the US in the foreign policy of all EU Member States, which is not the case. Finally, one would expect the closest ally of the US, the UK, to be the most ardent supporter of the CSDP. In reality, France has taken up this role (see Chapter 9), in spite of its foreign policy behaviour in which it sets itself regularly apart from Washington (see Pohl, 2013a, pp. 365–7).

Our criticism of the Neorealist account does not mean that external pressures do not play any role. They often do. However, the impact of external pressures is too diverse to offer a consistent explanation. The Liberal perspective, in which domestic processes play a key role, is better suited. It can include external pressure as an important determining factor for explaining the CSDP. Yet such external pressures are mediated through domestic political processes, which often translate identical pressures into very different responses across borders and time. We therefore disagree with Cladi and Locatelli (2013) that the ontological assumptions of Realism and Liberalism are incompatible. Both are Rationalist approaches to IR and foreign policy. The major difference is that Liberalism does not accept that the international system determines state behaviour, or even that external pressures are more important than domestic politics in shaping foreign policy choices. Taking these domestic processes as a point of departure, and allowing for the possibility that systemic pressure influence governmental interests and positions regarding foreign policy, allows us to better understand the CSDP.

Conclusion

In foreign policy analysis, the study of domestic factors in foreign policy-making has been advanced. This is not so much the case with respect to the CSDP. That is a serious omission if one accepts that the CSDP is about foreign policy-making in the EU Member States and that foreign policy-making cannot be understood without taking into account domestic factors. We argued that Moravcsik's New Liberalism in particular offers useful insights into the development of the CSDP, because it enables the student of the CSDP to take societal preferences and governmental interests as a starting point. We argued in favour of recognising the influence that domestic institutions have on the outcomes in the foreign policy decision-making process. We distinguished between parliamentary systems with coalition governments and single-party governments on the one hand, and (semi) presidential systems on the other. We also argued that it would be worthwhile to use the insights of representation studies in order to take the Liberal perspective one step further. The constitutional and political chain of delegation teaches us more about how governmental interests are influenced by domestic political processes. More in particular, the formal status of foreign policy-making, parliamentary mandate fulfilment and government mandate fulfilment offers a richer understanding of the CSDP. That being said, the presence of external pressures cannot simply be ignored. But unlike the Realist account, a Liberal perspective regards these external pressures as factors that are absorbed in the domestic political process.

The predominance of domestic factors in the development of the CSDP implies that there are serious constraints to the development of a common (grand) strategy. The relative autonomy of EU Member States in the CSDP means that EU foreign policy decisions are significantly influenced by governmental interests, rather than by national interests or by the EU's (collective) interests. New Liberalism holds that EU governments are above all concerned with electoral survival and may therefore opt for policy directions that contradict the EU's interests. That being said, the development of the CSDP shows that to a large extent the governmental interests of the individual 28 Member States correspond when it comes to the desire to strengthen peace and security.

Notes

1 One country's domestic crisis may of course constitute an international crisis for other states, as for example in the Syrian civil war. Yet third parties' responses are usually also a function of domestic political expediency, as the Syrian crisis again shows.
2 This strong dichotomy between the domestic and the international is primarily for the purpose of clarity. The boundaries between the two are often and increasingly blurred, for example where international media and think tanks directly impact on political choices outside their home country. Yet such transnational mechanisms still follow a domestic political logic because the impact or otherwise of an opinion piece is determined by the expected political outcomes for the respective government by its heeding, rejecting or ignoring it.
3 The Conservatives went as far as to put a demand for the abolition of the EDA into its 2010 general election programme. The EDA is a mechanism (among others) for voluntary

and rather limited cooperation between EU armies on joint procurement. Its annual budget is worth some €30 million – a burden distributed across 28 Member States.

References

Almond, G. A. (1950) *The American People and Foreign Policy*. New York: Praeger.

APSA (1950) Towards a More Responsible Two-Party System. *American Political Science Review*. 44 (3). pp. I–XI, 1–99.

Bäck, H., Debus, M. and Dumont, P. (2011). Who Gets What in Coalition Governments? Predictors of Portfolio Allocation in Parliamentary Democracies. *European Journal of Political Research*. 50 (4). pp. 441–78.

Baehr, P. R. (1974) Parliamentary Control over Foreign Policy in the Netherlands. *Government and Opposition*. 9 (2). pp. 165–88.

Baron, David P. (1998) Comparative Dynamics of Parliamentary Governments. *American Political Science Review*. 92 (3). pp. 593–609.

Beasley, R. K. and Kaarbo, J. (2014) Explaining Extremity in the Foreign Policies of Parliamentary Democracies. *International Studies Quarterly*. 58 (4). pp. 729–40.

Blais, A. and Bodet, M. A. (2006) Does Proportional Representation Foster Closer Congruence Between Citizens and Policy Makers? *Comparative Political Studies*. 39 (10). pp. 1243–62.

Budge, I. and Laver, M. (1993) The Policy of Government Coalitions: A Comparative Investigation. *British Journal of Political Science*. 23 (4). pp. 499–519.

Bueno de Mesquita, B., Smith, A., Siverson, R. M. and Morrow, J. D. (2005) *The Logic of Political Survival*. Cambridge, MA: MIT Press.

Canan-Sokullu, E. Ş. (2012) Domestic Support for Wars: A Cross-Case and Cross-Country Analysis. *Armed Forces & Society*. 38. pp. 117–41.

Carey, J. M. (2007) Competing Principals, Political Institutions, and Party Unity in Legislative Voting. *American Journal of Political Science*. 51 (1). pp. 92–107.

Cassese, A. (1980) *Parliamentary Control Over Foreign Policy*. Alphen aan de Rijn: Sijthoff & Noordhoff International Publishers BV.

Chandler, D. (2003) Rhetoric without Responsibility: The Attraction of 'Ethical' Foreign Policy. *The British Journal of Politics and International Relations*. 5 (3). pp. 295–316.

Chappell, L. (2009) Differing Member State Approaches to the Development of the EU Battlegroup Concept: Implications for CSDP. *European Security*. 18 (4). pp. 417–39.

Christensen, T. J. (1996) *Useful Adversaries: Grand Strategy, Domestic Mobilization, and Sino-American Conflict, 1947–1958*. Princeton, NJ: Princeton University Press.

Cladi, L. and Locatelli, A. (2013) Worth a Shot: On the Explanatory Power of Bandwagoning in Transatlantic Relations. *Contemporary Security Policy*. 34 (2). pp. 374–81.

Cladi, L. and Webber, M. (2011) Italian Foreign Policy in the Post-Cold War Period: A Neoclassical Realist Approach. *European Security*. 20 (2). pp. 205–19.

Cooper, R. (2003) *The Breaking of Nations – Order and Chaos in the Twenty-First Century*. London: Atlantic Books.

Downs, A. (1957) An Economic Theory of Political Action in a Democracy. *Journal of Political Economy*. 65 (2). pp. 135–50.

Doyle, M. W. (2008). Liberalism and Foreign Policy. In Smith, S., Hadfield, A. and Dunne, T. (eds) *Foreign Policy. Theories, Actors, Cases*. Oxford: Oxford University Press.

Duchêne, F. (1972) Europe's role in world peace. In Mayne, R. (ed.) *Europe Tomorrow: Sixteen Europeans Look Ahead*. London: Fontana.

Eichenberg, R. C. (2005). Victory Has Many Friends: US Public Opinion and the Use of Military Force, 1981–2005. *International Security*. 30 (1). pp. 140–77.

European Council (2003) *A Secure Europe in a Better World*. Brussels: European Union.

Evangelista, M. (1997) Domestic Structure and International Change. In Doyle, M. and Ikenberry, G. J. (eds) *New Thinking in International Relations Theory*. Boulder, CO: Westview Press.

Everts, P. (2002) *Democracy and Military Force*. Basingstoke, UK: Palgrave.

Everts, P. (1996) *Laat Dat Maar Aan Ons Over! Democratie, Buitenlands Beleid En Vrede*. Leiden: DSWO Press.

Freedman, L. (2000). Victims and Victors: Reflections on the Kosovo War. *Review of International Studies*. 26 (3). pp. 335–58.

Hofmann, S. C. (2013) *European Security in NATO's Shadow: Party Ideologies and Institution Building*. Cambridge: Cambridge University Press.

Hofmann, S. C. (2011) Why Institutional Overlap Matters: CSDP in the European Security Architecture. *Journal of Common Market Studies*. 49 (1). pp. 101–20.

Holmberg, S. (1999) Collective policy congruence compared. In Miller, W., Pierce, R., Thomassen, J., Herrera, R., Holmberg, S., Esaiasson, P. and Wessels, B. (eds) *Policy Representation in Western Democracies*., Oxford: Oxford University Press, pp. 87–109.

Holsti, O. R. (1992) Public Opinion and Foreign Policy: Challenges to the Almond-Lippmann Consensus. Mershon Series. *International Studies Quarterly*. 36 (4). pp. 439–66.

Huber, J. D. and Powell, G. B. (1994) Congruence Between Citizens and Policymaking in Two Visions of Liberal Democracy. *World Politics*. 46 (3). pp. 291–326.

Kaarbo, J. (2012) *Coalition Politics and Cabinet Decision Making: A Comparative Analysis of Foreign Policy Choices*. Ann Arbor, MI: University of Michigan Press.

Kaarbo, J. (2008) Coalition Cabinet Decision Making: Institutional and Psychological Factors. *International Studies Review*. 10 (1). pp. 57–86.

Kisangani, E. F. and Pickering, J. (2011) Democratic Accountability and Diversionary Force: Regime Types and the Use of Benevolent and Hostile Military Force. *Journal of Conflict Resolution*. 55 (6). pp. 1021–46.

Knecht, T. and Weatherford, M. S. (2006) Public Opinion and Foreign Policy: The Stages of Presidential Decision Making. *International Studies Quarterly*. 50 (3). pp. 705–27.

Knight, J. (1976) The Royal Prerogative and Foreign Policy: Notes on an Assumption. *Australian Outlook*. 30 (1). pp. 35–43.

Koga, J. (2011) Where Do Third Parties Intervene? Third Parties' Domestic Institutions and Military Interventions in Civil Conflicts. *International Studies Quarterly*. 55 (4). pp. 1143–66.

Krasner, S. D. (1978) *Defending the National Interest: Raw Materials Investments and US Foreign Policy*. Princeton, NJ: Princeton University Press.

Krotz, U. and Maher, R. (2011) International Relations Theory and the Rise of European Foreign and Security Policy. *World Politics*. 63 (3). pp. 548–79.

Laver, M. and Shepsle, K. A. (1996) *Making and Breaking Governments: Cabinets and Legislatures in Parliamentary Democracies*. New York: Cambridge University Press.

Louwerse, T. P. (2011) *Political Parties and the Democratic Mandate: Comparing Collective Mandate Fulfilment in the United Kingdom and the Netherlands*. Doctoral Thesis. Leiden: Leiden University.

Manners, I. (2002) Normative Power Europe: A contradiction in terms? *Journal of Common Market Studies*. 40 (2). pp. 235–58.

Mastanduno, M., Lake, D. A. and Ikenberry, G. J. (1989) Toward a Realist Theory of Action. *International Studies Quarterly*. 33. pp. 457–74.

Menon, A. (2011) Power, Institutions and the CSDP: The Promise of Institutionalist Theory. *Journal of Common Market Studies*. 49 (1). pp. 83–100.

Moravcsik, A. (2008) The New Liberalism. In Reus-Smith, C. and Snidal, D. (eds) *The Oxford Handbook of International Relations*. Oxford: Oxford University Press. pp. 234–54.

Moravcsik, A. (2000) The Origins of Human Rights Regimes: Democratic Delegation in Postwar Europe. *International Organization*. 54 (2). pp. 217–52.

Moravcsik, A. (1997) Taking Preferences Seriously: A Liberal Theory of International Politics. *International Organization*. 51 (4). pp. 513–53.

Moravcsik, A. (1993) Preferences and Power in the European Community: A Liberal Inter-governmentalist Approach. *Journal of Common Market Studies*. 31 (4). pp. 473–524.

Mueller, J. (1973) *War, Presidents, and Public Opinion*. New York: Wiley.

Müller, W. C. (2000) Political Parties in Parliamentary Democracies: Making Delegation and Accountability Work. *European Journal of Political Research*. 37 (3). pp. 309–33.

Oppermann, K. and Brummer, K. (2013) Patterns of Junior Partner Influence on the Foreign Policy of Coalition Governments. *The British Journal of Politics & International Relations*. 16 (4). pp. 555–71.

Owen, J. M. (2002) The Foreign Imposition of Domestic Institutions. *International Organization*. 56 (2). pp. 375–409.

Ozkececi-Taner, B. (2009) The Role of Ideas in Coalition Government Foreign Policymaking: The Case of Turkey between 1991 and 2002. *Republic of Letters*. Leiden: Brill.

Ozkececi-Taner, B. (2005) The Impact of Institutionalized Ideas in Coalition Foreign Policy Making: Turkey as an Example, 1991–2002. *Foreign Policy Analysis*. 1 (3). pp. 249–78.

Pohl, B. (2014) *EU Foreign Policy and Crisis Management Operations. Power, Purpose and Domestic Politics*. London: Routledge.

Pohl, B. (2013) Neither Bandwagoning nor Balancing: Explaining Europe's Security Policy. *Contemporary Security Studies*. 34 (2). pp. 353–73.

Pohl, B. and Van Willigen, N. (2015) Analytic Eclecticism and EU Foreign Policy (In)action. *Global Society*. Available at: www.tandfonline.com/doi/full/10.1080/13600826.2015.1029443

Power, S. (2002) *A Problem from Hell: America and the Age of Genocide*. New York: Basic Books.

Putnam, R. (1988) Diplomacy and Domestic Politics: The Logic of Two-Level Games. *International Organization*. 42 (3). pp. 427–60.

Risse Kappen, T. (1991) Public Opinion, Domestic Structure, and Foreign Policy in Liberal Democracies. *World Politics*. 43 (4). pp. 479–512.

Robinson, P. (2001) Theorizing the Influence of Media on World Politics: Models of Media Influence on Foreign Policy. *European Journal of Communication*. 16 (4). pp. 523–44.

Rosenau, J. N. (1961) *Public Opinion and Foreign Policy: An Operational Formulation*. New York: Random House.

Schimmelfennig, F. (2004) *The EU, NATO and the Integration of Europe. Rules and Rhetoric*. Cambridge: Cambridge University Press.

Schultz, K. (2013) Domestic Politics and International Relations. In Carlsnaes, W., Risse, T. and Simmons, B. A. (eds) *Handbook of International Relations*. London: Sage. pp. 478–502.

Schumpeter, J. A. (1976) *Capitalism, Socialism, and Democracy*. London: George Allen and Unwin.

Smith, M. E. (2012) Developing a 'Comprehensive Approach' to International Security: Institutional Learning and the CSDP. In Richardson, J. (ed.) *Constructing a Policy-Making State. Policy Dynamics in the EU*. Oxford: Oxford University Press. pp. 253–67.

Smith, M. (2004) Toward a Theory of EU Foreign Policy-Making: Multi-Level Governance, Domestic Politics, and National Adaptation to Europe's Common Foreign and Security Policy. *Journal of European Public Policy*. 11 (4). pp. 740–58.

Strøm, K. (2000) Delegation and Accountability in Parliamentary Democracies. *European Journal of Political Research*. 37 (3). pp. 261–89.

Strøm, K. and Müller, W. C. (1999) The Key to Togetherness: Coalition Agreements in Parliamentary Democracies. *The Journal of Legislative Studies*. 5 (3–4). pp. 255–82.

Taliaferro, J. W. (2009) Neoclassical Realism and Resource Extraction: State Building for Future War. In Lobell, S. E., Ripsman, N. and Taliaferro, J. W. (eds) *Neoclassical Realism, the State and Foreign Policy*. Cambridge: Cambridge University Press. pp. 194–226.

Telò, M. (2005) *Europe: A Civilian Power? European Union, Global Governance, World Order*. Basingstoke, UK: Palgrave Macmillan.

Thomson, R. (2001) The Programme to Policy Linkage: The Fulfilment of Election Pledges on Socio-Economic Policy In the Netherlands, 1986–1998. *European Journal of Political Research*. 40 (2). pp. 171–97.

Thomassen, J. J. A. (1994) Empirical Research into Political Representation: Failing Democracy or Failing Models? In Jennings, K. and Mann, T. E. (eds) *Elections at Home and Abroad, Essays in Honor of Warren Miller*. Ann Arbor, MI: Michigan University Press. pp. 171–97.

Timmermans, A. (2006) Standing Apart and Sitting Together: Enforcing Coalition Agreements in Multiparty Systems. *European Journal of Political Research*. 45 (2). pp. 263–83.

VanHoonacker, S. and Dijkstra, H. (2010) Understanding the Role of Bureaucracy in the European Security and Defence Policy: The State of the Art. *European Integration Online Papers*. 14 (1). pp. 1–33.

Walt, S. M. (1998) International Relations: One World, Many Theories. *Foreign Policy*. 110. pp. 29–44.

Warwick, P. V. (2001) Coalition Policy in Parliamentary Democracies: Who Gets How Much and Why. *Comparative Political Studies*. 34 (10). pp. 1212–36.

Weaver, R. K. (1986) The Politics of Blame Avoidance. *Journal of Public Policy*. 6 (4). pp. 371–98.

Zakaria, F. (1998) *From Wealth to Power. The Unusual Origins of America's World Role*. Princeton, NJ: Princeton University Press.

5 Beyond material factors?

Identity, culture and the foreign and security policy of the EU

Carla Monteleone

Since the seminal *The Culture of National Security. Norms and Identity in World Politics* (Katzenstein, 1996), it has been widely acknowledged that the strategic behaviour of states and their processes of defining security interests cannot be reduced to material factors such as military and economic power and its distribution. This is even truer in the case of the EU. Indeed, the evolution of European integration in the field of foreign, security and defence policy and the coordination practices established by EU Member States cannot be fully explained by looking at material factors only. This chapter will add to the picture the importance of identity, and, in particular, the *we-feeling* typical of belonging to a security community and security culture in the evolution of the practices adopted for the international projection of the EU and its Member States. In consideration of the importance that support of the UN has acquired since the 2003 ESS, both as a strategic priority and as a constitutive element of the EU identity, the chapter will then focus on the coordination practices adopted by EU Member States by looking at variations in their cohesion in the UNGA.

Identity and the foreign and security policy of the EU

Born immediately after the Second World War and after centuries of interstate wars among European states, the European integration process is in itself a security project aimed at redefining amity–enmity relations and the identity of Europe through institutional incentives, as well as at reshaping the identities and preferences of participating members. As suggested by Ruggie (1993, p. 172), changes in the context – and in particular the abandonment of territorial conflict – have been crucial in making the EU the first truly postmodern international political form: by reconfiguring their identity through the European integration process, EU Member States have started internalising the existence of the other members, and reimagining a European collective existence. The changed identity of European states shapes their preferences and interests (Katzenstein, 1996a, p. 518). Thanks to its durable success in avoiding wars among its members, over time the European integration process has started redirecting its focus from inward to outward, making possible the creation of a common foreign and security policy.

Looking only at material factors, the permanence of an area of peace among EU members, especially since the end of the Cold War, should not have been taken for granted, let alone their willingness to converge in their foreign and security policies, as Mearsheimer (1990) reminded us. On the contrary, Anderson and Seitz (2006) noticed that, from a military standpoint, the move towards the creation of a common defence policy defied logic. According to them, several factors were at play that should have worked against a common European defence. First, given the preponderant US contribution to European security through NATO, the creation of a common European defence could only be less efficient and effective. Second, it risked pushing the US out of Europe just as Germany was regaining power. Third, it risked weakening the apparent perception of unity, because Europeans differed on key strategic issues – including on the relationship with Russia (see Chapter 10). Finally, it required massive investment just as Europeans were reducing their defence spending and could not afford increases. According to them, the creation of a common foreign and security policy responded rather to the willingness to create cohesion and to strengthen the identity of a European *in-group*, in opposition to a potential *out-group*: it was a move taken in order to define the identity of the EU and to increase collective self-awareness.

Public opinion polls confirm the existence of a high correlation between European identity and European foreign and defence policy. They also suggest that, beyond the top-down intentions of political actors identified by Anderson and Seitz, a bottom-up incentive to reflect the emerging European identity in foreign and defence policy also existed. Despite variations in support towards the EU and several enlargement rounds that have challenged the EU to redefine its identity, since the early 1990s Eurobarometer data have regularly reported very strong support among Europeans for a common foreign policy, and even stronger support for a common defence policy.[1] This is remarkable, not only in that the two areas are normally included among the quintessential functions characterising states, but also in that defence is considered a higher priority and is included despite the absence of immediate military threats to the territorial integrity of any EU Member State. Making progress in the integration process in these areas is seen by Europeans as crucial for the definition of a European sense of role, mission and identity, and is necessary in order to increase support and legitimacy for the EU and for a process mostly perceived as elite-driven. The need to redefine a European identity should therefore be considered one of the drivers behind the creation of a common policy in the fields of foreign affairs, security and defence.

Such a driver is relevant because, as pointed out by Jepperson *et al.* (1996, p. 60), 'Identities both generate and shape interests', and 'Actors often cannot decide what their interests are until they know what they are representing – "who they are" – which in turn depends on their social relationships'. The development of a common foreign and security policy should be seen in relation to the attempt by the EU to affirm its identity, initially as an international actor, and later on as a global security actor. It should also be seen as the reflex of a 'we-feeling' developed by EU Member States as members of the same security community (Adler and Barnett, 1998), originally a Western European one, and then including new members following enlargement rounds. As Waever (1998, p. 77) noted, the strength of the community feeling is an important element, because 'the community works when the actors choose to act *as if* there is a community', and being part of the community becomes part of the self-conception of its members.[2] On the one hand, by rejecting homogenisation and choosing a common foreign and security policy, once the Cold War context in which the European integration process was born was over, Europe has also chosen to build an identity in the eyes of the others rather than from within. Accordingly, 'Europe can exist only if it has a "defense identity" and is a recognised actor on the international arena' (Waever 1998, p. 90). On the other hand, in a tightly coupled pluralistic security community like the European one, it is likely that shared identities and a high degree of trust will lead to cooperative and collective security and a high level of military integration (Adler and Barnett, 1998a, pp. 56–7). Indeed, being part of a security community creates a consultation habit that is reflected in practices of coordination among community members, and in the idea that it is *appropriate* to coordinate with the other community members rather than to move unilaterally. It also creates expectations (both in third parties and in other community members) regarding the behaviour of community members.

It is worth noting that, although EU Member States form a tightly coupled pluralistic security community, they are also part of the North Atlantic partly tightly coupled pluralistic security community, which includes the US. This is possible because each member of the community can hold multiple identities and multiple collective identities. Viewing the development of a foreign and security policy of the EU as an attempt to (re-)define a European identity does not necessarily mean that this is done in opposition to the US, although occasionally this may be the case. It is the evolution of the identity of the EU and the interaction between the two partially overlapping security communities, and therefore with the US, that helps in explaining variations in the preferences and interests of the EU, as well as in its security culture.

Security culture and the foreign and security policy of the EU

Closely related to identity, the security culture of the EU and its evolution is another important driver of the European integration process in foreign and security affairs. Krause (1999, p. 14) defined security culture as 'those enduring and widely shared beliefs, traditions, attitudes, and symbols that inform the ways in which a state's/society's interests and values with respect to security, stability and peace are perceived, articulated and advanced by political actors and élites.' Through socialisation processes, security culture provides decision-makers with a frame of core assumptions, beliefs and values about how security challenges can and should be dealt with (Williams, 2007, p. 256). By providing approaches to problem solving and strategic objectives, and by strengthening a collective sense of identity in terms of security, security cultures shape preferences for certain security instruments rather than others that are also available (Howorth, 2002; Attinà, 2006).

Like identity, security culture is subject to change over time and is influenced by the diffusion of new ideas, practices and experiences. European security culture has reflected changes in worldwide security culture. However, three Cold War experiences have been particularly important in shaping the security culture of Europe and its practices (Krause and Latham, 1999; Attinà, 2006). First, the experience of arms control negotiations convinced Europeans of the importance of security negotiations. They were effective in reducing the risk of violence. Moreover, by creating arms control communities, they helped create agreement 'on some basic but essential conceptual building blocks for the security-building and arms control effort' (Krause and Latham, 1999, p. 27), so that in the end, 'the *process* or dialogue mattered as much as the product' (Krause and Latham, 1999, p. 29). Second, the experience of the Helsinki process and the development of confidence building measures wiped away the secrecy of states in military affairs, affirmed the effectiveness of – and preference for – a cooperative approach to security, and led Europeans to believe that security is mutual. Alongside cooperative security, comprehensive security was introduced. Although the widening process took place in all Western countries, it was in Europe that it became a defining trait of security. The political and human dimension of security acquired new relevance (Attinà, 2006). Third, fed by the experience of war in Bosnia and instability at the European borders, in the 1990s the Cold War framing left room for a new discourse of threat focused on potential risks as sources of insecurity in Europe. The new reading of security 'transformed essentially contestable *interpretations* of danger ... into "objective" and incontestable *facts* regarding the sources of threat and insecurity in the international system' (Krause and Latham, 1999, p. 38). This has allowed the discourse of *new* threats and dangers in the European security culture to be present next to concepts of co-operative and comprehensive security (Attinà, 2006).

Scholars have wondered whether over time the EU has moved from having a security culture to also having a strategic culture (among others, Cornish and Edwards, 2001, 2005; Howorth, 2002). The debate among scholars of three generations, mostly on the methodological front and on whether strategic culture only shapes or also constitutes behaviour, has been lively (see, among others, Betts, 2000; Duffield, 1999; Gray, 1999, 2003; Johnston, 1999; Lantis, 2002; Legro, 1996; Poore, 2003). Moreover, several conceptions of strategic culture have been identified (Glenn, 2009). Nevertheless, the relation between ideational sets and strategy has been widely acknowledged. Originally defined as 'the sum total of ideas, conditioned emotional responses, and patterns of habitual behaviour that members of a national strategic community have acquired through instruction or imitation and share with each other with regard to nuclear strategy' (Snyder, 1977, p. 8), strategic culture has been redefined by three generations of scholars to refer to issues specifically related to war and the military.

In the 1980s, first generation scholars explained differences in states' strategy in relation to 'unique variations in macro-environmental variables such as deeply rooted historical experience, political culture, and geography' (Johnston, 1995, p. 36). Technology, organisational culture and traditions, historical strategic practices, political psychology, ideology and the international system structure could all be considered relevant explanatory variables, and these scholars believed that strategic culture – somehow homogeneous over time – pervades 'all levels of choice from grand strategy down to tactics' and by doing so delimits strategic options (Johnston, 1995, p. 37). For second-generation scholars, in the mid-1980s, strategic culture is a product of historical experience, but most of all is a declaratory strategy legitimising the authority of those in charge of decision-making, while strategic choices are constrained by the interests of hegemonic groups (Johnston, 1995, p. 40). In practice, though, strategic culture may have no causal effect on operational doctrine.

In the 1990s, third generation scholars saw strategic culture as a factor limiting decision-makers' options or as a lens altering the appearance and efficacy of potential choices, but it excluded behaviour as an element of the strategic culture and linked strategic culture to recent practices and experiences, therefore allowing it to vary (Johnston, 1995, p. 41). Trying to overcome shortcomings in previous definitions of strategic culture, Johnston came to the following definition:

> Strategic culture is an integrated 'System of symbols' (e.g. argumentation structures, languages, analogies, metaphors) which acts to establish pervasive and long-lasting strategic preferences by formulating concepts of the role and efficacy of military force in interstate political affairs, and by clothing these conceptions with such an aura of factuality that the strategic preferences seem uniquely realistic and efficacious.
>
> (1995, p. 46)

As Johnston makes clear, in this definition there are three quintessential elements of strategic culture: whether the role of war is considered inevitable or an aberration; whether the nature of the adversary and threat is considered as zero-sum or variable sum; and whether the use of force is considered effective to control outcomes and to eliminate threats, and the conditions under which applied force is considered useful. These elements provide shared information that reduces uncertainty about the strategic environment: strategic preferences vary according to variations in these elements and therefore affect behavioural choices. According to their preferences on these elements, different actors may have different strategic cultures, but variations in these elements may lead the same actor to vary its strategic culture. Strategic cultures are also strictly related to identity and to in-group identification. Accordingly, states sharing high levels of in-group identification will 'tend to share strategic cultures which exhibit hard *realpolitik* characteristics. Conversely, states with weak in-group identification, or states which perceive other states as sharing values characteristic of the in-group, are more likely to be influenced by *idealpolitik* strategic cultures' (Johnston, 1995, p. 60).

According to Rogers (2009, p. 833), Europe has had a grand strategy, that is, a theory about how to achieve security that identifies and prioritises threats and appropriate political and military remedies (Posen, 2004, pp. 33–4) or 'a community's prevailing compass for navigating world politics together' (Kornprobst, 2014, p. 7), since the very inception of the European Coal and Steel Community. Initially organised around its *civilian culture*, over time the grand strategy of the EU has abandoned the idea of a civilian power Europe to assume a progressively global role.

Thanks to the end of the Cold War (a shifting scene) and to an agreement on agency, purpose and means, in the early 1990s the EU managed to create a new grand strategy (Kornprobst, 2014). The 1993 European Council in Copenhagen acknowledged the importance of the success of political and economic reform in Central and Eastern Europe, and conceptualised Europe in terms of concentric circles, with EU members and prospective members forming the core. It also defined its identity as a community of values and invited the peripheries 'to join the EU if they abide by the EU's normative catalogue' (Kornprobst, 2014, p. 9) embodied in the Copenhagen criteria for accession: democracy, rule of law, human rights, minority group rights and market economics. By diffusing its norms, the EU set itself the goal to *EU-ise* the periphery through active socialisation of the political elites of candidate states into EU practices, and through economic incentives. From that moment on, the diffusion strategy 'became the seemingly self-evident anchor for making sense of the EU's relations with its neighbourhood' (Kornprobst, 2014, p. 9).

The war in the former Yugoslavia and the risks to the European project provided the rationale for a paradigm shift in the late 1990s and for a new vision of security and of the EU as a global power (Rogers, 2009). A discourse coalition of *euro-strategists* including Solana and a pan-European complex of institutions, think tanks, academic establishments and private organisations acted as brokers and mobilised to rearticulate the European grand strategy. If defining the EU as a civilian power identified the threat in a revival of a European war that could end European integration, redefining the EU as a global power meant acknowledging the existence of 'a cluster of interconnected challenges and threats to the security of the European Union as a unified territorial, political and economic space' (Rogers, 2009, p. 846). The new EU had to be strong and politically credible. In order to do that, it needed to acquire full instrumental power but it also had to be seen as legitimate. This translated into the combination of a greater activism with the promotion of *effective multilateralism* and the identification in the UN of an institutional point of reference. It also created a wider institutional apparatus in Brussels dealing with geopolitical issues, and new institutions capable of transforming the European power into a force for projection, among which were the HR, the EUMS, the Policy Unit (PU), the Joint Situation Centre (JSC), the Special Representatives (SR), the General Secretariat of the Council (GSC), the Committee for Civilian Aspects of Crisis Management (CCACM) and the EDA (Rogers, 2009, p. 853). The PSC, in particular, has been extremely important in promoting a trans-European strategic culture through normative socialisation (Howorth, 2010; Biava, 2011). From the early 2000s, the EU started being very active in launching its own peace operations. Nevertheless, whether the discourse on the EU as a global power managed to become hegemonic and to translate into a new grand strategy is still a matter of debate.

The 2003 ESS was an attempt in that direction. It included a diverse number of threats and challenges ranging from terrorism and organised crime to state failure, from nuclear proliferation to regional armed conflicts. Revisited in 2008, it highlighted that globalisation made the new threats and challenges to the security interests of the European Union more complex and interconnected. With the ESS, the EU made clear that, while territorial invasion is not realistic, the new European threats must be fought abroad, and a mixture of instruments, including military ones, was required. Effective multilateralism and a rule-based international order gained centre stage. Security and development were directly linked, but security was clearly acknowledged as a precondition for development. Nevertheless, according to Kornprobst (2014), contrary to the diffusion strategy of the 1990s, the ESS failed to become a grand strategy because it did not become a *commonplace*, that is it failed to become the natural starting point for reasoning and argumentation of the members of the community. Several important elements stand behind this failure. According to Kornprobst, EU Member States did not fully agree on what they meant by multilateralism, ranked their status in world affairs differently, had a different idea about the importance of special relations, but they also had different understandings of the appropriateness of the use of force. Therefore, despite its ambition to the contrary, the EU failed to transform itself from a regional actor into a global one.

Nevertheless, the idea that military instruments could be used – although with important caveats – was established, EU peace operations started introducing a military component, key documents were released and the Lisbon treaty confirmed the direction taken (Biava, 2011). The Petersberg tasks remained a reference point, but the Military Headline Goals, formulated over time, provided EU interventions with the task of covering the whole conflict cycle from prevention to peace consolidation, and with the possibility of using military assets. Although never deployed, EU Battlegroups were created, and reached full operational capacity in 2007. Moreover, the national strategic cultures of EU Member States started converging with regard to prevalent strategic norms under the influence of changing threat perceptions, institutional socialisation, shared experiences from joint missions, similar threat assessments among epistemic communities, elite socialisation in common institutions, societal learning from crises and the increasing demand for out-of-area operations (Meyer, 2005; Giegerich, 2006; Meyer and Strickmann, 2011). Existing differences reflect the fact that strategic culture can be heterogeneous and contested, because it reflects a majoritarian view which can be subject to both internal and external forces of contestation and change (Meyer, 2005, p. 529). As a result of the socialisation of high level officials within the new EU institutions – the PSC above all – and of the conformity pressure exerted on the newcomers, shared visions and expectations among actors and a growing acceptance of the EU as a framework for defence cooperation developed (Meyer, 2005; Biava, 2011; Howorth, 2010). In particular, the actors involved put an emphasis on the 'necessity to find a constructive consensus in the name of a more general European interest and according to the principle of solidarity' as an important driver of their behaviour (Biava, 2011, p. 52). In addition, the same effects of socialisation were found in military cultures and even in the military ethos of EU Member States (King, 2006; Koivula, 2009). Interestingly, one of the cornerstones of the emerging military ethos is 'Pretend to be warlike but don't fight', reflecting the ambiguous attitude of and differences among EU Member States regarding the use of force (Koivula, 2009).

As Biava (2011) highlighted, there are some elements of divergence in the strategic culture of EU Member States. Among them were whether or not there should be geographical limits to the CSDP engagement, whether EU intervention should cover the entire temporal spectrum of a crisis, and whether the typology of intervention should be prevalently civilian or military. But there are also many elements of convergence that characterise the emergent EU strategic culture as being based on: the principle of the projection of forces within a multilateral framework; the principle of international legitimacy and the implementation of local ownership; the reliance on a flexible, comprehensive, dynamic, and long-term approach, based on an ad hoc and integrated (including civil–military) use of multidimensional instruments; and a restricted use of military means, deployed on the basis of a mandate limited in time and space, and foreseeing an exit strategy (Biava, 2011, p. 57). As Biava *et al.* (2011) have pointed out, thanks to these elements of convergence, the EU has elaborated strategic guidelines, identified its threats, developed a capacity to act and shared norms on the legitimacy of action. The socialisation and learning-by-doing processes have then contributed to spreading and institutionalising these norms, ultimately shaping the EU's strategic framework.

EU Member States' practices and cohesion in the UN General Assembly

Socialisation of high-level Member States' officials within EU institutions has played an important role in advancing the creation of common norms and in strengthening the *we-feeling* as members of the same community. Through frequent interactions, processes of arguing, persuasion and social learning, EU Member States' officials learnt to internalise new norms and rules of appropriateness in order to become *members in good standing* of that community and they redefined their national interests accordingly (Finnemore and Sikkink, 1998; Checkel, 1999; Borzel and Risse, 2003, p. 66). Indeed, frequent interactions within institutionalised settings such as intergovernmental organisations over time affect processes of interest (re-)definition to the point of leading to interest convergence (Bearce and Bondanella, 2007). In the case of the EU, despite the lack of enforcement mechanisms, since the EPC an increasingly binding set of behavioural standards has emerged and norms of behaviour have been progressively reinforced (Ginsberg, 2001; Tonra, 2000; Major, 2005).

The UNGA represents a useful forum in which changes in EU Member States' practices of coordination in foreign and security affairs can be analysed. It represents a strategic priority and a constitutive element of the EU identity, and all EU Member States are present, so it is possible to look at variations in their voting behaviour to see how cohesively EU members act. Because in the UNGA the principle *one state one vote* creates more incentives to defect than to cooperate, voting cohesion is normally the result of coordination among EU Member States. Indeed, until the 1990s, EU members rarely voted as a bloc, unless the level of disagreement in the UNGA was high. In particular, when a cohesive vote by EU Member States was unlikely to change the outcome of a resolution, the coordination process seemed to be limited and specific national interests could prevail over the majority position of the EU. However, the EU is the only regional organisation that, since the 1980s, has acquired such a high level of coordination and strategic voting behaviour that it has become capable of increasing its level of voting cohesion in contested votes (Burmester and Jankowski, 2014).

Since the launch of the EPC, EU Member States have made increasing attempts not only at consulting each other but also at institutionalising their consultations at the UN. Although not binding, especially on the UNSC permanent members (France and the United Kingdom), these measures represented a step forward in creating a distinct European presence based not only on common interests but also on a common identity at the UN. The importance ('It is vital') for the EU of speaking at the UN with one voice and for EU Member States to coordinate was stressed in the 1999 Framework Agreement between the UN and the EU. But it was the EU's political choice of effective multilateralism with a strong UN at its heart that made the EU Member States' practice of coordination at the UN important, not only as a political goal per se but also as instrumental to supporting the effectiveness of the UN. As stated in the 2003 ESS, 'Strengthening the United Nations, equipping it to fulfil its responsibilities and to act effectively, is a European priority'. In this respect, EU Member States' practice of coordination at the UN is both an outcome and the reflection of an ongoing process of redefinition of the identity and strategic culture both of the EU and of its Member States.

Laatikainen and Smith (2006, p. 9) have pointed out the existence of three processes at the UN: the development of institutional capability for coordinating the policies of EU Member States; the adaptation of EU Member States to ensure the consistency and effectiveness of the EU voice; and an external diffusion process of European ideas and institutions. Acting as a single political voice at the UN is not only a choice of EU Member States: they are expected to be a unified actor (Paasivirta and Porter, 2006, p. 35; Laatikainen, 2004, p. 4). The practice of coordination at the UN, and especially the UNGA, means that 'Debate about the particular policy question or agenda item is continued until all members of the EU group without any exception agree to the direction and wording of the policy to be endorsed' (Dedring, 2004, p. 2). The practice of preparing the position on UN issues before each UNGA session before the entry into force of the Lisbon treaty and the upgrading of EU status in the UNGA is described in detail by Paasivirta and Porter (2006) and confirmed by Laatikainen (2004). It involved the circulation by the Presidency of a draft paper outlining the basic line to take on the agenda of the forthcoming UNGA session, sometimes drawn from conclusions issued by the Council ahead of major UN meetings.[3] The draft paper was then submitted for EU coordination in the framework of the Council, triggering 'a coordination process in the relevant Council Working Groups' and feeding into the EU position in New York (Paasivirta and Porter, 2006, p. 40). Statements delivered by the Presidency were often prepared through the New York Office of the Council's Secretariat system of EU circulars, and meetings of the EU convened in the Council's offices enabled *real time* coordination on a constant basis (Paasivirta and Porter 2006, p. 41). These meeting were of utmost importance in accommodating the EU position and made it possible to respond to the need to find support or to keep on negotiating.

Over 1,300 EU coordination meetings (Member States and Commission) are organised annually in New York alone,[4] with heads of missions meeting at least weekly to discuss the most important or difficult issues. The local electronic mailing system is used to pass messages to convene the coordination meetings and circulate documents to the relevant experts (Paasivirta and Porter, 2006, p. 42). These meetings also have the function of sharing information that not all missions have access to and, especially in the case of the smaller missions, which lack the resources to follow the issues in the political agenda of the day, can help in forming a position (Interview 1). The EU position is normally delivered by the Presidency and, when EU Member States speak, they normally refer to the Presidency statement. As Paasivirta and Porter note,

> The EU coordination process has thus become a central feature of the daily working life of all EU diplomats posted to New York.... What is certain is that the reflex and culture of coordination is now well and truly entrenched in the approaches of all EU Member States at the United Nations. Indeed, the will of the Member States to achieve a common position on issues before the UNGA and ECOSOC almost always prevails over any single national concern.
>
> (2006, p. 43)

Furthermore,

> The culture of EU cohesion ... is founded upon intensive common preparation, a unified and strategic external identity, and the ways and means of presenting EU positions with one voice. The culture stems from a combination of a common institutional framework and practical working habits.... The sense of the EU as a single actor has evolved to the extent that it is a

familiar sight to all partners at the UN, and is the pattern of behaviour which is now expected of the EU.

(Paasivirta and Porter, 2006: 47)

Coordination among EU Member States at the UN works so well not only because it is 'ingrained in the working habits' of EU diplomats in New York and supported by common rules and a common space, but also because there is 'a substantive and realistic judgment that more is achieved by the EU's Member States when acting together than any state could manage alone' (Paasivirta and Porter, 2006, p. 48). This situation has only changed slightly with the entry into force of the Lisbon treaty, which led the EU delegation to the UN to progressively assume the role of the rotating Presidency and to be responsible for the day-to-day coordination of the EU position, and the upgrading in 2011 of the EU status in the UNGA.

There is still considerable variation in the degree of adaptation of EU Member States toward EU diplomacy (Laatikainen and Smith, 2006) and remarkable differences have been registered on some issues (Luif, 2003), reminding us that EU Member States tend to defect when it comes to vital national issues. However, the increase in EU Member States' voting cohesion at the UNGA is generally considered evidence of the coordination practice. Starting from the 1990s, coordination efforts drove to a marked increase in EU states' voting cohesion, showing that voting cohesion was not only to be associated with similar interests among European states, but was also the result of the intense work done in Brussels and New York (Luif, 2003; Laatikainen, 2004; Paasivirta and Porter, 2006; Hosli *et al.*, 2011). EU Member States since the second half of the 1990s have managed to increase the level of unanimous votes to around 80 per cent and to drastically reduce two-way and three-way splits (Johansson-Nogués, 2004, p. 72). Moreover, EU cohesion levels are generally higher than those for the full UNGA and differences in cohesion levels are not necessarily registered on *high politics* issues (Hosli *et al.*, 2011).

This does not mean that the EU acts as a single voice through its Member States yet, nor that full convergence has been achieved. Indeed, an analysis of the voting cohesion of EU Member States in the UNGA from the 59th until the 66th session (Figure 5.1) shows that, on average, EU Member States are divided in the UNGA in about a third of the roll call votes. They more often split into two groups, occasionally into three groups, very rarely into four.[5] In particular, in the period under consideration, EU Member States were divided in a percentage of votes that ranges from 42 per cent in the 62nd session, to 24 per cent in the 66th session. The trend is, however, stable. Nevertheless, considering that splits in two groups are by far the prevailing mode when EU Member States are not cohesive, it is worthy of note that most of the two-way splits are caused by the defection of one or two EU Member States only, while the rest of the EU Member States manages to maintain voting cohesion (Figure 5.2). It is also worthy of note that, in the period under consideration, only France and the UK have defected from EU Member States' voting cohesion in more than 40 per

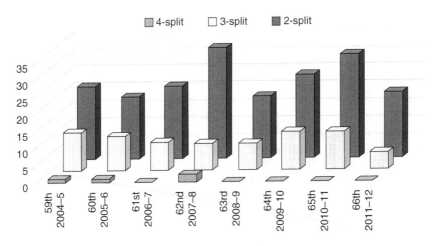

Figure 5.1 Percentage of split votes of EU member states 2004–12 (source: author's elaboration of UN data).

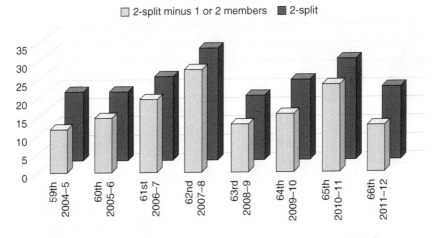

Figure 5.2 Comparison between two-split votes and two-split votes with only one or two members defecting from EU cohesion (absolute numbers) (source: author's elaboration of UN data).

cent of their votes. Considering that they often tend to vote alike, this is the reflection of their special status as permanent members of the UNSC. Cyprus has also defected in just over 30 per cent of its votes, very often in isolation. All the other EU Member States, though, have tended to restrict their behaviour, and have coordinated regularly and to a large degree to present themselves as a single bloc.

What emerges at the UNGA is that EU Member States have started inten-
sively coordinating despite a context in which it is national sovereignty that ultimately really counts. They have made institutional and procedural changes to
adapt, because they have realised the importance of the politics of scale in that
forum, but also because they felt they were part of a group, had internalised
norms and rules, and were feeling internal and external pressure to behave as
good members of the group. Moreover, they have acted cohesively in support of
an institution that they consider a priority in the ESS. However, fragmentation is
always possible, as only EU states can vote at the UN and they have repeatedly
defected in order to guard their vital interests. In particular, the international economic crisis that started in late 2007, and even more the Eurozone crisis in 2010
that shocked Southern European countries and put into doubt the idea of European solidarity, could have a negative impact not only on the resources and the
structure of opportunities of the affected EU Member States, but also on their
we-feeling and therefore on their incentives to follow and act through the group.
Likewise, the Ukraine conflict could put to the test the capacity of the EU
Member States closer to Russia to maintain a common position (see Chapter 10).

Conclusions

The process of European integration in the field of foreign, security and military
affairs has been influenced not only by material factors, but also by processes of
redefinition of the European identity and of European security culture. In both of
these processes, the interaction between top-down and bottom-up inputs is
important. The attempt to strengthen the identity of a European *in-group* could
build on the very favourable public opinion polls in support of a foreign and
defence policy and on the existing *we-feeling* as members of a mature security
community that, having developed a high degree of trust among its members,
naturally moves on towards a high level of military integration. The attempt to
move from a security culture to a strategic culture could build on a wider long-
term process of redefinition of threats and challenges that reflected a partially
changing attitude towards the nature of the adversary and the use of force. As
Johnston (1995) noted, the interaction between identity and security culture is
also important. Indeed, the move from an EU strategic culture based on idealpolitik to one including military elements is in itself a reflection of a stronger in-
group identification.

The practice of coordination among EU Member States reflects changes in both
identity and strategic culture. By looking at coordination practices and at variation
in voting cohesion, it has clearly emerged that, despite the absence of enforcement
mechanisms, EU Member States tend to be bound by their belonging to the same
community. Given that all actors simultaneously hold multiple identities and that
security strategy reflects a majoritarian view, which can be subject to contestation,
defection is possible and, indeed, although limited, it takes place.

However, in the process of building a foreign, security and defence policy,
both the move to strengthen a European identity and the move from security to

strategic culture have been only partially successful. Indeed, top-down inputs have not fully matched advancements in *feeling European* among European citizens, highlighting the existence of important differences and revealing a gap. Likewise, the top-down attempts to promote a strategic culture and a global role for the EU have met with some resistance. The Eurozone crisis has put to the test the *we-feeling*, especially in the Southern European countries, and the conflict in Ukraine could put to the test the emerging European strategic culture. Overcoming the legitimacy deficit that might arise as a result of this gap and resistance, and building on existing common elements may be necessary to pass both tests.

Notes

1 Asked between 1992 and 2010 the question

> Irrespective of other details of the Maastricht Treaty, what is your opinion on each of the following proposals? Please tell me for each proposal whether you are for it or against it. One common foreign policy among the Member States of the European Union, towards other countries

a percentage in favour ranging from a minimum of 62.7 to 72 was regularly obtained. Asked in the same period the question

> Irrespective of other details of the Maastricht Treaty, what is your opinion on each of the following proposals? Please tell me for each proposal whether you are for it or against it. A common defence and security/military policy among the European Union Member States

a percentage in favour ranging from a minimum of 68 to a maximum of 80 was regularly observed (the only exception is a 60 per cent obtained in 1996). See http://ec.europa.eu/public_opinion/cf/showchart_line.cfm?keyID=280&nationID=16,&startdate=1992.10&enddate=2010.06 and http://ec.europa.eu/public_opinion/cf/showchart_line.cfm?keyID=281&nationID=16,&startdate=1992.10&enddate=2008.10 [accessed: 30 January 2015]. Moreover, asked between 2011 and 2014 the question

> What is your opinion on each of the following statements? Please tell me for each statement whether you are for it or against it. (One answer per line) A common foreign policy of the 27 Member States of the EU

percentages in favour ranged from 61 to 66. Interestingly, also in this period, defence seemed more important to Europeans. Asked 'What is your opinion on each of the following statements? Please tell me for each statement whether you are for it or against it. (One answer per line) A common defence and security policy among EU Member States', percentages in favour ranged from 71 to 76. See http://ec.europa.eu/public_opinion/cf/showchart_line.cfm?keyID=3786&nationID=16,&startdate=2011.05&enddate=2014.11 and http://ec.europa.eu/public_opinion/cf/showchart_line.cfm?keyID=3787&nationID=16,&startdate=2011.05&enddate=2014.11 [accessed: 30 January 2015].

2 Germany, for instance, has clearly redefined its identity as a member of the European Community.

3 Conclusions are prepared by the relevant Council Working Group in Brussels. It is here that experts from EU Member States meet Commission representatives and the Council Secretariat (Paasvirta and Porter, 2006, p. 40).

4 www.eu-un.europa.eu/articles/en/article_9389_en.htm [accessed: 4 September 2013].

5 All roll call votes taken in the UNGA (not in its committees) were included in the analysis

and absences are counted as expression of a separate position. Data were taken from the UNGA website www.un.org/en/ga/ in relation to resolutions and from the UN website UNBISNET unbisnet.un.org, and the meeting records and/or press releases were analysed for each session [accessed: 23 August 2014].

References

Adler, E. and Barnett, M. (eds) (1998) *Security Communities*. Cambridge: Cambridge University Press.

Adler, E. and Barnett, M. (1998a) A framework for the study of security communities. In Adler, E. and Barnett, M. (eds) *Security Communities*. Cambridge: Cambridge University Press, pp. 29–65.

Anderson, S. and Seitz, T. R. (2006) European Security and Defense Policy Demystified. Nation-Building and Identity in the European Union. *Armed Forces and Society*. 33 (1). pp. 24–42.

Attinà, F. (2006) The Building of Regional Security Partnership and the Security Culture Divide in the Mediterranean Region. In Adler, E., Crawford, B., Bicchi, F. and Del Sarto, R. (eds) *The Convergence of Civilizations. Constructing a Mediterranean Region*. Toronto: University of Toronto Press. pp. 239–65.

Bearce, D. H. and Bondanella, S. (2007) Intergovernmental Organizations, Socialization, and Member-State Interest Convergence. *International Organization*. 61 (4). pp. 703–33.

Betts, R. K. (2000) Is Strategy an Illusion? *International Security*. 25 (2). pp. 5–50.

Biava, A. (2011) The Emergence of a Strategic Culture within the Common Security and Defence Policy. *European Foreign Affairs Review*. 16 (1). pp. 41–58.

Biava, A., Drent, M. and Herd, G. P. (2011) Characterizing the European Union's Strategic Culture: An Analytical Framework. *Journal of Common Market Studies*. 49 (6). pp. 1227–48.

Börzel, T. A. and Risse, T. (2003) Conceptualizing the Domestic Impact of Europe. In Featherstone, K. and Radaelli, C. M. (eds) *The Politics of Europeanization*. Oxford: Oxford University Press. pp. 57–80.

Burmester, N. and Jankowski, M. (2014) Reassessing the European Union in the United Nations General Assembly. *Journal of European Public Policy*. 21 (10). pp. 1491–1508.

Checkel, J. T. (1999) *International Institutions and Socialization*. (ARENA Working Paper 5).

Cornish, P and Edwards, G. (2005) The Strategic Culture of the European Union: A Progress Report. *International Affairs*. 81 (4). pp. 801–20.

Cornish, P. and Edwards, G. (2001) Beyond the EU/NATO Dichotomy: The Beginnings of a European Strategic Culture. *International Affairs*. 77 (3). pp. 587–603.

Dedring, J. (2004) Reflection on the Coordination of the EU Member States in Organs of the United Nations. *CFSP Forum*. 2 (1). pp. 1–3.

Duffield, J. S. (1999) Political Culture and State Behavior: Why Germany Confounds Neorealism. *International Organization*. 53 (4). pp. 765–803.

Finnemore, M. and Sikkink, K. (1998) International Norm Dynamics and Political Change. *International Organization*. 52 (4). pp. 887–917.

Giegerich, B. (2006) *European Security and Strategic Culture*. Baden-Baden: Nomos.

Ginsberg, R. (2001) *The European Union in International Politics: Baptism by Fire*. Lanham: Rowman & Littlefield.

Glenn, J. (2009) Realism versus Strategic Culture: Competition and Collaboration? *International Studies Review*. 11 (3). pp. 523–51.

Gray, C. S. (2003) In praise of strategy. *Review of International Studies*. 29 (2). pp. 285–95.

Gray, C. S. (1999) Strategic Culture as Context: the First Generation of Theory Strikes Back. *Review of International Studies*. 25 (1). pp. 49–69.

Hosli, M. O., Moody, R., O'Donovan, B., Kaniovski, S. and Little, A. G. H. (2011) Squaring the Circle? Collective and Distributive Effects of United Nations Security Council Reform. *Review of International Organizations*. 6 (2). pp. 163–87.

Howorth, J. (2010) The Political and Security Committee: a Case Study in 'Supranational Intergovernmentalism'. *Les Cahiers Européens*. 1/2010.

Howorth, J. (2002) The CESDP and the Forging of a European Security Culture. *Politique européenne*. 8. pp. 88–109.

Interview 1, Interview with a European Diplomat in Washington, Washington, 9 June 2010.

Jepperson, R. L, Wendt, A. and Katzenstein, P. J. (1996) Norms, Identity, and Culture in National Security. In Katzenstein, P. J. (ed.) *The Culture of National Security. Norms and Identity in World Politics*. New York: Columbia University Press. pp. 33–75.

Johansson-Nogués, E. (2004) The Fifteen and the Accession States in the UN General Assembly: What Future for European Foreign Policy in the Coming Together of the 'Old' and 'New' Europe? *European Foreign Affairs Review*. 9 (1). pp. 67–92.

Johnston, A. I. (1999) Strategic Cultures Revisited: Reply to Colin Gray. *Review of International Studies*. 25 (3). pp. 519–23.

Johnston, A. I. (1995) Thinking about Strategic Culture. *International Security*. 19 (4). pp. 32–64.

Katzenstein, P. J. (ed.) (1996) *The Culture of National Security. Norms and Identity in World Politics*. New York: Columbia University Press.

Katzenstein, P. J. (1996a) Conclusion: National Security in a Changing World. In Katzenstein, P. J. (ed.) *The Culture of National Security. Norms and Identity in World Politics*. New York: Columbia University Press. pp. 498–537.

King, A. (2006) Towards a European Military Culture? *Defence Studies*. 6 (3). pp. 257–77.

Koivula, T. (2009) Towards an EU Military Ethos. *European Foreign Affairs Review*. 14 (2). pp. 171–90.

Kornprobst, M. (2014) Building Agreements Upon Agreements: The European Union and Grand Strategy. *European Journal of International Relations*. First published on June 27, 2014 as doi:10.1177/1354066114535273. pp. 1–26.

Krause, K. (1999) Cross-Cultural Dimensions of Multilateral Non-Proliferation and Arms Control Dialogues: An Overview. Krause, K. (ed.) *Culture and Security. Multilateralism, Arms Control and Security Building*. London and Portland: Frank Cass Publishers. pp. 1–22.

Krause, K. and Latham, A. (1999) Constructing Non-Proliferation and Arms Control: The Norms of Western Practice. In Krause, K. (ed.) *Culture and Security. Multilateralism, Arms Control and Security Building*. London and Portland: Frank Cass Publishers. pp. 23–54.

Laatikainen, K. V. (2004) Assessing the EU as an Actor at the UN: Authority, Cohesion, Recognition and Autonomy. *CFSP Forum*. 2 (1). pp. 4–9.

Laatikainen, K. V. and Smith, K. E. (eds) (2006) *The European Union at the United Nations. Intersecting Multilateralisms*. Houndmills and New York: Palgrave.

Lantis, J. S. (2002) Strategic Culture and National Security Policy. *International Studies Review*. 4 (3). pp. 87–113.

Legro, J. W. (1996) Culture and Preferences in the International Cooperation Two-Step. *American Political Science Review*. 90 (1). pp. 118–37.

Luif, P. (2003) *EU Cohesion in the UN General Assembly*. (EU Institute of Security Studies Occasional Paper no. 49).

Major, C. (2005) Europeanisation and Foreign and Security Policy – Undermining and Rescuing the Nation State? *Politics*. 25 (3). pp. 175–90.

Mearsheimer, J. J. (1990) Back to the Future: Instability in Europe After the Cold War. *International Security*. 15 (1). pp. 5–56.

Meyer, C. O. (2005) Convergence Towards a European Strategic Culture? A Constructivist Framework for Explaining Changing Norms. *European Journal of International Relations*. 11 (4). pp. 523–49.

Meyer, C. O. and Strickmann, E. (2011) Solidifying Constructivism: How Material and Ideational Factors Interact in European Defence. *Journal of Common Market Studies*. 49 (1). pp. 61–81.

Paasivirta, E. and Porter, D. (2006) EU Coordination at the UN General Assembly and ECOSOC: A View from Brussels, a View from New York. In Wouters, J., Hoffmeister, F. and Ruys, T. (eds) *The United Nations and the European Union: An Ever Stronger Partnership*. The Hague: T. M. C. Asser Press. pp. 35–48.

Posen, B. (2004) The European Security Strategy: Practical Implications. *Oxford Journal on Good Governance*. 1 (1). pp. 33–8.

Poore, S. (2003) What is the Context? A Reply to the Gray–Johnston Debate on Strategic Culture. *Review of International Studies*. 29 (2). pp. 279–84.

Rogers, J. (2009) From 'Civilian Power' to 'Global Power': Explicating the European Union's 'Grand Strategy' Through the Articulation of Discourse Theory. *Journal of Common Market Studies*. 27 (4). pp. 831–62.

Ruggie, J. G. (1993) Territoriality and Beyond: Problematizing Modernity in International Relations. *International Organization*. 47 (1). pp. 139–74.

Snyder, J. L. (1977) *The Soviet Strategic Culture: Implications for Limited Nuclear Operations*. Santa Monica, CA: RAND.

Tonra, B. (2000) Denmark and Ireland. In Manners, I. and Whitman, R. (eds) *The Foreign Policies of European Union Member States*. Manchester: Manchester University Press. pp. 224–42.

Waever, O. (1998) Insecurity, Security, and Asecurity in the West European Non-war Community. In Adler, E. and Barnett, M. (eds) *Security Communities*. Cambridge: Cambridge University Press. pp. 69–117.

Williams, P. D. (2007) From Non-Intervention to Non-Indifference: The Origins and Development of the African Union's Security Culture. *African Affairs*. 106 (423). pp. 253–79.

6 How to explain the transnational security governance of the European Union?

Kamil Zwolski[1]

Introduction

The relationship between EU studies and the broader field of IR remains problematic and somewhat awkward. Although both fields could benefit enormously from each other's theoretical and empirical insights, they tend to be indifferent to one another. On the one hand, EU scholars often consider their subject so unique that new theories and frameworks have to be (re)invented each time they want to understand or explain an empirical phenomenon. On the other hand, IR scholars are often disinterested in EU studies, thus omitting empirical evidence relevant for different IR questions, such as those concerning global governance (Warleigh-Lack, 2011) or New Regionalism (Warleigh, 2004; Warleigh-Lack and Rosamond, 2010). As a result, EU studies risk becoming self-referential as well as ignored by IR and broader Political Science (Rosamond, 2006). This is also problematic for advancing our capacity to explain European security policy, because – as this chapter suggests – there are valuable theories and concepts originating from outside the immediate field of European Studies.

This chapter argues that the empirical developments in the EU offer unexploited opportunities for both drawing from and enriching the scholarship on the Sociology of (international) Bureaucracy, Global Security Governance and IR. An important attempt at utilising IR theory to explain European security has been undertaken by the editors of this volume, and this chapter aims to contribute to this discussion. It does not engage with IR theories *sensu stricto*, such as Realism, Liberalism or Social Constructivism, although this exercise is also very important, if only to bring European studies closer to the mainstream debates in IR. While theories of integration, such as Neofunctionalism, have served (and perhaps still do serve) us well in studying the dynamics of European integration, this fact may have contributed to the disconnect between European studies and the wider IR. Realism has perhaps been the least intuitive approach to adopt to study European integration (see Chapter 1), with Liberalism and Constructivism regularly providing analytical tools, concepts and frameworks.

This chapter, although it does not engage with IR theory, contributes to broadening the discussion on explaining European security from a perspective which is not necessarily intuitive for the European studies scholar. As such, the argument in this chapter has been partially inspired by two invitations. First, Per M. Norheim-Martinsen (2010) has invited scholars to fully embrace 'governance' as a framework to better understand the dynamics of the EU's CSDP. The governance approach, as he has argued, directly challenges Realist and Inter-Governmentalist theories about the nature of the EU's security co-operation, because it assumes a much greater importance of international institutions and transnational networks. In contrast to Norheim-Martinsen's focus on CSDP and military co-operation, this chapter suggests, as an illustration of the theoretical point, that the EU's policy on CBRN matters offers even more fertile ground for incorporating the governance approach.

Second, Alex Warleigh-Lack and Ben Rosamond (2010) have called for a more explicit dialogue between the studies on European integration and New Regionalism. Elsewhere, Warleigh-Lack (2011) has also pointed out that although European Studies can offer valuable insights to scholars studying the processes of global governance, it is partially the responsibility of EU scholars to initiate the exchange of ideas across intellectual borders. The aim of this chapter is to foster such exchange by demonstrating how the EU's transnational security governance on CBRN risk mitigation can be explained by a story which is not derived from EU studies.

It has become a commonplace to explain the international behaviour of the EU through narratives involving the concepts of *civilian* (Duchêne, 1972) or *normative* (Manners, 2002; Whitman, 2011a) power in Europe. Although they are very different, both concepts presume that the character of the EU's external activities is unique.[2] The EU studies-based explanation helps to uncover insightful patterns in the EU's external behaviour. However, it can also reinforce the $N=1$ problem when studying the EU, that is the perception of the EU as an 'N' of 1. This is why it is also helpful to explore alternative explanations, which depict the EU's international security policy as normal for an international bureaucracy. To this end, the chapter engages with the scholarship on the Sociology of Bureaucracy and bureaucratic behaviour in IR, potentially opening the space for comparative analysis with non-EU cases.

The chapter begins with the constitutive argument conceptualising an important part of the EU's policy on CBRN risk mitigation as an example of the transnational security governance approach. This exercise in descriptive synthesis will shed more light on a unique case study of CBRN Risk Mitigation Centres of Excellence (CoE). The CBRN CoE is an innovative project launched by the EU in 2009, with the purpose of 'developing comprehensive tailored training and assistance packages' in the field of CBRN risk mitigation (European Commission, 2009, p. 8). These training and assistance packages are directed at the regions considered by the EU as vulnerable, currently including different parts of Africa, the Middle East, South East Asia and South East Europe (CBRN-CoE, 2015). In terms of policy practice, the EU has established a number of regional secretariats, which act as focal points for coordinating national and regional project development and for establishing long-term, transnational networks of CBRN experts. The initiative is financed through the EU's Instrument for Stability (IfS).

In the second part, this chapter proposes an explanation of the EU's transnational security governance approach which derives from the study of domestic bureaucracy in sociology and international bureaucracy in IR. In this narrative, the EU, together with other International Organisations (IOs), is considered an international bureaucracy (Barnett and Finnemore, 2004). As a bureaucracy, the EU must be expected to develop a set of practices typical for this form of organisation. The third part brings together the descriptive and analytical arguments of the chapter by addressing the following question: what are the implications for the concept of security governance if we conceptualise IOs as international bureaucracies? By incorporating the insights from the scholarship on IR and the Sociology of Bureaucracy, this chapter offers a practical example of how intellectual bridges can be developed across social sciences borders, as an illustration of the empirical point. The benefits and possible research programmes stemming from this rapprochement are further discussed in the conclusion.

The EU's transnational security governance and CBRN risk mitigation

The constitutive argument conceptualising the EU's CBRN CoE as an example of transnational security governance is developed in two stages. In the first stage, the chapter reflects on the value of the security governance framework in studying the EU's international security policy. In the second stage, the chapter incorporates the security governance framework, as originally developed by Webber *et al.* (2004) and further operationalised by Norheim-Martinsen (2010), to introduce the key attributes of the CBRN CoE project. The empirical discussion in this chapter is brief and certainly does not exhaust the topic of the EU's role in CBRN risk mitigation policies. However, its main purpose is to demonstrate a more theoretical point about the EU's policy as an example of security governance, which can in turn be explained with reference to the theories of bureaucratic legitimacy.

European security governance beyond CSDP

Why has the governance approach become so popular among scholars researching the dynamics of the EU's international security policy? The short answer is that governance in the scholarship on the EU's international security policy reflects the broader trend in the study of international security cooperation, with the growing focus on horizontal processes and non-state actors (Krahmann, 2003; Webber *et al.* 2004; Kirchner, 2006; Kirchner and Sperling, 2007; Schroeder, 2011). Schroeder (2011, p. 31) neatly encapsulates the key characteristics of *governance* as referring to 'a mode of political decision-making beyond hierarchical government of a traditional interventionist state'. This is a very broad definition, but in fact it may even be too restrictive, because governance does not have to take place only at the *decision-making* stage. As Rosenau (1995) argues, governance may include *systems of rule*, which entail *control* and *steering.* Schroeder (2011, p. 31) further notes that governance 'provides a framework for understanding the fragmentation of authority to new actors and levels, and it enables a comprehensive analysis of interactions in a sector characterised more by complex decision-making and nested responsibilities for action'. While consensus seems to have emerged that *governance* is well suited to analyse the EU's international security policy-making (see the literature on EU security governance), it is unclear *what parts* of the EU's institutional apparatus should be included in the analysis.

Following the EU's own post-Maastricht vocabulary, the second pillar, and particularly the CSDP framework, has occupied a central place in the scholarship on the EU's role in international security (Knodt and Princen, 2003, p. 2). For example, Norheim-Martinsen (2010), while aiming to contribute to the literature on the EU's security governance, focuses on only one aspect, i.e. the CSDP. Although each effort to better our understanding of the EU's international security apparatus is to be valued, the EU's security governance is a term that is more encompassing than is often acknowledged in the literature. In its external dimension, the security governance of the EU must also include longer-term and structural elements, most notably the IfS (Gänzle, 2009; Whitman and Wolff, 2012; Zwolski, 2012, 2012a). Consequently, although Norheim-Martinsen (2010) aimed for his analysis of the CSDP governance to challenge Intergovernmentalism, we cannot truly achieve this objective without the inclusion of longer-term, financial instruments, such as the IfS (article 4), in the analysis. Furthermore, as this chapter demonstrates, the budgetary instruments on the verge of security and development assistance make the EU's security governance genuinely *transnational.* Consequently, while not neglecting CSDP, any meaningful analysis of the EU's role in international security must also include relevant financial instruments.

Admittedly, a truly comprehensive approach to studying the EU's international security role is challenging. Nonetheless, we cannot ignore consistent empirical developments that trespass the boundaries dividing the CSDP and the former Community pillar policies and instruments (Keukeleire and MacNaughtan, 2008; Smith, 2008; Kaunert and Zwolski, 2013). Even more importantly, we cannot ignore such developments when incorporating the 'governance' approach. As already hinted, there are different conceptualisations of security governance, including various attempts at summarising this strand of the scholarship (Kirchner and Domínguez, 2011, pp. 5–11; Sperling, 2009, pp. 4–6; Schroeder, 2011, pp. 30–6).

The most common approach is to adapt the *governance turn* in IR (Rosenau and Czempiel, 1992), European Studies (Kohler-Koch and Rittberger, 2006) or national politics (Rhodes, 1997) to the problem of security cooperation. Some important recent contributions have made an effort to take the security governance scholarship to the next analytical level. Notably, Sperling and Webber (2014) argue that systemic factors have been neglected at the expense of agency in this strand of scholarship. Thus, they ask 'how and why security actors behave in the aggregate and whether that behaviour reflects wider systemic properties'

(2014, p. 1). Ehrhart *et al.* (2014) aim to deepen the analytical value of security governance by transforming this concept into critical questions and enhance it as a critical tool.

All these contributions, and especially the recent ones, are important in evaluating how security governance works in practice, including the opportunities it offers and its limitations. It also invites scholars to link the discussion of security governance with some of the other discussions in IR. One such possibility is to explore the opportunities which transnational security governance may offer for the recent strand of IR scholarship concerning international practices (Adler and Pouliot, 2011). The inductive focus on international practices, defined as competent performances, promises to 'broaden the ontology of world politics, serves as a focal point around which IR theory can be structured, and can be used as a unit of analysis' (Adler and Pouliot, 2011, p. 1). The transnational security governance approach of the EU meets the basic attributes of international practices, including its patterned character, its embeddedness in a particular organisational context, and its social development through learning and training. Taking into account the growing body of research on the EU's security governance, European studies has potential to offer fundamental empirical contributions to the programme of international practices research, which itself aims at building bridges across different traditions in IR.

It is impossible here to identify all the approaches to the security governance concept. Instead, the chapter incorporates the model developed by a group of scholars (Webber *et al.*, 2004) and revisited by Norheim-Martinsen (2010), who has identified the EU's security governance as (a) consisting of multiple centres of power, each involved in addressing contemporary security challenges, (b) including the interaction of multiple actors, including non-state public and private actors, (c) containing formal and informal institutionalisation, which affects actors' room for manoeuvre, (d) including ideational relations between actors, including shared norms and ideas; and (e) involving collective purpose, which can be understood as a structure and process. All of these attributes require the broadening of the scholarly focus, to include also transnational instruments such as the IfS.

Security governance and the EU's CBRN network-based approach

The argument of this section is that the conceptual benefits of the security governance approach can only be fully exploited when moving beyond the CSDP framework and military co-operation in the EU. In fact, the CBRN non-proliferation, identified at the top of the EU's international security agenda, requires instruments and policies other than those related to the military. In this context, the CBRN CoE initiative has emerged as the flagship EU approach to CBRN risk mitigation, as the result of two factors. First, CBRN non-proliferation was allocated the largest proportion of the IfS budget under Article 4, defining the EU's assistance in the stable conditions for co-operation (€266 million for the years 2007–13 = 13 per cent of the total budget) (European Commission,

2007). Second, in the pool available for CBRN non-proliferation, the CBRN CoE initiative is defined as the 'number one' priority area for the EU (European Commission, 2009, 2012). This is unsurprising, considering that the EU has long planned to move its assistance beyond the former Soviet Union and the CBRN CoE enabled the EU to go global (judging by the scope of regional actors involved). Further, in the light of the criticism directed towards its previous assistance programmes (Sodupe and Benito, 1998), the EU planned to change the methodology of its assistance by decentralising it and focusing on 'local ownership'. Moreover, CBRN CoE reflect the priorities of the UNSC Resolution 1540, which provides the international context for the EU's initiative.

How can the concept of security governance synthesise the attributes of the EU's transnational CBRN policy? The aforementioned five features of the security governance concept are incorporated into the analysis. With respect to the question of heterarchy, *multiple centres of power* are inevitable in the system of transnational security governance, regardless of how depoliticised it may appear. Indeed, we can expect the existence of multiple centres (and relations) of power at different levels in the case of CBRN CoE. At the EU institutional level, the Council of Ministers has been slowly growing into coordinating its policies vis-à-vis international non-proliferation regimes, such as the Review Conferences of the Non-Proliferation Treaty (Portela, 2004; Müller, 2005). In parallel, the European Commission has been involved in low-key non-proliferation activities in the former Soviet Union since the early 1990s (Zwolski, 2011, 2011a). The Lisbon Treaty reforms offer opportunities to bring more coherence to the CBRN policy of the EU.

With regards to the *multiple actors* dimension of security governance, CBRN CoE involve a broad variety of stakeholders at all levels. This is not surprising, because 'cooperation and coordination between all levels of government and international partners' is at the core of the IfS in the area of CBRN matters (European Commission, 2011, p. 6). Within the EU, the project is coordinated by the European Commission (Joint Research Centre, Development and Cooperation-EuropeAid) and the EEAS, with the potentially greater role of the Member States (Dupré and Servais, 2012). The United Nations Interregional Crime and Justice Research Institute (UNICRI) is involved in the implementation. At the national level, the CBRN CoE are developed and implemented through the co-operation of the so-called National Focal Points of the Partner Countries, which are countries outside the EU participating in the networks. They develop regional CBRN risk mitigation projects through the aforementioned Regional Secretariats (Mignone, 2013).

The EU's CBRN risk mitigation approach does not just include, but is defined by, *formal and informal institutionalisation*. Informal institutionalisation is at the core of CBRN CoE, with hundreds of experts and policy-makers meeting at regional workshops and preparing joint applications for CBRN risk mitigation resources (Schmidt, 2013). Informal institutionalisation overlaps with formal institutionalisation in the network-based system such as CBRN CoE. The already-mentioned National Focal Points of the Partner Countries can comprise a variety of actors as diverse as first responders, police, customs, CBRN agencies, ministries, academia and intelligence (Winfield, 2011, p. 50). They form teams of around 20–30 experts, representing a country at the regional level through co-operation with regional secretariats. Such teams may play important integrative roles, because 'in many cases it is the first time that many of the representatives that cover the whole of CBRN in a country have sat down and talked to each other' (Winfield, 2011, p. 50).

Security governance also includes *relations between actors that are ideational*. Importantly, there already exists a significant body of scholarship concerning the role of norms in the EU's international security policy (Risse-Kappen, 1997; Whitman, 1998; Manners, 2002). It is therefore important to broaden the outlook in order to identify the ideational challenges facing the EU in its arguably innovative approach to transnational security governance. These challenges concern the fact that the co-operation with partner countries is voluntary; it involves important matters of security risks; and the countries are asked to think through the lens of regional needs, not merely national interests. This approach is fundamentally different from the traditional role of IOs facilitating interstate co-operation. States, rather than just having an institutional setting to cooperate, are invited to engage in CBRN risk-mitigating projects with other states. These projects, in turn, are implemented by actors such as the German Office of Economics and Export Control.

This approach requires national leaders in the Middle East, North Africa, South East Europe, South East Asia and the African Atlantic Façade to adjust their thinking about preventing CBRN risks. Leaders in these regions are implicitly asked by the EU and UNICRI to operate under the assumption that their interests in CBRN matters are not as different as to prevent them from developing joint security projects, even if mutual trust has not been developed yet. In fact, building local and regional trust is the intended original contribution of the EU's CBRN CoE to the environment where different nuclear research and technical centres already exist. In fact, project coordinators argue that in such a sensitive field as CBRN, trust and confidence are pivotal for improving security in the long term: 'We will not make a real difference in threat/risk reduction on the mere substance of our projects. Something has to come first: *Trust and Confidence Building Measures* [original emphasis] (Dupré and Servais, 2012, p. 2). The EU's methodology in this respect may indeed be considered innovative, but – as this chapter argues at the latter stage – it can be explained when the EU is considered an international bureaucracy utilising its key sources of legitimacy.

A sense of *collective purpose* is the final attribute of the security governance approach. It is a result of both structure and process. From the structural perspective, purpose is the outcome of institutionalisation, because institutions 'entrench particular forms of behaviour among their participants by prescribing rules of entry, norms of interaction and constraints on behaviour' (Webber *et al.*, 2004, p. 8). There are questions about the 'sense of purpose' in the EU's CBRN transnational security governance, particularly after the Lisbon Treaty reshuffled the decision-making apparatus by moving the parts of the European Commission and the Council Secretariat to the newly established EEAS. Institutional cultures have been long established in both the Commission and the Council, and it may take a while for the new culture to emerge (Whitman, 2011a). From the process perspective, governance is underpinned by policy outcomes, including how they take shape. In CBRN CoE, the outcomes will be affected by a number of factors, including the commitment of EU Member States; access to relevant expertise; interaction by different project teams; the ability to establish geographical and thematic priorities; establishing an accurate verification mechanism and communicating the outcomes to a wider audience (Dupré and Servais, 2012; Mignone, 2013).

Synthesising the attributes of the EU's CBRN risk mitigation policy under the concept of transnational security governance can, in itself, lead to interesting observations. At the same time, however, the constitutive mode of argumentation in this case provides little theoretical value for uncovering the driving factors behind the EU's approach to security governance. As a result, the synthesis on its own provides an important first step to explaining the EU's transnational security governance approach, but it subsequently must be subjected to the question 'of what is this an instance?' (Rosenau and Durfee, 1995, p. 183).

One proposition derives from European studies, where scholars tend to portray the EU as a *sui generis* international security actor with a unique international identity. In other words, the EEC, and currently the EU, is a *power* with a qualifying adjective. Among numerous efforts to qualify the EU as a power, *civilian* (Duchêne, 1972) and *normative* (Manners, 2002; Whitman, 2011) have become the most widely accepted labels capturing the nature of the EU's international role. As a result of this unique international identity of the EU, we can expect that the international security objectives and policy of this organisation will reflect a certain set of norms that are different from the norms of other powers. Although some scholars have argued for incorporating non-EU cases into the civilian and normative power narrative (e.g. Maull, 1990; Diez, 2005; Tocci, 2008), this story has predominantly been applied to the EU's international role.

This narrative seems to be able to suitably explain the transnational security governance of the EU, in the form of the CBRN CoE project. If, however, this were the only possible explanation, the benefit for an IR scholar of studying the EU would be unclear. Equally, European studies would risk becoming self-referential, with little introduction of intellectual fresh air into the discipline. In this light, the remaining part of this chapter suggests that the EU's leading CBRN-related project, involving the creation of CBRN CoE, constitutes an expected outcome of normal bureaucratic politics. In order to further explore this explanation, the chapter must turn to sociological and IR insights concerning the nature of bureaucracy, particularly its sources of authority. Max Weber's (1978) insights on bureaucratic authority are significant in this narrative, because they help to better explain why the EU, *or any other* international bureaucracy, would adopt an approach to international security that is purely managerial, with experts and expertise at its core. Furthermore, Social Constructivist insights can help to better embed this story in the IR vocabulary by incorporating Weberian ideas about bureaucracy into how we understand modern IOs (Barnett and Finnemore, 2004).

The EU as a normal bureaucracy

The idea that IOs are bureaucracies has been put forward by Social Constructivist scholars Michael Barnett and Martha Finnemore (2004). They have advanced their arguments against the dominant view that IOs mostly do what states want them to do, and thus studying their autonomous intentions and behaviour is bound to be an unfruitful endeavour. If IOs are bureaucracies, then we should expect them to follow a range of impersonal rules – building blocks of bureaucracies. Barnett and Finnemore (2004) identify four effects that bureaucratic rules have on IOs. First, rules prescribe actions for an organisation both internally and externally. Internally, rules dictate the type of behaviour that is considered 'normal'. Externally, IOs develop new sets of rules aimed at other international actors, such as countries in conflict. Second, rules define how IOs perceive, organise and interpret the world. Third, rules are used by IOs to create or constitute the social world; predictably the world created by IOs is typically amenable to intervention by IOs themselves. Fourth, rules can be constitutive of the organisation's identity. For example, the UN emphasises the importance of consent in its approach to conflict resolution.

The sole fact that IOs are bureaucracies, however, offers an incomplete explanation of the transnational security governance approach of the EU. To obtain a more insightful picture, we must examine what kind of authority the EU has to undertake action at the international level. The scholarship on the legitimacy of organisations, including international bureaucracies, is heavily indebted to Max Weber (1978) who distinguished among charismatic, traditional and legal (rational) authority. In particular, the third ideal type of authority has been subsequently incorporated into the study of organisations. In this context, Richard Scott (2008) has identified two distinctive approaches. The first approach emphasised the relationship between legitimacy and the goals of organisations, asking whether these goals are congruent with social norms and values (Parsons, 1960; Pfeffer and Salancik, 1978). The second approach, in contrast, has focused on the organisations' structures and procedures (Meyer and Rowan, 1977). The argument here is that 'organizational success depends on factors other than efficient coordination and control of productive activities' (Meyer and Rowan, 1977, p. 352). Instead, the prospects for the survival of organisations are directly related to their highly elaborated institutional environments and how isomorphic with these environments organisations become (Meyer and Rowan, 1977). As the rest of this chapter demonstrates, these organisational structures and procedures offer valuable insights into explaining the EU's particular approach to international security policy.

The moral authority of international bureaucracies

Applying Weberian arguments about legitimacy to IR, Barnett and Finnemore (2004) have identified three sources of the IOs' authority: delegated authority, moral authority and expert authority. While the first source is important, because it refers to the authority delegated to IOs by states, it is the other two sources that can shed most light on the practices of the EU in international security. In particular, the case of CBRN CoE, as an intended impartial network of experts in CBRN matters very broadly construed, requires strong authority to secure the commitment of regions and countries as divergent as Jordan, Morocco, Ukraine and Singapore. This challenge seems to be recognised by EU project coordinators, who emphasise the importance of trust and confidence building (Dupré and Servais, 2012, p. 2), local resources and expertise (Winfield, 2011, p. 48) and the voluntary character of CBRN networks (Van der Meer, 2013, p. 3).

Moral authority refers to the intended neutral, impartial and even depoliticised behaviour of IOs vis-à-vis self-interested states. How do IOs develop moral authority? As Meyer and Rowan (1977) argue, organisations gain legitimacy, resources and stability through adhering to certain myths. These myths are simply institutional rules that lead to the formalisation of organisational structures. The myths have two attributes. First, they 'identify different social purposes as technical ones and specify in a rule-like way the appropriate means to pursue these technical purposes rationally' (Meyer and Rowan, 1977, pp. 343–4). Arguably, building on the fact that bureaucracies draw their authority from their very nature of being impersonal, they are subsequently in a better position than states to frame even the most sensitive national security problems in more neutral, depoliticised terms. When security problems are framed by international bureaucracies, mostly in technical rather than political terms, IOs can more credibly position themselves as legitimate authorities possessing, or capable of organising, the necessary resources to address such problems.

Second, the myths enabling the formalisation of organisations are highly institutionalised, and thus 'beyond the discretion of any individual participant or organization' (Meyer and Rowan, 1977, p. 344). For example, the myth of 'expert knowledge' is highly institutionalised by the established Western educational system. This myth is very important as a source of the IOs' authority and thus it requires treatment in a separate, following section. Here, it is primarily mentioned for its property of making political problems seem less contentious and more neutral (Eriksen, 2011). Similarly, the myth of 'transnational policy networks' as a desirable form of governance is highly institutionalised by the 'governance turn' in international co-operation, enabling non-hierarchical structures and multiple actors (Krahmann, 2003a). Such underlying myths contribute to the legitimacy of international bureaucracies and shape the way in which their practices become formalised. In the case of the EU's transnational security governance, the ambition to frame problems as technical in nature is further amplified by the sensitivities associated with security policy. The myths or institutional rules concerning *expert knowledge, transnational networks* or *international prestige* all work to the IOs' advantage in the process of formalising policy structures such as CBRN CoE.

The expert authority of international bureaucracies

In addition to the delegated and moral authority of IOs, Barnett and Finnemore (2004) also distinguish expert authority. Max Weber has observed that, essentially, bureaucracy is 'domination through knowledge' (1978, p. 225), which consists of technical knowledge – itself an important source of power – but also of knowledge stemming from experience in service. Writing his contribution over ninety years ago, Weber (1978, p. 975) has already noted that '[t]he more complicated and specialized modern culture becomes, the more its external supporting apparatus demands the personally detached and strictly objective *expert*'. Weber was writing about the growing complexity of culture long before the digital age revolutionised the sources and nature of security risks, introducing new levels of complexity and technological progress (Giddens, 1990; Beck, 1999). In consequence, we require experts to address these risks at least as much as states needed tanks to conduct warfare in the twentieth century.

The reliance on different kinds of expertise provides IOs with a significant source of authority. It is also an important basis of their power due to the growing gap between experts and those who depend on experts' knowledge and experience (Scott, 2001, p. 108). Nowhere is this need for expertise as apparent as in the field of CBRN security, involving a myriad of technical and political challenges. CBRN CoE, as a form of transnational security governance, aims to fill the need for expertise at national and regional levels. Among the key objectives of the initiative are (a) to provide CBRN training to participating countries; (b) to support participating countries in developing legal, administrative, and technical measures; and (c) to provide a coherent package of training and assistance covering CBRN matters such as export control, illicit trafficking, crisis response and redirection of scientists (European Commission, 2009). At the same time, however, the highly specialised expertise required puts a strain on the availability of human resources in the EU and in participating countries (Mignone, 2013, p. 7). Furthermore, with twenty-nine projects implemented by eighteen entities in forty-two different countries, as was the case in mid-2013 (Schmidt, 2013, p. 1), there is a risk that the expertise which is available will not be optimally utilised (Mignone, 2013, p. 7).

Notwithstanding their access to and ability to mobilise external technical expertise, bureaucracies also appear legitimate because they typically have a long time to develop their practices (Weber, 1978). This experience-based expertise is particularly important in comparison to democratic states, where officials often have to step down when, after four or five years, they have just achieved fluency in their area of competence. In contrast, civil servants often have the opportunity to spend more time with the institutions and policies they are involved in. We can find this (often tacit) experience-based expertise in every formal organisation. We can also find it in the EU in the field of preventing

CBRN-related threats. As early as the beginning of the 1990s, the European Community initiated technical assistance—known as the Technical Aid to the Commonwealth of Independent States (TACIS)—with the security and safety of nuclear installations constituting an important component of this assistance. The low profile of the Community's activities channelled through TACIS allowed the European Commission to develop its assistance relatively uncontested, apart from the criticism directed at the actual effectiveness of TACIS (Sodupe and Benito, 1998). When, in 2009, the European Commission first outlined the rationale for CBRN CoE, it was building on its experience of managing TACIS: 'Taking into account the lessons learned through the TACIS programme and the first IfS IP [Indicative Programme], the IP 2009–2011 intends to move away from an "ad hoc", centralized approach to promoting coherent, integrated regional networks' (European Commission, 2009, p. 7). The long experience of the European Commission's Join Research Centre with CBRN matters, according to Heyes (2012), makes it a 'centre of excellence' even if the actual CBRN CoE have not existed long enough to label them 'excellent'.

To sum up, as Figure 6.1 encapsulates, the above analysis has indicated the relevance of this IR-derived story in explaining the EU's approach to international security governance. In this narrative, the EU does not have to be unique as compared to other international actors in order to develop transnational security governance structures. Instead, the transnational security governance approach of the EU *stems naturally* from its character as a bureaucracy. In other words, because the EU can be conceptualised as an international bureaucracy, its behaviour is natural for this form of social organisation, particularly considering the sources of bureaucratic authority. IOs legitimise their international activities through the apparent neutrality of their expertise and impersonal rules guiding their behaviour. Consequently, it is more difficult for the governments participating in CBRN CoE to resist this co-operation on the grounds that the EU serves particularistic interests of a given state or individual. Equally, the transnational security governance approach of the EU *results* from its technical and experience-based expertise. Importantly, the EU by itself, like other international bureaucracies, does not possess sufficient expertise to fully address complex security risks. It has learned, however, through many years of experience, to draw

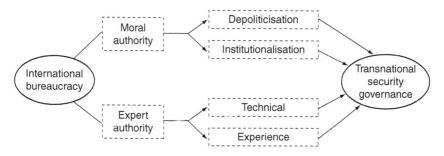

Figure 6.1 The EU as an International Bureaucracy.

the necessary resources from the outside. The ability of international bureaucracies to pool outside expertise in the service of their own objectives gives them enormous leverage over states which typically have more constrained resources and a shorter-term focus.

International bureaucracy and security governance

The previous sections have reinforced the scholarly argument that the international security policy of the EU can be conceptualised as a system of security governance. Further, they have suggested that the transnational security governance of the EU in the area of CBRN risk mitigation can be depicted as predictable for an international bureaucracy, because bureaucracies draw their authority from their intended neutral character and expertise. The broader question that still needs addressing, however, is what the implications for the concept of security governance are if we conceptualise IOs as international bureaucracies.

No one has influenced our conception of modern bureaucracy more than Max Weber. At the same time, however, the Weberian model of a unitary state with its effective bureaucracy appears incongruent with how governance is defined in the literature. The German sociologist is rarely referenced in the governance scholarship. When references are made, they mostly serve the purpose of reinforcing the dichotomy between the Weberian ideas of hierarchy and unity on the one hand, and heterarchy and fragmentation characterising governance systems on the other hand (Pierre and Peters, 2000, p. 81; Sellers, 2011, p. 127). This tendency is unsurprising when we consider the nation-state as the starting level of analysis, and only then try to assess how decentralised, or how fragmented, the regional or global governance system has become. Zürn (2013, pp. 416–17) talks in this context about methodological nationalism. Enroth (2011, p. 31) concludes that even as a governance-oriented approach network theory 'is confined to its nation-state origins'.

The alternative route, and the one taken in this chapter, is to start the analysis at the level of IOs (Martin and Simmons, 2013). When an IO, and not just states, is conceptualised as a bureaucracy, we can consider it a 'distinctive social form of authority with its own internal logic and behavioural proclivities' (Barnett and Finnemore, 2004, p. 3). As a result, we can more easily identify a growing number and scope of clusters of institutions, which lead to the creation of transnational networks. Such networks can include both formal and informal organisations. Importantly, networks of international institutions also mean networks of memberships in IOs, which can 'magnify the possibilities for cooperation and expanded joint gains among members' (Martin and Simmons, 2013, p. 341).

While the question of how fragmented and decentralised nation-states have become divides scholars of governance, IOs as bureaucracies are *defined* by formal and informal networks, as well as different degree of institutionalisation. What becomes particularly interesting for scholars of security governance is, however, when IOs develop networks strategically, in order to achieve their policy objectives. The concept of security governance, as defined by Webber *et al.*

(2004) and adopted by Norheim-Martinsen (2010), seems to fit particularly well to better our understanding of the system in which IOs develop such networks. This does not mean, however, that there are no tensions between various attributes of the governance system and some of the components of the IOs' authority.

The principle of heterarchy, which entails the existence of multiple centres of power, has challenged the hierarchical notion of centralised nation-states. When the state is taken as a basic unit of analysis, heterarchy helps to account for the influence of non-state actors at different levels, in order to obtain a more accurate image of collective self-organisation. Heterarchy becomes more problematic, however, in the governance system with international bureaucracies and their clusters at the centre of analysis. Here, we have to recognise the intention of IOs to present their action as depoliticised, which contrasts with the very political nature of intra- and inter-institutional relations. This tension becomes particularly apparent in security matters and has been recognised in the case of CBRN CoE, where multiple centres of power are evident.

The other attributes of the governance approach, as discussed in this chapter, are less contentious and better suited to understand the self-organising, transnational system, with international bureaucracies as the primary unit of analysis. While the principle of 'multiple actors' is important for the understanding of security governance, which recognises states as the basic units (Krahmann, 2003; Weber *et al.* 2004), it is *definitional* for the transnational networks of IOs. It includes actors at all levels, with experts becoming especially prominent in the fields such as CBRN. The same observation concerns formal and informal institutionalisation; IOs *are* formal institutions which constantly create other formal *and* informal institutions, such as, as discussed in this chapter, CBRN CoE.

The remaining two attributes concern norms underpinning the governance system and the nature of the collective purpose. Non-materialist accounts of security governance stress the importance of norms and ideas underpinning international cooperation (Katzenstein, 1996). Equally, norms are crucial for transnational governance systems. As the case of the CBRN CoE demonstrates, international bureaucracies may even recognise that certain norms, such as trust and confidence, are central for achieving policy objectives. Finally, both state-centric and transnational approaches to security governance must recognise the contested nature of *purposefulness*, conceptualised as the outcome of structure and process. Inevitably, self-organising governance structures involving multiple centres of power and many different actors will struggle when a common decision or action must be taken. International bureaucracies may have the advantage, however, with their experience-based authority and intra-institutional tacit knowledge.

Conclusion, research programme and benefits to European studies

Theorizing European security has been hampered, to some extent, by insufficient dialogue between those working in the field of European studies, and those engaged in IR. This chapter has suggested one possible avenue to foster intellectual exchange across academic boundaries. It has started with the argument of a constitutive nature, conceptualising the EU's policy on CBRN risk mitigation as transnational security governance. In contrast to most studies theorising and conceptualising the EU's international security policy, this chapter has demonstrated that noteworthy empirical developments take place beyond the military-focused CSDP. In particular, the chapter has identified the CBRN CoE project as an example of the transnational security governance approach, primarily because of its reliance on networks and experts. Following on from this constitutive argument, the chapter has presented a story explaining the development of the CBRN CoE by the EU.

This story, however, is not embedded in EU studies and does not depict the EU as a unique international actor. Instead, the chapter has argued that the EU can be conceptualised as a normal bureaucracy. In this narrative, derived from IR and the Sociology of Bureaucracy, IOs are conceptualised as international bureaucracies. They draw authority from their rational legal character and expertise, not only from the act of delegation by states. Consequently, *all* IOs intend to act impartially and apolitically, drawing on a wide range of expertise. This explanation has proved feasible in explaining the EU's transnational security governance approach in the form of CBRN CoE. Moreover, it carries the benefit of potentially opening the door for comparative analysis, which is the first proposition concerning a future research programme.

The door for comparative analysis, when the study of the EU's transnational security governance is involved, is opened *potentially*, because we may initially not know whether non-EU case studies exist. As Rosamond (2006) argues, however, this is not a problem when we relax the assumption about the EU as a benchmark case. In the area of transnational security governance, treating the EU as a normal bureaucracy contributes to such relaxation, by suggesting that its approach to international security policy is potentially no different from that of other IOs. The broader community of IR scholars may find such a move helpful in order to incorporate insights from European studies to compare the EU's approach to security with other confirmed or potential cases of a similar approach in other parts of the world. Potential case studies may include, for example, the initiatives developed under the auspices of the International Atomic Energy Agency (IAEA), such as the International Nuclear Security Education Network, or coordinated by the IAEA such as the International Network for Nuclear Security Training and Support Centres (IAEA, 2012).

Finally, it must be stressed that, rather than being weakened, EU studies would benefit substantially from engaging more directly with the broader discipline of IR on a more regular basis (Warleigh, 2004; Warleigh-Lack, 2011). As this chapter has suggested, the transnational security governance of the EU offers substantial opportunities for this engagement, encouraging EU studies to actively shape IR debates concerning, for example, International Bureaucracy and Global Security Governance. At the same time, academic bridge building would also encourage researchers to seek and explore empirical cases beyond

Europe, further improving our understanding of what we can observe in the EU. All these benefits would contribute, in turn, to refining the theories and approaches derived from EU studies, such as these concerning the civilian or normative character of the EU's power.

Notes

1 A modified version of this chapter was originally published in *JCMS (Journal of Common Market Studies)*, 52(4). An earlier version was presented at the EISA 8th Pan-European Conference on International Relations in Warsaw (September 2013). I wish to thank Mai'a K. Davis Cross, Jonathan Havercroft and Åsne Kalland Aarstad for their very helpful comments.
2 It must be noted that non-EU cases are increasingly explored in the context of the *normative power* narrative. See, for example, Maull (1990); Diez, (2005); Special Issue on Normative Power Europe in *Cooperation and Conflict*, 48(2).

References

Adler, E. and Pouliot, V. (2011) International Practices. *International Theory.* 3(1). pp. 1–36.
Barnett, M. and Finnemore, M. (2004) *Rules for the World: International Organizations in Global Politics.* Ithaca, NY: Cornell University Press.
Beck, U. (1999) *World Risk Society.* Cambridge: Polity.
CBRN-CoE (2015) About CoE. Available from: www.cbrn-coe.eu/AboutCoE.aspx [accessed: 23 February 2015].
Diez, T. (2005) Constructing the Self and Changing Others: Reconsidering 'Normative Power Europe'. *Millennium—Journal of International Studies.* 33(3). pp. 613–36.
Duchêne, F. (1972) Europe's Role in World Peace. In Mayne, R. (ed.) *Europe Tomorrow: Sixteen European Looks Ahead.* London: Fontana. pp. 32–47.
Dupré, B. and Servais, P. (2012) The EU CBRN Risk Mitigation Centres of Excellence. *CBRN CoE Newsletter*, 4, October. Available from: www.cbrn-coe.eu/Portals/0/cbrn-coe-public-documents/cbrn%20coe%20newsletter%20volume%204%202012.pdf [accessed 23 February 2015].
Ehrhart, H-G., Hegemann, H. and Kahl, M. (2014) Towards Security Governance as a Critical Tool: a Conceptual Outline. *European Security.* 23(2). pp. 119–25.
Enroth, H. (2011) Policy Network Theory. In Bevir, M. (ed.) *The SAGE Handbook of Governance.* London: SAGE. pp. 19–35.
Eriksen, E. O. (2011) Governance Between Expertise and Democracy: The Case of European Security. *Journal of European Public Policy.* 18(8). pp. 1169–89.
European Commission (2012) Multi-annual Indicative Programme 2012–13 for Assistance in the Context of Stable Conditions for Cooperation under the Instrument for Stability', C(2012) 5584 final, 20 August. Available from: eeas.europa.eu/ifs/docs/ifs_mip_2012_13_en.pdf [accessed: 23 February 2015].
European Commission (2011) *Long-term Responses to Global Security Threats: Contributing to Security Capacity Building in Third Countries through the Instrument for Stability* (Brussels: European Commission). Available from: http://ec.europa.eu/europeaid/node/11181_en [accessed: 23 February 2015].
European Commission (2009) The Instrument for Stability – Multi-annual Indicative Programme 2009–2011. C(2009) 2641, 8 April. Available from: www.eeas.europa.eu/ifs/docs/mip_2009_2011_en.pdf [accessed: 23 February 2015].

European Commission (2007) The Instrument for Stability: Strategy Paper 2007–2011 (Brussels: European Commission). Available from: www.eeas.europa.eu/ifs/docs/ifs_strategy_2007-2011_en.pdf [accessed: 23 February 2015].

Gänzle, S. (2009) *Coping with the 'Security-Development Nexus': The European Community's Instrument for Stability—Rationale and Potential.* Bonn: German Development Institute.

Giddens, A. (1990) *The Consequences of Modernity.* Cambridge: Polity, in association with Blackwell.

Heyes, A. (2012) An Assessment of the Nuclear Security Centres of Excellence. *The Stanley Foundation,* May. Available from: www.stanleyfoundation.org/resources.cfm?id=481 [accessed: 23 February 2015].

IAEA (2012) Nuclear Security Report 2012. International Atomic Energy Agency, GOV/2012/41-GC(56)/15, 31 July.

Katzenstein, P. (ed.) (1996) *The Culture of National Security: Norms and Identity in World Politics.* New York: Columbia University Press.

Kaunert, C. and Zwolski, K. (2013) *The EU as a Global Security Actor: A Comprehensive Analysis Beyond CFSP and JHA.* Basingstoke, UK: Palgrave.

Keukeleire, S. and MacNaughtan, J. (2008) *The Foreign Policy of the European Union.* Basingstoke, UK: Palgrave.

Kirchner, E. (2006) The Challenge of European Union Security Governance. *Journal of Common Market Studies.* 44(5). pp. 947–68.

Kirchner, E. and Domínguez, R. (2011) Regional Organizations and Security Governance. In Kirchner, E. and Domínguez, R. (eds) *The Security Governance of Regional Organizations.* Abingdon, UK: Routledge. pp. 1–22.

Kirchner, E. and Sperling, J. (2007) *EU Security Governance.* Manchester: Manchester University Press.

Knodt, M. and Princen, S. (2003) Introduction: Puzzles and Prospects in Theorizing EU's External Relations. In Knodt, M. and Princen, S. (eds) *Understanding the European Union's External Relations.* Abingdon, UK: Routledge. pp. 1–16.

Kohler-Koch, B. and Rittberger, B. (2006) Review Article: The "Governance Turn" in EU Studies. *Journal of Common Market Studies.* 44(S1). pp. 27–49.

Krahmann, E. (2003) Conceptualizing Security Governance. *Cooperation and Conflict.* 38(1). pp. 5–26.

Krahmann, E. (2003a) National, Regional and Global Governance: One Phenomenon or Many? *Global Governance.* 9(3). pp. 323–46.

Manners, I. (2002) Normative Power Europe: A Contradiction in Terms? *Journal of Common Market Studies.* 40(2). pp. 235–58.

Martin, L. L. and Simmons, B. A. (2013) International Organizations and Institutions. In Carlsnaes, W., Risse, T. and Simmons, B. A. (eds) *Handbook of International Relations.* London: SAGE. pp. 326–51.

Maull, H. W. (1990) Germany and Japan: The New Civilian Powers. *Foreign Affairs.* 69 (5). pp. 91–106.

Meyer, J. W. and Rowan, B. (1977) Institutionalized Organizations: Formal Structure as Myth and Ceremony. *American Journal of Sociology.* 83 (2). pp. 340–63.

Mignone, A. (2013) The European Union's Chemical, Biological, Radiological and Nuclear Centres of Excellence Initiative. *Non-Proliferation Papers,* 28 June.

Müller, H. (2005) *The 2005 NPT Review Conference: Reasons and Consequences of Failure and Options for Repair.* Stockholm: The Secretariat of the Weapons of Mass Destruction Commission.

Norheim-Martinsen, P. M. (2010) Beyond Intergovernmentalism: European Security and Defence Policy and the Governance Approach. *Journal of Common Market Studies.* 48(5). pp. 1351–65.

Parsons, T. (1960) *Structure and Process in Modern Societies.* London: Collier Macmillan.

Pfeffer, J. and Salancik, G. R. (1978) *The External Control of Organizations: A Resource Dependence Perspective.* Hagerstown, MD: Harper & Row.

Pierre, J. and Peters, B. G. (2000) *Governance, Politics and the State.* Basingstoke, UK: Palgrave.

Portela, C. (2004) The EU and the NPT: Testing the New European Nonproliferation Strategy. *Disarmament Diplomacy.* No. 78, July/August.

Rhodes, R. A. W. (1997) *Understanding Governance.* Buckingham: Open University Press.

Risse-Kappen, T. (1997) *Cooperation Among Democracies: The European Influence on US Foreign Policy.* Princeton, NJ: Princeton University Press.

Rosamond, B. (2006) The Future of European Studies: Integration Theory, EU Studies and Social Science. In Eilstrup-Sangiovanni, M. (ed.). *Debates on European Integration.* Basingstoke, UK: Palgrave. pp. 448–60.

Rosenau, J. N. (1995) Governance in the Twenty-first Century. *Global Governance.* 1(1). pp. 13–43.

Rosenau, J. N. and Durfee, M. (1995) *Thinking Theory Thoroughly: Coherent Approaches to an Incoherent World.* Boulder, CO: Westview Press.

Rosenau, J. N. and Czempiel, E. O. (eds) (1992) *Governance without Government: Order and Change in World Politics.* Cambridge: Cambridge University Press.

Schmidt, K. (2013) Introduction. *CBRN CoE Newsletter.* No. 6, June.

Schroeder, U. C. (2011) *The Organization of European Security Governance: Internal and External Security in Transition.* Abingdon, UK: Routledge.

Scott, J. (2001) *Power.* Cambridge: Polity Press.

Scott, W. R. (2008) *Institutions and Organizations: Ideas and Interests.* London: SAGE.

Sellers, J. M. (2011) State–Society Relations. In Bevir, M. (ed.) *The SAGE Handbook of Governance.* London: SAGE. pp. 51–64.

Smith, K. (2008) *European Union Foreign Policy in a Changing World.* Malden, MA: Polity.

Sodupe, K. and Benito, E. (1998) The Evolution of the European Union's TACIS Programme, 1991–96. *Journal of Communist Studies and Transition Politics.* 14 (4). pp. 51–68.

Sperling, J. A. (2009) Introduction: Security Governance in a Westphalian World. In Wagnsson, C., Sperling, J. A. and Hallenberg, J. (eds) *European Security Governance: The European Union in a Westphalian World.* Abingdon, UK: Routledge. pp. 1–15.

Sperling, J. and Webber, M. (2014) Security Governance in Europe: A Return to System. *European Security.* 23 (2). pp. 126–44.

Tocci, N. (2008) *Who is a Normative Foreign Policy Actor? The European Union and its Global Partners.* Brussels: Centre for European Policy Studies.

Van der Meer, A. (2013) Interview with the new Head of Unit DEVCO B5. *CBRN CoE Newsletter.* No. 6, June.

Warleigh, A. (2004) In Defence of Intra-disciplinarity: 'European Studies', the 'New Regionalism', and the Issue of Democratisation. *Cambridge Review of International Affairs.* 17(2). pp. 301–18.

Warleigh-Lack, A. (2011) Obsolete if Obstinante? Transforming European Union Studies in the Transnational Era. In Wunderlich, J.-U. and Bailey, D. J. (eds) *The European Union and Global Governance.* Abingdon: Routledge. pp. 13–18.

Warleigh-Lack, A. and Rosamond, B. (2010) Across the EU Studies–New Regionalism Frontier: Invitation to a Dialogue. *Journal of Common Market Studies.* 48 (4). pp. 993–1013.

Weber, M. (1978) *Economy and Society.* Berkley, CA: University of California.

Webber, M., Croft, S. and Howorth, J. (2004) The Governance of European Security. *Review of International Studies.* 30(1). pp. 3–26.

Whitman, R. G. (ed.) (2011) *Normative Power Europe: Empirical and Theoretical Perspectives.* Basingstoke, UK: Palgrave.

Whitman, R. G. (2011a) The Rise of the European External Action Service: Putting the Strategy into EU Diplomacy?. Available from: www.euce.org/eusa/2011/papers/8l_whitman.pdf. [accessed: 15 February 2015]

Whitman, R. G. (1998) *From Civilian Power to Superpower? The International Identity of the European Union.* Basingstoke, UK: Palgrave.

Whitman, R. G. and Wolff, S. (eds) (2012) *The European Union as a Global Conflict Manager.* Abingdon, UK: Routledge.

Winfield, G. (2011) The Network of Excellence. *CBRNe World.* Spring, pp. 47–52. Available from: www.cbrn-coe.eu/Portals/0/cbrn-coe-public-images/the_network_of_excellence.pdf [accessed: 23 February 2015].

Zürn, M. (2013) Globalization and Global Governance. In Carlsnaes, W., Risse, T. and Simmons, B. A. (eds) *Handbook of International Relations.* London: SAGE. pp. 401–25.

Zwolski, K. (2012) The EU and a Holistic Security Approach After Lisbon: Competing Norms and the Power of the Dominant Discourse. *Journal of European Public Policy.* 19(7). pp. 988–1005.

Zwolski, K. (2012a) The EU as an International Security Actor After Lisbon: Finally a Green Light for a Holistic Approach? *Cooperation and Conflict.* 47 (3). pp. 68–87.

Zwolski, K. (2011) The External Dimension of the EU's Non-proliferation Policy: Overcoming Inter-institutional Competition. *European Foreign Affairs Review.* 16(3). pp. 325–40.

Zwolski, K. (2011a) Unrecognised and Unwelcome? The Role of the EU in Preventing the Proliferation of CBRN Weapons, Materials and Knowledge. *Perspectives on European Politics and Society.* 12(4). pp. 477–92.

Part II

On the limits of IR theories for understanding the CSDP

7 Of politics and policies

Thinking strategically about the EU

Olivier Schmitt

Introduction

The institutionalisation of the European Union's (EU) external relations has attracted a lot of attention from International Relations (IR) and EU scholars. The main schools of IR theories have been invoked to explain this puzzling situation, in particular Structural Realism, Neoliberalism and Constructivism. Other researchers have looked at the gradual institutionalisation of the EU's external relations apparatus through the socialisation of its main actors in Brussels, trying to open the black box of the decision-making processes. Overall, there is no shortage of theoretical explanations attempting to make sense of the EU's external relations, and this book is a contribution to an empirically and theoretically rich literature. Logically, the large majority of this production is dominated by the *why?* question: how can we best account for the rise of the EU's external action? However, few analyses focus on the *what for?* and explore the strategic meaning of this new institutional/political framework. One of the few academic works to explicitly engage with this issue concluded in 2009:

> a picture emerges of a European strategy in the making, albeit one that is so far mostly modest as well as partial. There appear to be certain structural factors at work that allow for, even facilitate, a slow but incremental process of accruing actor properties at the core of the complex web of European institutions.
>
> (Engelbrekt and Halleberg, 2009, p. 211)

In 2012, another edited volume similarly concluded that the EU's role in international security was limited, only partly effective, and always in the making (Ginsberg and Penska, 2012).

How can we account for this state of affairs? Can the EU be considered to possess strategic characteristics? Is it still, as Adrian Hyde-Price suggested, a 'neurotic centaur' (2006, p. 153), or has the EU improved its capacity to act strategically? Based on an analysis derived from classical authors in strategic studies, this chapter suggests that it has not. In fact, I would go even further and argue that the notion of a European strategy is an impossibility: with strategy and politics being ontologically related, the absence of a European political project logically leads to the absence of a European strategy. At best, the EU's external relations are a number of *policies*, but cannot be a strategy. Asking the *what for?* question has a number of consequences for the *why?*; in particular, I argue that a fruitful way to look at the EU's external relations would be to apply the tools of Public Policy Analysis and the Sociology of Bureaucracy, as demonstrated in Chapters 4 and 6 in this volume. In the absence of politics, IR theories have a limited analytical power, apart from drawing on Classical Realism in order to explain this very lack of politics, as is explained in the closing section of this chapter.

This chapter is organised as follows. First, I define my understanding of strategy and make the argument that strategy and IR go hand in hand. Second, I apply the strategic analytical framework to the EU's external relations, and observe that, in the absence of a political project, the EU cannot have a strategy. Third, I argue that while Classical Realism explains the absence of politics, it is probably better to analyse the EU's external relations through the tools developed by public policy analysis. The conclusion summarises the argument and the chapter.

What is strategy? A framework for assessing the EU's external action

Clearly delineating the distinction between strategy and IR is a difficult but nevertheless important task, as the relationship that is established between the two has important consequences, which directly impact upon the assessment of European foreign policy. The key difficulty is ontological and concerns the extent to which strategy and IR are interrelated. Two different views can be offered. The first one treats IR and strategy as two parallel subfields of Political Science and resists the idea of treating strategic studies as a subfield of IR. If we consider that strategic studies focus on the role of armed forces in international politics, this position might seem odd, especially because the issues of war and peace were so critical in the establishment of the academic discipline of IR after World War I. The argument, put forward most notably by Robert Ayson (2008), is the following: the key difference between strategic studies (as a subfield of Political Science alongside IR) and security studies (as a subfield of IR) is, to put it in Raymond Aron's words from his masterpiece *Peace and War Among Nations* (1962), the *praxeology* (the science of action): security studies are more analytical, and strategic studies more directed towards practical action. In Ayson's words:

> security studies is at times the more passive side of the coin – a study of the conditions of the international security system and theories on the nature of that system. Strategic studies has a stronger interest in action and decision – what are states and other actors doing as they interact strategically, what choices do they face, and what choices ought they take?
>
> (Ayson, 2008, p. 572)

Security studies would be concerned with describing the landscape, while strategic studies would be about how to act and reshape this landscape in an instrumental way. While the distinction seems to make sense a priori, it is highly doubtful that such a sharp ontological distinction can be established between strategy and security studies, and even more so between strategy and IR.

The first problem with this argument stems from a misunderstanding of Max Weber's *axiological neutrality*. Axiological neutrality refers to the double warning that it is impossible to deduce a value judgement from factual propositions, and that it is impossible to deduce a factual proposition from a value judgement. In short, the social scientist must strive to achieve value neutrality in the establishment of causal mechanisms, and enters a different realm when making policy prescriptions derived from analysis. When making policy prescriptions, social scientists would be sacrificing the scientific component of their work for a normative part, which would be un-scientific and thus open to political debate. However, this understanding of the social scientists' work is too limiting and over-interprets Weber (who was merely giving advice on how to properly collect data and establish causal mechanisms) while discouraging social scientists from participating in public debates because of the risk of losing their *scientificity* (Kalberg, 2013, p. 15). In fact, it is possible to ground a social scientist's participation in public debates in reason, because of the difference between the past and the present on the one side, and the future on the other. The past and the present are finished and, in theory, open to *total knowledge*. Events are finished and, with sufficient data, it would in theory be possible to reconstruct the causal mechanisms that led to certain events or class of events. On the other hand, the future is contingent and open. The role of the social scientist is then to try to interpret causal mechanisms occurring with a certain regularity, in order to reasonably assess the likely results of an action and contribute to the normative debates about the course of action that must be chosen. To summarise, the role of the social scientist is to 'understand the world in order to change it' (Favre, 2005, p. 1). As such, it is incorrect to set the allegedly more descriptive *security studies* against the purposeful *strategic studies*.

Second, all theories of IR, whether explicitly or not, have a relationship with strategy. Liberal theories of IR have a long history of engaging with topics directly covered by strategic thought, such as the relationship between maritime power, free trade and wealth (covered by Mahan and Corbett); ideological and economical containment (covered by Liddell Hart) and the strategic objective of humanitarian interventions (Seybolt, 2007). Whenever Liberals acknowledge that the use of force is necessary, be they reluctant, or calling for it in the case of humanitarian interventions, they are engaged in a dialectical relationship with strategy, as uncomfortable as it may be for them (Howard, 1989). Constructivists have long studied the normative and cultural determinants of military actions (Katzenstein, 1996; Finnemore, 2003), also showing how decision-makers can strategically manipulate facets of their own culture in order to achieve favourable political outcomes (Farrell, 2005; Schmitt, 2012). Realists also have a direct engagement with strategy, although not as obvious a one as it might appear at first glance. In fact, the very notion of strategy contradicts the notion of balance of power (used to explain outcomes in the international system, in particular the outcome of wars), which is so critical to many Realist approaches (Reiter, 1999), as strategy supposes a purposeful action and a degree of agency denied by the more traditional structural approaches of IR. Nevertheless, strategic thinking has had an influence on several Realist concepts, such as deterrence theory (Schelling, 1966; Morgan, 2003) and the offence–defence balance (Lynn-Jones, 1995; Glaser and Kaufmann, 1998), and the most recent work in Structural Realism successfully integrates the distribution of power in the international system with the strategy adopted by the unipolar state in order to explain international outcomes (Monteiro, 2014). Strategic theory is then fundamentally the cornerstone of any theory of IR: instead of separating IR and strategy or considering strategy as a subfield of IR, it is better to conceptualise strategic theory as *the* theory of international action (Vennesson, 2013). The best example of such integration is Raymond Aron, who acknowledged that his conceptualisation of IR in his masterpiece *Peace and War amongst Nations* was directly shaped by his engagement with Clausewitz's *On War*. As long as IR include the risk of war between actors in the system (be they states or other actors), strategy, with its focus on the use or the threat of use of force, will remain a cornerstone of any sound understanding of the international scene.

Finally, and elaborating on the previous point, strategy is fundamental to politics itself. Politics, in its broadest sense, is the activity through which people make, preserve and amend the general rules under which they live. Politics is then fundamentally about cooperation and conflict about normative rules and the proper distribution of limited resources among members of a given community. The regulatory instrument of politics is power, in its multiple forms (Mann, 1986, 1993, 2012), which is exactly the purpose of strategy, defined by one of the contemporary giants in the field as 'the art of creating power' (Freedman, 2013, p. 8). As a journal on strategy explains:

> Strategy, is an eternal and ubiquitous function that all security communities have required, past, present, and we can anticipate with extremely high confidence, future also. Human security communities – extended families, clans, tribes, states, even gangs of bandits – have to do strategy, functionally understood, because they all have purposes (political ends) that need protecting or advancing by choice of effective methods (strategic ways), using whatever instruments of coercion (military means), they have or can acquire.
>
> (*Infinity Journal*, 2013)

To summarise, without strategy, there is no meaningful use of power, and thus no politics. As such, political scientists or IR scholars who overlook strategy are thus condemning themselves to understand little or nothing of the object they study. Although it is frequently mistakenly used in this way in daily speech, it is important to understand that strategy cannot be reduced to the *rational attempt to achieve a goal.* In this very limited understanding, any behaviour could be strategic: from the individual drinking coffee in the morning in order to wake up to the company designing a plan to market a new product. Strategy cannot be reduced to *purposeful action*: it is ontologically related to politics, as politics is about the existence of conflict and strategy about how to generate power (military, social, economic, diplomatic, etc.) in order to prevail in a conflict. There is no politics without strategy, but there can also be no strategy without politics.

Once the critical role of politics in understanding strategy is established, it is necessary to set up an analytical framework for assessing the EU's foreign policy. As Colin Gray (2010) explains, strategy is the bridge that connects politics with policy. As such, strategy can best be conceptualised as composed of three main categories (*People and Politics*, *Preparation for War* and *War Proper*), comprising seventeen dimensions of strategy. The category *people and politics* examines people, society, culture, politics and ethics. The category *preparation for war* includes economics and logistics, organisation, military administration, information and intelligence, strategic theory and doctrine, and technology. Finally, the category *war proper* consists of military operations, command, geography, friction, the adversary, and time. While this framework is a useful heuristic tool to analyse the multiple dimensions of strategy, it is important to understand that these dimensions are interrelated, and that the study of strategy is incomplete if it is considered in the absence of any of the elements above.

Some readers might be concerned about the fact that these analytical categories are overly focussed on war as an instrument of policy. After all, some analysts see the EU as a *normative power*, or a *civilian power* (for a review of the debate, see Orbie, 2006) trying to transcend the old ways of international politics, and will probably argue that I establish an unfair test for the EU's external policy, as the criteria for assessing a strategy could not capture the originality of the EU's external action. This potential criticism is easy to dismiss on several grounds. First, as mentioned above, strategy and politics are ontologically related, and it is impossible to imagine a form of politics that would not have power as a regulatory instrument and thus strategy as a way of efficiently creating and using power. Second, given the potential of war as an enduring and probably unavoidable feature of the international system (Cocker, 2014), it is simply normal to include a military dimension in the analysis. The fact that the EU is inventing a new form of foreign policy and that the *old ways* of diplomacy are obsolete still remains to be demonstrated. As Reich and Lebow (2014) have argued, it is correct that the EU has been comparatively efficient in agenda setting, but this is only one of the three dimensions of power and influence they identify (the two others being custodial economic management and security sponsorship). The EU could be lamentably failing on the other dimensions of power, in particular the military one. The recent Russian resurgence and aggressive behaviours in Georgia and Ukraine analysed in Chapter 10 as well as the increasing difficulties of accommodating a rising China in the international system (Coker, 2015) are further evidence that other actors do not endorse the new form of foreign policy the EU is supposed to promote (see also Chapter 11). In that case, the criteria used to assess whether the EU behaves strategically or not logically include the military dimension of power.

Based on the conceptualisation of strategy elaborated above, the next section analyses the EU's action. By using this systematic framework, it is possible to assess the degree to which the EU's actorness on the international scene can be characterised as strategic or not.

A strategy or a policy? The EU and strategic action

People and politics

Arguably, the category *people and politics* is the most critical to establish a strategic action, but is also problematic for the EU. Because of its specific organisation, the EU is neither an integrated political unit, nor an intergovernmental organisation. The specificities of the EU integration process have fascinated political scientists for decades, with several mechanisms being identified regarding integration and several consequences for political theory being drawn from the EU experience (e.g. the idea of a post-modern political community that would divorce the polity from its national base or the potential emergence of a new *European* identity). However, no matter how we look at the EU integration process (especially on economic issues), one is forced to acknowledge that states, through the European Council, still have the upper hand on foreign relations and defence issues, an aspect reinforced and confirmed by the Lisbon treaty. This means that it is technically improper to speak about *the EU* per se, but instead it should be more accurate to analyse the aggregation of the Member States' preferences. Of course, being a group decision-making process, the EU's external relations face the problem long identified in social choice theory from Condorcet to Arrow, which is to satisfy all the stakeholders' normative and practical/instrumental expectations about the way collective decision making *ought* to work. This is what is commonly expressed as *finding the lowest common denominator*, a traditional feature of Liberal Intergovernmentalism, best illustrated by the work of Andrew Moravcsik and detailed in this volume's third chapter. Group decision-making processes are not an impediment to strategy-making per se: every decision a polity makes involves a degree of collective decision-making. But generally, there are, in national systems, specific figures that are institutionally entitled to make the final decision, for example the President in the US or the Prime Minister in the UK. However, no such figure exists in the EU political system, as the High Representative of the Union for Foreign Affairs and Security Policy can only implement decisions and is under strict instructions by the Member States not to overreach his/her limited prerogatives. The establishment of the European External Action Service, while it is likely to facilitate the coordination of the EU's external instruments, does not change this basic point: it is a tool of implementation, not of decision-making.

In the absence of an authoritative figure able to make the ultimate decision, the EU can hardly be described as engaged in strategy making. This has strong consequences, as the EU is absent from the major challenges facing its environment. This was best illustrated lately by the complete absence of political consensus regarding the Libyan insurrection (which was eventually managed by NATO despite the adoption of a late arms embargo) or the revolution in Ukraine. While Russia has redefined by force the borders of a European state, for the first time in Europe since 1945, the EU has been unable to reach a consensus on the issue, torn as it was between the Member States' conflicting priorities. Characteristically, the EU's reaction to the Ukraine crisis was to reemphasise the second goal of the Common Foreign and Security Policy: 'consolidate and support democracy, the rule of law, human rights and the principles of international law' (Treaty on EU, art 21 para 2), which was the lowest common denominator amongst Member States. The EU assured Russia that it had no agenda in Ukraine apart from the promotion of the rule of law and human rights, which was exactly what Vladimir Putin perceived as a direct threat to his authoritarian rule and intended to push back (Zimmerman, 2014). The naivety with which the EU dealt with Russia on this issue reveals how impossible it finds it to think dialectically (a characteristic of strategic thinking), which stems from an institutional obligation to find the lowest common denominator amongst Member States.

This institutional impossibility of devising a strategy is the symptom of a much more fundamental problem, which is the current absence of any political project for the EU. During the Cold War, protected by the American military umbrella, European states could focus on trade agreements, and a number of institutional innovations such as the creation of the European Parliament. From the 1980s onwards, and following the neoliberal revolution, the creation of a unified economic market became a political project in itself (Jabko, 2009). After the adoption of the Maastricht treaty, which established the Euro as a common currency for a number of states, the third political project became the reunification of the European continent, nearly achieved after the EU enlargement of 2004. Since then, no overarching political project that could bring Europeans together has emerged. The most striking example of the absence of a political project was the management of the financial crisis after 2008. The crisis has been managed in two ways. First, the European Central Bank (ECB) went way beyond its original mandate of controlling inflation and improvised a number of financial fixes in order to save the Euro. Second, a Franco-German condominium, later replaced by a German-only domination after France's loss of political influence following the degradation of her economic situation, imposed a specific management of the crisis at a high social cost, especially in Greece. This perfectly encapsulates the two fundamental issues in relation to the EU and strategy: a financial institution with no elective mandate and an informal agreement legitimising a hierarchy of states managed the crisis, thus lacking legitimacy to enforce a political vision in the long run. This is where the much-lamented *democratic deficit* of the EU matters: in the absence of a popular base for the policies, it is impossible to establish a strategy, as such actions would be unsustainable in the long term. The reaction to this popular disenchantment towards the EU was translated in electoral terms during the Parliamentary elections of May 2014, during which political parties from both the far-right and the far-left[1] and populist parties willing to drastically alter EU policies and the EU integration process obtained a large number of votes, even coming ahead of traditional parties in countries such as France (Front National), the UK (UKIP) and Greece (Syriza). In addition to sending to the European parliament a growing number of MPs actually opposed to the EU, the latest European elections have also once again demonstrated that the predominant drivers of votes are national, and not European, which means that no matter how hard some scholars try to establish the existence of a supranational *European* citizenship (for the latest example, see Pullano, 2014), the electoral body is still defined in national terms. In short, there is no European demos.

To summarise, the very notion of an EU strategy is an ontological impossibility. This stems from the observation that the EU institutional system is a polity leaning towards Intergovernmentalism and thus preventing a figure or, as Colin Gray would put it, a strategist as *hero* (2011) from making strategic decisions. This system is the direct consequence of the absence of a political project and the absence of a European demos, which ultimately displays the absence of any form of EU politics. Because there is no politics, there can be no strategy, but only a number of policies.

Preparation for war

Assessing the *preparation for war* dimension of the EU is a matter of seeing the glass half full or half empty. If we consider the progress made since 1999, there is a clearly observable improvement in terms of command structures, coordination mechanisms and military readiness. If we consider what would be necessary to qualify the EU as a strategic actor, the gap is staggering. The following assessment acknowledges the gradual development of institutional tools pertaining to the preparation of war, but highlights their limitations and their disconnection from actual needs.

The EU officially adopted a grand strategy in 2003 (slightly updated in 2008), the *European Security Strategy: a Secure Europe in a Better World*. This document highlights the main threats the EU is supposed to face: terrorism, proliferation of Weapons of Mass Destruction (WMDs), regional conflicts, state failure and organised crime. The strategy addresses a number of ways to deal with these issues, in particular engagement with regional actors, promotion of international law and humanitarian action. A conceptualisation of the use of the military tool is lacking in the document, apart from a general statement calling for the 'need to develop a strategic culture that fosters early, rapid, and when necessary, robust intervention' (European Council, 2003, p. 11). This means that the EU only understands military power in terms of power projection, following the interventionist and *transformationist* credo that was widespread between the end of the twentieth and the beginning of the twenty-first centuries (Forster, 2006; Locatelli, 2007; Locatelli and Testoni, 2009; Farrell *et al.*, 2013). Most notably, this also reflects the fact that collective territorial defence is not handled by the EU, but is NATO's responsibility: EU crisis management is understood as a way to intervene in a conflict between two non-EU actors, which singularly limits the scope of EU autonomy and strategic action. The EU has established a number of procedures in order to translate this grand strategy into guidance for specific operations, in particular the establishment of a Crisis Management Concept, which is supposed to establish a plan to integrate all relevant means in order to form a coherent solution to a given crisis. Once the Crisis Management Concept is agreed upon, military strategic planning is the responsibility of the EU Military Committee, supported by the EU Military Staff, working under the political control and guidance of the Political and Security Committee. The final product, the *initiating military directive* forms the basis for the planning established by the designated operation commander. This brief description of the process necessary to establish an operation highlights the fact that the EU has managed to create a number of structures relevant for strategy making.

In terms of strategy of resources, two actions must be noted. The first is the establishment of the European Defence Agency (EDA) in 2004. According to its website, the goal of the EDA is 'to improve the EU's defence capabilities through cooperative projects and programmes'. In short, the EDA aims at rationalising the research and acquisition programmes of the Member States' armed forces. Other ad hoc or European-wide programmes of cooperation in the realm of training or education must also be noted. Moreover, the EU has agreed to establish the *Battlegroups*, which aim to keep at all times two 1500-strong battlegroups ready for immediate action, should the European Council decide to use them. The battlegroups rotate every six months, and are supposed to have sufficient firepower and reach for a quick intervention in the theatre of operations, before reinforcements arrive.

So it seems that the EU has managed to establish a number of mechanisms and institutional tools relevant for the conduct of strategy especially pertaining to preparation for war. However, when looked at in detail, the picture is less rosy. First, the strategic thinking of the EU is utterly obsolete. To be fair, it reflects the world of 2003, when terrorism was top of the list of security issues following the 9/11 attacks, and WMDs were a concern in the run-up to the Iraq war. But in 2015, the grand strategy established by the EU misses important potential security threats, such as the re-emergence of a hostile Russia, the establishment of authoritarian and aggressive regimes in the Middle East, the threat to critical structures overseas or the disruption of economic sea lanes, which are critical for the European economy. All these security threats require large military forces and a willingness to wage high-intensity operations. In that regard, the EU scorecard is dramatic. Related to the point identified above that states are the primary actors of the EU's external action, the fall in European defence budgets and cuts in the size of the European armed forces has been uncoordinated, brutal and looks like a collective race to the bottom, with only

France, the UK and to some extent Germany retaining relatively credible military forces. A report by the EU Institute for Security Studies provides a grim picture for the future of European armed forces:

> In 3–5 years – 'bonsai' armies: existing troop formations will increasingly shrink, and so will their capability range. Bigger countries may manage to preserve some sort of full spectrum capabilities but at the price of decreased sustainability. For smaller ones, entire capabilities will be abandoned. As a result, major functional gaps will emerge, with immediate effects on the overall capacity to launch joint and combined missions.
>
> In 5–8 years – defence industrial exodus: the current and foreseeable financial situation of most EU countries render the launch of new large-scale defence industrial/technological projects highly unlikely. As developments over the past few years show, given the expansion of extra-EU defence markets, Europe-based defence contractors will try to increase their foreign presence through a mix of export, cooperation, joint ventures and acquisitions. EU dependency on non-EU partners and suppliers will inevitably ensue.
>
> In 8–12 years – loss of technological leadership: decreasing R&T funds will impact negatively on Europe's current relative technological edge, rendering the required minimum of 'strategic autonomy' a pipedream. In prospect, this could lead to a de facto 'de-industrialisation' of European defence.
>
> (Missiroli, 2013, p. 12)

This brutal degradation of the military tool means that the EU will be incapable of imposing its will (and thus creating power – the definition of strategy), being short of the means to do so. Even the alleged success of the EU Battlegroup Concept reveals an absence of military thinking: 1,500 uniformed soldiers are either too many or too few. They are too many for a humanitarian assistance operation (which mostly requires logistical means rather than troops), but they are too few for an initial coercive action: lessons learned from Afghanistan or Mali reveal that a battlegroup of between 4,000 and 5,000 soldiers (the size of the French and German contingents in Afghanistan or the size of the French contingent in Mali) would be a more appropriate format as it gives the force commander enough flexibility by drawing on a variety of military means. In addition to a faulty military strategy, the political will is lacking. The classic example is the fact that the EU battlegroups have never seen any action, because of the absence of a political consensus on their deployment. If they exist only for the sake of claiming that Europe is doing something, they are just another proof that the CSDP is a policy but certainly not a strategy. EU military instruments are purely decorative, mostly because it is impossible to find a consensus on strategic and military options amongst the *Big Three* (France, Germany and the UK) in European defence, a situation that is unlikely to change anytime soon (Pannier and Schmitt, 2014).

To summarise, it is true that the EU has launched a number of initiatives aimed at increasing its capacity for strategic action when it comes to the preparation for war. However, the result is definitely insufficient. The EU grand strategy, encapsulated in the ESS, is wholly inadequate and outdated. In the meantime, the military strategy is limited, based on poorly conceived military tools (the EU Battlegroup Concept) and subject to the goodwill of European states, which seem to be engaged in a race to the bottom by sacrificing their military instruments. In short, the EU also fails to pass the requirement for the *preparation for war* dimension of strategy.

War proper

The assessment of the *war proper* dimension of strategy for the EU logically flows from the two other dimensions. To put it bluntly, the EU has never seen any war. Yes, there have been a number of crisis management operations, but on such a limited scale that they are more akin to robust policing than to war. This limited engagement is the direct consequence of the lack of political consensus and lack of military instruments with which the EU is confronted. The remainder of this section briefly surveys the operations that the EU is engaged in, revealing their limits. This focus on ongoing missions is justified by the fact that, being the more recent, they should be benefitting from the experience accumulated by the EU. I show that this is not the case, which serves to reinforce my point that it is ontologically impossible for the EU to have a strategy.

As of 2013, the EU was engaged in four military operations and thirteen civilian missions.

As the table illustrates, the vast majority of the EU missions and operations consists of training activities. The most intensive operations in terms of potential military engagements are EUFOR Althea, a peacekeeping operation, and EU NAVFOR Atalanta, a naval policing operation. Considering the low intensity of the operations the EU is engaged in (and was engaged in, EUFOR Congo and EUFOR Chad were also peace-keeping operations), it is fair to say that the EU has never seen war. The absence of any form of coercive engagement is partly related to the lack of a political project mentioned above (thus preventing the definitions of objectives worth using military force for), but also to a division of labour between the EU and other organisations, thus delegating to others the *war proper* dimension of strategy. In several instances, the EU conducts operations or missions that are supposed to complement the actions of another international actor. For example, the EUPOL Afghanistan mission operates in an environment where NATO and the United Nations carry the bulk of the effort. The same is true of EUTM Mali, where France is the primary actor and pushed for the creation of an EU-led training mission in order to avoid the traditional accusations of neocolonialism (Notin, 2014). The same can be said of the missions in Iraq, Congo, Kosovo and Sudan. In all cases, the primary actors are a multinational coalition conducting military operations, i.e. the UN or NATO. The dynamic is interesting: as most NATO members are also EU members, it is a conscious

Table 7.1 EU missions and operations (2013)

	Name	Location	Personnel	Duration
EU Operations	EUFOR Althea	Bosnia and Herzegovina	600	Since 2004
	EU NAVFOR Atalanta	Horn of Africa	1200	Since 2008
	EUTM Somalia	Somalia	125	Since 2010
	EUTM Mali	Mali	560	Since 2013
EU Missions	EUBAM Rafah	Palestinian territories	7	Since 2005
	EUBAM	Moldova and Ukraine	220	Since 2005
	EUJUST LEX	Iraq	66	Since 2005
	EUSEC	RD Congo	41	Since 2005
	EUPOL COPPS	Palestinian territories	95	Since 2006
	EUPOL	Afghanistan	491	Since 2007
	EUPOL	RD Congo	50	Since 2007
	EUMM	Georgia	405	Since 2008
	EULEX	Kosovo	2,065	Since 2008
	EUCAP Sahel	Niger	64	Since 2012
	EUCAP Nestor	Kenya, Djibouti, Somalia, Seychelles	72	Since 2012
	EUAVSEC	South Sudan	47	Since 2012
	EUBAM	Libya	44	Since 2013

Source for Data: EEAS.

choice by Member States to use NATO for the *real work* (for example in Afghanistan) and the EU for smaller tasks. Multiple reasons can explain this state of affairs (ranging from Member States' individual preferences to the institutional flexibility that NATO structures provide, not to mention the American support), but it is the dynamic that matters here: wherever intensive coercive operations take place, the EU is a mere civilian force auxiliary to the intervention. Of course, anyone looking at the details of the programmes implemented by the EU would probably find that, here and there, the EU has had a positive effect. For example, it is regularly mentioned that the EU mission in Afghanistan was a good complement to the American trainers. I do not dispute that fact (doing something is probably better than doing nothing in most cases), but it is the broader picture that matters: the fact remains that in such cases, the EU does little and its presence is anecdotic. Even where large military interventions do not take place, the EU action is limited: about 100 trainers in the Palestinian territories, forty-four in Libya, 220 in Moldova and Ukraine, etc. In principle, such actions would make sense: securing and helping build a Libyan state (for example) is a direct European interest. But the means and the actions are wholly inadequate and condemned to ineffectiveness, as demonstrated by the political evolutions of Libya or Ukraine, to take these two examples. Once again, such actions are more akin to *showing the flag* (hence a policy) rather than a thought-through long-term action designed to secure the EU's interests in these areas. The closest the EU comes to a strategically meaningful action is with the EU NAVFOR operation: securing maritime traffic is important for the European economy, and it is only logical that the EU attempts to secure its interests. However, once again, the intensity of the operation makes it more akin to a robust policing action than to a war-like engagement. Since there is still no *war proper* dimension to the operation, it is difficult to call EU NAVFOR *strategic*, but it is probably as close as it gets to strategic behaviour; the real test will be if the ships engaged in the mission find themselves in a combat situation.

To summarise, the EU scorecard on the *war proper* dimension of strategy is also very limited, for the simple reason that the EU has never seen war, and has always acted as a small auxiliary to interventions facing war-like conditions (such as in Afghanistan or Mali) or at best as a robust cop in other places. But this failure is not surprising, as it is the direct result of the absence of a political project and of available means.

Overall, the above analysis shows that, because of the absence of politics, EU external action is not, because it cannot be, a strategy. It is at best a number of policies. Once the absence of strategy is established, it is important to assess how the EU's external action can be better explained from the vantage point of IR theories.

Theoretical perspective on the absence of strategy

From a theoretical perspective, the emergence of the CSDP is puzzling only because it seems redundant. As is well known, the CSDP is by no means the furnisher of security in Europe, as a complex web of institutions and practices concerned with European security, the first and foremost being obviously NATO, already exists. The relations between NATO and the EU have been the subject of countless articles, conferences and reports. After a decade of debates on the proper scope and focus of both institutions, the hard truth remains: NATO means the United States, which means military capabilities and reassurances incommensurate with those which any aggregation of European states could generate. If security means territorial defence, then NATO is European security. This hard fact is the only reason why the emergence of the CSDP is such a puzzle: the European initiative seems redundant, and has more to do with party ideologies than with a real strategic rationale (Hofmann, 2013). Instead of being a case of *soft balancing* (Pape, 2005; Jones, 2006), the CSDP is better explained by looking at national party preferences about multilateralism, sovereignty and Europe. As such, the EU security policy is not about European security. Even the French have become disillusioned with the CSDP as the report written by Hubert Védrine about the French reintegration to NATO shows (Védrine, 2012). European security must be thought of as a case of embedded organisations, furnishing different capabilities fit for different needs. In that sense, Pohl (2014) is entirely right: the CSDP is an inconsistent application of a liberal principle vaguely aimed at showing the EU's interest in the security of its neighbourhood. As explained above, there has been a lot of policies (including missions), but nothing substantially political at the EU level, which confirms Pohl's findings that the operations and missions are mostly directed towards Member States' internal audiences instead of reflecting strategic thinking of the EU in trying to shape its security environment.

Being short of a political project, the EU has no strategy for its CSDP, which ends up being limited to easy low-intensity missions and financial aid without even making an effort to articulate military, economic and diplomatic resources into broader political action. If one wants to look to IR theories to explain this weakness, the reference should not be to Structural Realists but to Classical Realists instead. When he wrote *The Concept of the Political* in French while in Geneva, Hans Morgenthau (1933) distinguished between two notions of power. *Pouvoir* was the traditional Weberian understanding of power as relation, the stronger actor (in terms of material resources and/or *authority*) imposing its will. But he also used the term *puissance*, which referred to a normative aspect of power, based on a political project. As he explained, 'political action can be defined as an attempt to realise moral values through the medium of politics, that is, power' (Morgenthau, 1962, p. 110). When Morgenthau wanted to *speak truth to power*, he was emphasising the necessary realisation by political elites of the transformative potential of power. Right now, the EU may have some *pouvoir*, but clearly lacks *puissance*, being short of a political project that would serve as a micro-foundation for strategic behaviour. As long as the EU will not learn how to articulate political ends, ways to achieve them and available means (in short, learn to think strategically), the CSDP will remain a policy occupying a few hundred policy-makers and think-tankers in Brussels and the capitals, having little impact on broader European security concerns.

As such, the relevant theoretical tool to analyse EU external relations might well be Public Policy Analysis, as used in Chapter 4 of this volume, instead of IR theories. Looking at the EU's external actions with the theoretical tools of Public Policy Analysis – such as agenda-setting, the advocacy-coalition frame-work, the stages approach, blame avoidance, policy narrative, policy network or path dependence – is fruitful, as it helps explain why and how certain *policies* are established, maintained or terminated. But, in the absence of a political project, and therefore in the absence of strategy as identified in this chapter, IR theories may not be the most appropriate theoretical framework, apart from drawing on Classical Realism in order to understand why the EU lacks *puissance*, the transformative/normative dimension of power.

Conclusion

This chapter began with the observation that, after fifteen years of continuous publications, the characterisation of what the EU is doing on the international stage is still puzzling, with analysts being divided between enthusiasts emphasis-ing the major progress since 1999 and sceptics highlighting the limited impact of

EU actions. In theoretical terms, all major IR theories have been mobilised to explain the rise of European security cooperation. This chapter has attempted to take a step back, and, instead of exploring why and how the CFSP came to existence, it tried to explore its strategic meaning. In order to do so, I delineated my understanding of strategy, arguing that it is ontologically related to politics (and thus to IR), before putting the EU's external relations to the test according to the three main dimensions of strategy: people and politics, preparation for war and war proper. Following this framework, I have argued that, because of the lack of a European political project, there could be no European strategy. Instead, there are a number of policies, more or less effective, but which together cannot qualify as a strategy. This limitation is inherent in the institutional design of the European institutions, the ambivalent political regime that is the EU (neither a federal state, nor an intergovernmental organisation, but one which leaves large autonomy to states in the realm of defence and foreign policy), and the existence of a complex web of organisations and practices concerned with European security, first and foremost NATO. As such, the relevant theoretical tool to explore the EU's external relations could well be Public Policy Analysis, rather than IR theories.

Note

1 This observation does not mean that the far right and the far left offer similar arguments regarding the needs and the ways to alter EU policies.

References

Aron, R. (1962) *Paix et Guerre entre les Nations*. Paris: Calmann-Lévy.
Ayson, R. (2008) Strategic Studies. In Reus-Smith, C. and Snidal, D. (eds) *The Oxford Handbook of International Relations*. Oxford: Oxford University Press.
Cocker, C. (2014) *Can War be Eliminated?* Cambridge: Polity Press.
Coker, C. (2015) *The Improbable War. China, the United States, and the Logic of Great Power Conflicts*. London: Hurst Publishers.
Engelbrekt, K. and Hallenberg, J. (2009) Conclusion: a Strategic Actor Under Permanent Construction? In Engelbrekt, K. and Hallenberg, J. (eds) *The European Union and Strategy. An Emerging Actor*. Abingdon, UK: Routledge.
European Council (2003) *A Secure Europe in a Better World*, 2003. www.eeas.europa.eu/csdp/about-csdp/european-security-strategy/ (accessed: 25 February 2015).
Farrell, T. (2005) World Culture and Military Power. *Security Studies*. 14 (3). pp. 448–88.
Farrell, T., Rynning, S. and Terriff, T. (2013) *Transforming Military Power since the Cold War*. Cambridge: Cambridge University Press.
Favre, P. (2005) *Comprendre le Monde pour le Changer. Epistémologie du Politique*. Paris: Presses de Sciences Po.
Finnemore, M. (2003) *The Purpose of Intervention. Changing Beliefs about the Use of Force*. Ithaca, NY: Cornell University Press.
Forster, A. (2006) *Armed Forces and Society in Europe*. Basingstoke, UK: Palgrave.
Freedman, L. (2013) *Strategy: a History*. Oxford: Oxford University Press.

Ginsber, R. H. and Penksa, S. E. (eds) (2012) *The European Union in Global Security. The Politics of Impact*. Basingstoke, UK: Palgrave Macmillan.

Glaser, C. L. and Kaufmann, C. (1998) What is the Offense-Defense Balance and Can We Measure It? *International Security*. 22 (4). pp. 44–82.

Gray, C. S. (2011) The Strategist as Hero. *Joint Forces Quarterly*. 62(3). pp. 37–45.

Gray, C. S. (2010) *The Strategy Bridge. Theory for Practice*. Oxford: Oxford University Press.

Hofmann, S. C. (2013) *European Security in NATO's Shadow*. Cambridge: Cambridge University Press.

Howard, M. (1989/1978) *War and the Liberal Conscience*. New Brunswick: Rutgers University Press.

Hyde-Price, A. (2006) A Neurotic 'Centaur': the Limitations of the EU as a Strategic Actor, in Engelbrekt, K. and Hallenberg, J. (eds) *The European Union and Strategy. An Emerging Actor*. Abingdon, UK: Routledge. pp. 153–67.

Infinity Journal (2013) What is Strategy?, *IJ Brief*. www.infinityjournal.com/article/91/What_is_Strategy/ (accessed: 25 February 2015).

Jabko, N. (2009) *L'Europe par le Marché. Histoire d'une Stratégie Improbable*. Paris: Presses de Sciences Po.

Jones, S. G. (2006) *The Rise of European Security Cooperation*. Cambridge: Cambridge University Press.

Kalberg, S. (2013) *Max Weber's Comparative-Historical Sociology Today*. Farnham, UK: Ashgate Publishing.

Katzenstein, P. J. (ed.) (1996) *The Culture of National Security: Norms and Identity in World Politics*. New York: Colombia University Press.

Locatelli, A. (2007) The Technology Gap in Transatlantic Relations: a Cause of Tension or a Tool of Cooperation? *Journal of Transatlantic Studies*. 5 (2). pp. 133–54.

Locatelli, A. and Testoni, M. (2009) Intra-Allied Competition and Alliance Durability. The Case for Promoting a Division of Labour among NATO Allies. *European Security*. 18 (3). pp. 345–62.

Lynn-Jones, S. M. (1995) Offense-Defense Theory and its Critics. *Security Studies*. 4 (4). pp. 660–91.

Mann, M. (2012) *The Sources of Social Power*. Volume III. Cambridge: Cambridge University Press.

Mann, M. (1993) *The Sources of Social Power*. Volume II. Cambrige: Cambridge University Press.

Mann, M. (1986) *The Sources of Social Power*. Volume I. Cambridge: Cambridge University Press.

Missiroli, A. (ed.) (2013) *Enabling the Future. European Military Capabilities 2013–2025: Challenges and Avenues*. Paris: European Union Institute for Security Studies.

Monteiro, N. (2014) *Theory of Unipolar Politics*. Cambridge: Cambridge University Press, 2014.

Morgan, P. (2003) *Deterrence Now*. Cambridge: Cambridge University Press.

Morgenthau, H. J. (1962) Decision-Making in the Nuclear Age. *Bulletin of the Atomic Scientists*. 18 (10). pp. 105–17.

Morgenthau, H. J. (1933) *The Concept of the Political*. Translation Vidal, M. (2012). Abingdon, UK: Palgrave Macmillan.

Notin, J. C. (2014) *La Guerre de la France au Mali*. Paris: Tallandier.

Orbie, J. (2006) Civilian Power Europe. Review of the Original and Current Debates. *Cooperation and Conflict*. 41(1). pp. 123–28.

Pannier, A. and Schmitt, O. (2014) Institutionalised Cooperation and Policy Convergence in European Defence: Lessons from the Relations between France, Germany and the UK. *European Security.* 23 (3). pp. 270–89.

Pape, R. A. (2005) Soft Balancing Against the United States. *International Security.* 30 (1). pp. 7–45.

Pohl, B. (2014) To What Ends? Governmental Interests and European Union (non-) Intervention in Chad and the Democratic Republic of Congo. *Cooperation and Conflict.* 49 (2). pp. 191–211.

Pullano, T. (2014) *La Citoyenneté Européenne. Un Espace Quasi-Etatique.* Paris: Presses de Sciences Po.

Reich, S. and Lebow, R. N. (2014) *Good-Bye Hegemony. Power and Influence in the Global System.* Princeton, NJ: Princeton University Press.

Reiter, D. (1999) Military Strategy and the Outbreak of International Conflict. *Journal of Conflict Resolution.* 43 (3). pp. 366–87.

Schelling, T. (1966) *Arms and Influence.* Yale, CT: Yale University Press.

Schmitt, O. (2012) Strategic Users of Culture: German Decisions for Military Action. *Contemporary Security Policy.* 33(1). pp. 59–81.

Seybolt, T. B. (2007) *Humanitarian Military Intervention. The Conditions for Success and Failure.* Oxford: Oxford University Press.

Védrine, H. (2012) *Report for the President of the French Republic on the Consequences of France's Return to NATO's Integrated Military Command, on the Future of Transtlantic Relations, and the Outlook for the Europe of Defence,* 14 November. Available from: www.defense.gouv.fr/content/download/190042/2094793/file/Rapport%20V%C3%A9drine_GBR_DEU.pdf [accessed: 29th May 2014].

Vennesson, P. (2013) La Stratégie. In Balzacq, T. and Ramel, F. (eds) *Traité de Relations Internationales.* Paris: Presses de Sciences Po.

Zimmerman, W. (2014) *Ruling Russia: Authoritarianism from the Revolution to Putin.* Princeton, NJ: Princeton University Press.

8 The EU-NATO conundrum in perspective

Luis Simón

Introduction

Realism appears to be clawing its way back into the European security debate (Rosato, 2011; Rynning, 2011; Cladi and Locatelli, 2012, 2013; Dyson, 2013). This is hardly surprising, given the growing uncertainty about the future of European integration (Kahn and Kupchan, 2013), the renewed preference of most European countries for bilateral and sub-regional forms of security cooperation (Jones, 2011), or recent intra-European divergences over how to deal with the Libyan crisis (Menon, 2011). All these developments seem to challenge the notion of an 'ever closer union', and speak directly to Realist assumptions about the supremacy of the national interest and the immanence of conflict and competition in international politics. In this regard, Russia's unilateral annexation of Crimea in March 2014 can only help amplify the current sense of gloom about European security (see Chapter 10).

The question marks that surround Europe's future are symptomatic of deeper geopolitical trends. In the early 1990s, Kenneth Waltz already warned that if Europe and the world were at peace and international norms and institutions reigned supreme, it was only because of US/Western global military and geopolitical hegemony (Waltz, 1993). Today, as the US faces mounting challenges around the world and a decade of inconclusive wars and the economic rise of Asia underscore the relative decline of the West, there is a growing sense of contestation about the (Western-made) global order (Kupchan, 2012). Insofar as Europe is concerned, the US retreat towards a less pro-active foreign policy course (see Chapter 9) is both animating and aggravating regional geopolitical uncertainties (Simón and Fiott, 2014).

Admittedly, post-11 September US unilateralism and the 2003 Iraq War already provided a handy hook for Neorealist accounts of European security cooperation back in the early 2000s. A Common Security and Defence Policy (CSDP), the Neorealist logic went, was the best way for Europeans to mitigate the prospect of excessive US power (Posen, 2004, 2006). However, post-11 September US unilateralism was a rather short-lived phenomenon. As the US retreated towards a more multilateral and less interventionist approach to foreign policy from the mid-2000s (Haass, 2005), references to European balancing of

US power began to subside. In fact, more recent Neorealist accounts of European security cooperation have turned to the idea that unipolarity leads Europeans to bandwagon on, not balance, US power. The fact that security cooperation in a EU framework has not led to a diminishing European reliance on NATO, the bandwagoning thesis goes, leads to the conclusion that the CSDP is primarily aimed at strengthening Europe's 'bargaining power' vis-à-vis the US, and therefore poses no direct threat to Transatlantic cohesion (Cladi and Locatelli, 2012, 2013; Dyson, 2013).

Arguably, the main problem with (most) Neorealist-inspired analyses of European security cooperation has been their clinging to the assumption that global dynamics have a rather homogeneous impact across Europe (Posen, 2004, 2006; Jones, 2007; Cladi and Locatelli, 2012, 2013). As much as European countries may hold different foreign and security perspectives, the reasoning goes, a world of continent-sized superpowers is a world that underscores Europe's geopolitical decline. And that world calls for European security cooperation. Whether that is to balance against excessive US power or to get a better negotiating position at the NATO table is a question that comes later. What really matters is that geopolitical decline leads to European security cooperation. Such a parsimonious narrative transcends Neorealism, and enjoys widespread appeal amongst European security scholars (Grevi, 2009; Howorth, 2010). The link between geopolitical decline and cooperation may well explain part of the European security puzzle. However, it ignores a key fact: European countries might indeed be subject to common security challenges, but they disagree more often than not about how to cope with them. In other words, while their many similarities often lead them to cooperate, their differences and specificities translate into conflicting priorities over how to arrange the terms of cooperation (Simón, 2014).

Part of the problem with most Neorealist analyses of European security has been methodological. By ignoring how specific debates within CSDP or NATO play out, most Neorealist analyses of European security have failed to properly grasp the nature and extent of inter-European conflict. Given the proliferation of new institutions, concepts and capabilities, some scholars have concluded that the CSDP was largely characterised by strong patterns of cooperation (Posen, 2004, 2006; Hyde-Price, 2006; Jones, 2007). However, whether a given institution was created (i.e. the European Defence Agency, EDA), new capabilities were being developed (i.e. the Battlegroup Concept) or missions were launched tells us very little in itself about the nature of the CSDP. The same goes for NATO. Conflicting national priorities mean CSDP and NATO initiatives can be ambiguous, inefficient or irrelevant, and often are all of those things at the same time. Only by looking at how national priorities play out in the context of specific initiatives or debates can we uncover the contradictory nature of CSDP and NATO, characterised by both cooperation and conflict. Very often, it is only when it comes to organising the specific terms of cooperation that conflicting priorities surface.

Drawing on Classical Realism (Morgenthau, 1948, 1985), this contribution aims at shedding light on the tension between conflict and cooperation that lies at the heart of the EU-NATO conundrum. Classical Realism's emphasis on nation-states, we contend, allows us to unpack the otherwise opaque (Neorealist) notion of *structural change* and assess how individual European countries process change at the systemic level. Moreover, by focussing on power instead of security, Classical Realism allows us to transcend the hollow notion that cooperation is inherently positive for all European countries. If a European country is to maximise its power or influence, the CSDP and NATO must develop in a direction that reflects its own specific interests. And insofar as European countries possess different strengths, they hold different visions over the direction the CSDP or NATO ought to take. This highlights the importance of the regional level of the balance of power and intra-European frictions, otherwise largely neglected by (most) Neorealist accounts of European security.

This contribution examines the interplay between a dynamic international context and the evolving strategic priorities of Britain, France and Germany towards the CSDP and NATO. The first part of the chapter identifies the main shortcomings associated with most Neorealist analyses of European security cooperation, namely their disregard for intra-European relative gain considerations and their lack of clarity in delineating the differences between security and power. The second section offers an empirical analysis of the interplay between systemic change, the evolving strategic priorities of Britain, France and Germany and the evolution of CSDP and NATO between 2001 and 2014. The third and final section offers some concluding observations about Classical Realism's potential to enhance our understanding of the EU-NATO conundrum.

The politics of European security: between conflict and cooperation

Admittedly, the link between national power and European security has not been missing from the literature. In the 1990s, a handful of Realist scholars identified intra-European balance of power dynamics as the key driver of European security cooperation – or lack thereof (Mearsheimer, 1990; Grieco, 1995; Art, 1996). However, ever since the launch of the CSDP in the late 1990s, most Neorealist discussions on European security cooperation have gravitated around one main question: whether European security calculations are driven by a will to balance against US unipolarity or bandwagon with the US (Posen, 2004, 2006; Hyde-Price, 2006; Jones, 2007; Cladi and Locatelli, 2012, 2013; Dyson, 2013).

Confining the European security debate to the US factor is problematic, for neither do Europeans think with one mind about the US, nor is the US the only thing in their minds. More broadly, the focus on unipolarity restricts the discussion on the structure of the international system to the global level, to the detriment of the regional (European) one. This might well be explained by the global bias inherent in Structural Realism, as formulated by Waltz (1979).

Confining the European security debate to the US factor is problematic, because European countries disagree more often than not about how to deal with the US. This might be a useful operating assumption. However, it offers little empirical value, not least as it fails to accommodate the idea that different regions feature their own balance of power dynamics that is relatively autonomous from global ones. While during the Cold War the global nature of US–Soviet competition tended to mask regional geopolitical variations or subtleties, the early 1990s presided over a period of increasing scholarly attention to regional security dynamics (Buzan and Waever, 2003). Ultimately, the relative importance of the global and regional levels of international politics varies depending on the context of dynamic international context. In contrast to Waltz's emphasis on the global level of the international system, the balance-of-threat brand of Neorealism highlights the importance of regional dynamics in accounting for states' foreign and security policy calculations (see Chapter 2). For Stephen Walt (1987), states balance against threat (not power), and therefore pay attention primarily to their immediate geographical environment and to the balance between offensive and 'defensive' capabilities (1987).

The balance-of-threat brand of Neorealism brings an important perspective to the question of European security cooperation (or lack thereof). According to Ringsmose (2013), regional strategic considerations are at the heart of intra-European foreign and security policy differences. In a similar vein, Dyson has argued that variations in geographical position and degrees of exposure to different areas of the globe for energy security have an important impact upon the calculations of different European countries vis-à-vis NATO and CSDP (2013; see also Chapter 2). Unfortunately, neither Ringsmose nor Dyson get to operationalise those differences by tracing their impact on specific NATO or CSDP debates. This might be explained by the fact that these two authors are primarily concerned with how such differences may relate to European attitudes towards US power. In any event, by insisting on the need to bring the regional level into the picture, these works constitute an important qualification to existing Neorealist analyses of European security cooperation.

Ultimately, the question of whether the regional level trumps the global (or vice-versa) is an empirical one, and can only be addressed by examining the interplay between a dynamic international environment and the evolving strategic priorities of Europe's most powerful countries – for it is they who largely delineate the nature and pace of European security cooperation. Paradoxically, having systematically prioritised the global level over the regional one, most Neorealist analyses of European security cooperation seem to have betrayed the very added-value of Neorealism; by concentrating on Europe's geopolitical decline vis-à-vis others (chiefly the US) they have implicitly assigned Europe the status of an independent analytical unit. This has led them to reduce the problem of relative gains (Grieco, 1988) to European calculations vis-à-vis US power, and to dismiss the intra-European side of the relative gains problem altogether.

Geopolitical decline and European security cooperation

As already argued, most Neorealist accounts of European security cooperation have concentrated most of their attention on the question of European geopolitical decline, and this has often led them to treat Europe as a coherent geopolitical actor (Posen, 2004, 2006; Jones, 2007). This is not to say that these analyses are unaware of intra-European differences. Cladi and Locatelli do acknowledge the existence of such differences, but dismiss them as secondary – and effectively superfluous. After all, they contend, 'systemic pressures (power imbalances in particular) make bandwagoning with the US a rational behaviour' (Chapter 1). Posen (2006, p. 58) adopts a similar line in arguing that although '(f)our Western European powers ... possess significant capability relative to most other international actors' each of them individually is 'much weaker than the United States'. Again, the corollary is that weakness brings European countries together and trumps any differences they may have.

Hyde-Price (2006, pp. 229–31) has addressed the question of intra-European security differences in a direct fashion. However, he has done so only to discount their importance. In his view, Europeans do not care about their own differences and frictions because they inhabit a stable regional context and are therefore 'secure' (2006, p. 230). If all that European states care about is security and they are indeed secure, it remains unclear why they would want to engage in security cooperation in the first place.

Given that most Neorealist-inspired analyses of CSDP argue precisely that Europeans cooperate to downplay their *geopolitical decline*, we are only left with the implication that they care deeply about their competition with third parties (and in particular the US) but not (or much less so) about their competition for power and influence within Europe. This would explain the tendency of most European countries to see the EU as a power multiplier (Treacher, 2001). That is indeed what Hyde-Price (2006), Posen (2004, 2006) and Jones (2007) seem to be driving at. However, this would also be a problematic assumption, for a European state can hardly safeguard its relative power in relation to third actors without taking into account how powerful it is in relation to its fellow Europeans (i.e. within the power multiplier). Surely, both levels must be interdependent: in order for a medium-sized European state to narrow the (power) gap with a third party (i.e. the US), the thriving of the (EU) power multiplier does not suffice. It is just as important that the state in question thrives within the multiplier. This means that it is the duty of each state to ensure that cooperation in the framework of the power multiplier occurs in a way that highlights its own comparative advantages.

In other words, a state's power depends both on the prosperity of the multiplier as well as on its own (relative) position within the multiplier. And the latter is a battle that needs to be fought against fellow Europeans who, by virtue of their respective strengths and comparative advantages, hold different preferences regarding the directions the power multiplier ought to take. Thus, while Posen (2004, 2006), Hyde-Price (2006) or Jones (2007) are indeed correct to argue that European states are increasingly weak in relative terms, they have downplayed the fact that they are differently weak, by virtue of their different strengths (military, diplomatic, other forms of *soft power*, bilateral alliances, position within various international organisations, etc.). Whereas their common weakness represents an incentive towards cooperation, their specific strengths and comparative advantages translate into conflicting priorities over the terms of cooperation. CSDP and NATO are therefore mixed games, characterised by the existence of both cooperation and conflict (Schelling, 1958).

Insofar as their preoccupation with the success of the power multiplier cannot be separated from their own ability to affect the development of the multiplier, European states will tend to simultaneously observe both their positions vis-à-vis third parties and power and the competition for power and influence with their fellow Europeans. Britain's traditional perception of NATO as a means to *keep the Germans down, the Americans in and the Russians out* is most illustrative in this regard (Baylis, 1993). Perhaps the intra-European relative gain dimension is most visible in the case of France, a country that has continuously advocated for European security cooperation ever since the end of the Second World War. France's initial impulse to create a European Defence Community in 1950 was largely explained by its desire to exercise some degree of influence over West German rearmament (Dwan, 2001). Likewise, the Fouchet plans I and II were part of a broader French effort aimed at reversing the supranational trend taken by the European integration project, which was seen in Paris as benefitting West Germany in the long term (Nuttall, 1992).

In a more contemporary context, France's push for the CSDP and the European Monetary Union during the Maastricht Treaty negotiations in the second half of 1991 must be largely seen as a reaction to German reunification, the logic being that a strong multilateral (EU) setting should help mitigate the prospect of an increasingly autonomous and powerful Germany (Baun, 1995/6). Most recently, France's reintegration within NATO's military structure and attempts to strengthen its bilateral strategic ties with the US and the UK must be partly seen as a result of its growing frustration with the failure of military CSDP and Germany's increasing influence over the EU's political direction (Simón, 2013).

Admittedly, one should not blame Neorealism for the fact that certain scholars decided to confine the debate on European security cooperation to the US factor. As Rynning (2011) has rightly argued, Realist thought is sufficiently rich and diverse to accommodate a wide array of interpretations about European security cooperation – or lack thereof. Indeed, Mearsheimer's portrayal of European security cooperation as a means to contain German power, rather than balance the US, bears testament to this fact (2001). Rynning himself has reclaimed the tradition of Intergovernmental approaches to the study of European integration (Hoffmann, 1966) to point to the potential of Classical Realism to explain European security cooperation. As Rynning (2011) contends, Classical Realism would allow us to portray the CSDP as an evolving institution with no end-state, whose purpose is rescuing the (waning) power of the nation-state.

Its emphasis on power maximisation and influence sets Classical Realism apart from Neorealism and its focus on security. Hyde-Price's assertion that European states strive for security and not 'power maximisation' (2006) is most illustrative in this regard. If all European states care about is 'security' and they are indeed 'secure' (2006, p. 230) it remains very much unclear why they would choose to cooperate in the first place. If Europeans worried only about security in a narrow sense, why worry about US power? An excessively powerful US could certainly undermine European autonomy or influence, but surely, it would not endanger the physical survival or formal sovereignty of its European allies? The literature on the indirect and liberal nature of US hegemony would seem to contradict this implication (Ikenberry, 1998). A focus on power, understood as a nation's ability to act and assert itself against any forces that might threaten its autonomy, would allow such questions to be overcome. Not least, it would help transcend the *balancing vs bandwagoning* debate (Cladi and Locatelli, 2012, 2013) and reflect the mixed picture of European security politics, characterised by patterns of cooperation and conflict.

The question, therefore, is not whether Europeans cooperate or they do not (they do), but, rather, the extent, nature and limitations of their cooperation. And understanding the evolving strategic priorities of Europe's most powerful states is critical to addressing such questions. After all, it is they who, in an attempt to maximise their power through a calculated resort to the CSDP and NATO, account for the inherent contradictions that inform European security politics. States' calculations towards the CSDP and NATO are not fixed: they are informed by the opportunities and challenges offered by a dynamic international context. Therefore, only by looking at the interplay between a dynamic international context and the evolving strategic priorities of Europe's most powerful countries can one grasp the nature of the contradictions that define European security politics. The next section examines the relationship between a dynamic international environment and the evolving strategic priorities of Britain, France and Germany towards NATO and the CSDP between 2001 and 2014.

International change, the *big three* and the CSDP-NATO conundrum

The 2001–2014 period can be separated into two distinct analytical units: the *post-11 September* years (2001–5) and the *post-Iraq* years (2005–14). The *post-11 September* years saw a return to a return of direct threats to Western hegemony in the form of Islamist terrorism and rogue states; an increasing emphasis on expeditionary military warfare in the West; the adoption of a markedly unilateral and militaristic approach to foreign policy on the part of the US hegemon; and a substantial US geostrategic shift towards Central Asia and the Middle East, away from Europe. In turn, during the *post-Iraq* years the US adopted a more multilateral and less militaristic approach to foreign policy, which broadly coincided with George W. Bush's second presidential term (2005–9). Following Obama's arrival to power in 2009, war fatigue and a growing emphasis on domestic economic reform further conspired to harden Washington's aversion to military interventions and penchant for multilateralism. In turn, Obama's announcement of a pivot to Asia in 2011 and successive cuts in the US defence budget from 2013 onwards would seem to further compound Washington's geostrategic shift away from Europe.

Whilst *post-11 September* and *post-Iraq* arguably constitute rather fluid categories, 2005 would seem to be an appropriate cut off point. For one thing, that year witnessed the beginning of George W Bush's second presidential term, which coincided with an important move towards multilateralism in US foreign policy (Haass 2005; Calleo 2009. For another, it was in 2005 when Dutch and French voters rejected a Draft Constitutional Treaty, thus casting the EU into a two-year period of reflection. The 2005–7 years epitomised a historical transition, from an EU centred around Western Europe into one in which the admission of ten new members from Central and Eastern Europe seemed to underscore Germany's increasing centrality and influence in the European integration process (Szabo, 2004).

The post-11 September years (2001–5)

If the 1990s were the era of the post-Cold War peace dividend, the 11 September attacks on US soil were a reminder of the existence of direct threats to Western security and shifted US attention to the triad of international terrorism, failed states and WMD proliferation (Walt, 2001; McInnes, 2003). Against this backdrop, the post-11 September years led to an increased emphasis on high-end networked expeditionary military capabilities in the US (Freedman, 2003; Londsdale, 2003). In terms of foreign policy, Washington adopted a markedly unilateral and militaristic stance, leaving behind the multilateralism of the 1990s (Ikenberry, 2002; Jervis, 2003). Additionally, the emphasis on the War on Terror and the campaigns in Afghanistan and Iraq saw a shift in US strategic attention away from Europe (Coker, 2003).

11 September raised important challenges for Europeans. From a military–strategic viewpoint, the growing threat posed by rogue states and international terrorism underscored the importance of expeditionary concepts and capabilities (Lindley-French, 2002). In turn, Washington's response to the 11 September attacks posed two important questions: how to deal with an increasingly unilateral and condescending US (Heisbourg, 2003) and how to grapple with the prospect of a US geostrategic reorientation away from Europe (Coker, 2003). These challenges led Britain, France and Germany to pay increasing attention to expeditionary concepts and capabilities (nationally as well as within the CSDP and NATO frameworks), but also to promote and embrace initiatives aimed at mitigating or tempering US unilateralism (Press-Barnathan, 2006). However, their specific interests resulted in conflicting visions regarding these two questions. Such conflicting visions permeated specific CSDP and NATO debates.

Britain wanted to be part of the post-11 September process of military transformation that the US had embarked on (Howorth 2003), not least as it promised to strengthen the strategic edge and global geopolitical reach of the West (UK Ministry of Defence, 2003). On the other hand, London understood that US unilateralism and condescension towards Europe posed a threat to Transatlantic cohesion – and therefore to its own status as a geostrategic bridge between America and Europe. However, it was Britain's conviction that the best way to mitigate the problem of US unilateralism was for Europeans to make themselves more useful to the US (Kramer, 2003; Wither, 2007). In his address to the House of Commons on 18 March 2003, Prime Minister Tony Blair argued that 'the best way to deal with' US unilateralism 'is not rivalry but partnership ... if our plea is for America to work with others, to be good as well as powerful allies, will our retreat make them multilateralist? Or will it not rather be the biggest impulse to uniltateralism there could ever be' (2003). Thus, in Britain's mind, it was of fundamental importance that the European allies were pushed to develop those expeditionary capabilities that would ensure their ongoing interoperability with the US (Interview 1).

After 11 September, Britain made it a priority to invest in the kind of network-enabled expeditionary capabilities the US valued, and to push Europeans down that same expeditionary route. London actively used NATO and the CSDP to promote such objectives. In NATO, Britain advocated for initiatives such as Allied Command Transformation (ACT), the Prague Capabilities Commitment (PCC) and the NATO Response Force (NRF), all of which were aimed at promoting European military transformation and pushing Europeans into a more expeditionary direction (Interview 1). Insofar as the CSDP is concerned, Britain was the main advocate of the EU Battlegroup Concept, hammered out at a bilateral summit with France in London in November 2003 and later supported by Germany (Interview 2). The Battlegroup Concept would constitute the cornerstone of the 2010 Military Headline Goal, which put forward an expeditionary conception of the military instrument and emphasised the importance of high readiness (Lindstrom, 2007). Additionally, and in reaction to Franco-German calls for a European armaments agency in late 2002, Britain insisted that it would only support the establishment of a defence agency if it were to focus on promoting expeditionary concepts and capabilities and keep its role in armaments and industrial cooperation to a minimum (Interview 3). Thus, at their bilateral summit in Le Touquet (France) in February 2003, Britain and France agreed on a template for a future EDA, whose main emphasis would indeed be on capability development (Interview 4).

Finally, its will to preserve Western political and strategic cohesion led Britain to promote a more globally oriented NATO (hoping to make the Alliance more attractive to Washington) and resist those CSDP initiatives aimed at strengthening the EU's political and strategic autonomy from the US and the Atlantic Alliance. In that vein, Britain proved to be a strong supporter of ACT, the PCC and the NRF during the 2002 NATO Prague Summit; constantly argued in favour of a greater NATO role in Afghanistan; and even partnered the US in support of deploying the NRF to that country during the 2004 NATO Istanbul Summit (Interview 5). In a CSDP context, London resisted any (French) calls for an EU Operational Headquarters and opposed the idea of giving the EDA programme management prerogatives and a higher budget, in order to make sure that the agency's role in promoting European armaments and defence-industrial cooperation was minimal (Interview 3).

For France, US unilateralism and condescension towards European (read French) global interests emphasised more than ever the need for European strategic autonomy (Chirac, 2003). Interestingly, however, the post-11 September international context offered Paris a double opportunity in this regard. On the one hand, the return of direct threats to Western security and the post-11 September solidarity with the US generated momentum in favour of European capability development, which had been a longstanding French priority (Dumoulin, 2006; Durand 2007). The French were particularly wary of the disregard most European countries had for military force, and of their tendency to identify themselves with civilian power (Interview 4). They understood that the development of Europe as a strategic actor required expeditionary military power and believed that, given their global strategic reach and their excellence in the realm of military-strategic assets, they were set to reap many of the political benefits of European strategic autonomy (Durand, 2007).

The attacks of 11 September and the ensuing wave of European solidarity towards the US offered France the opportunity to canvass political support for capability development – and thus redress Europe's civilian power biases. The French sought to exploit this opportunity by pushing the military transformation agenda both within NATO and the CSDP. To that end, Paris joined forces with Washington and London at the 2002 NATO Prague Summit in support of ACT, the PCC and the NRF (Interview 7). All those initiatives were largely aimed at using NATO as a transmission belt for US expeditionary concepts and capabilities into European militaries. In a CSDP context, France partnered Britain to promote the Battlegroup Concept and agreed to make capability development central to the EDA's mandate (Interview 8).

Beyond the question of capability development, the French saw a unilateral and militaristic US as the best lure to sell the idea of EU political (and strategic) autonomy in other European capitals – and help Berlin overcome its traditional Atlanticist reflex in particular (Interview 6). During the post-11 September years, Paris actively promoted initiatives aimed at enhancing the EU's political and strategic autonomy within the CSDP framework and sought to resist Washington's attempts to turn NATO into a global political actor. In this vein, France argued earnestly in support of creating an EU Operational Headquarters for the planning and conduct of CSDP military operations (Simón, 2010) and resisted EU–NATO cooperation at the operational and capability development levels (Morel, 2004).

The French also insisted that the EDA should focus not only on capability development, but also on stimulating European armaments cooperation and promoting the emergence of a European Defence Technological and Industrial Base. On that point, they found in Germany a consistent ally (Interview 9). Additionally, France played a leading role in the launch of EUFOR Artemis in 2003, the first CSDP military operation autonomous from NATO (Ulrikssen *et al.*, 2004). As far as NATO was concerned, France teamed up with Germany at the 2004 Istanbul Summit to block the deployment of the NRF to Afghanistan (Interview 7). For the French, the NRF was merely a training concept whose main purpose was to assist the development of (expeditionary) military capabilities in Europe, and not to boost the Alliance's standing as a global strategic and political actor (Dumont, 2007).

The post-11 September context posed several puzzles for Germany. For one thing, its traditional attachment to the Transatlantic relationship and post-11 September sense of solidarity led Berlin to lend diplomatic support to Washington's attempts to push the question of capability development in a NATO context, and give the nod to initiatives such as ACT, PCC and the NRF (Overhaus, 2007). However, such support was both reluctant and limited. While Germany had been historically comfortable with the Alliance's collective defence mission, a NATO shift to expeditionary warfare represented a direct challenge to its own civilian power narrative. Such narrative was premised upon the identification of military force with defence and the rejection of the military constituted a regular foreign policy instrument (Harnisch and Maull, 2001). This partly explains why Berlin would constantly drag its feet on military transformation (Meiers, 2007), but also why it insisted on limiting the use of the NRF – and opposing its deployment to Afghanistan during the 2004 NATO Istanbul Summit (Interview 10).

Germany was also concerned about Washington's increasingly unilateral and militaristic approach to foreign policy, as well as the prospect of a US decoupling from European security. These concerns partly explain Berlin's increasingly open attitude to French calls for EU strategic autonomy during the post-11 September years, illustrated by its diplomatic support of the concepts of an EU OHQ and European armaments cooperation (Interview 11). Admittedly, a strategically autonomous EU presupposed a stronger military instrument, and that clashed with Germany's own conception of a 'civilian power Europe' (Berenskoetter and Giegerich, 2010). However, Britain's reluctance about EU military and strategic autonomy (and Washington's absence in the EU) meant that the CSDP framework would prove far more prone to German political influence (than NATO) and allow Berlin considerable leeway in terms of regulating the pace and extent of militarisation. This was in fact demonstrated by Germany's ambiguous support for the idea of an EU military OHQ (Simón, 2010), and by its insistence that the EU Battlegroups develop more of a civilian–military focus and their deployment be subject to UN approval (Berenskoetter and Giegerich 2010).

European security politics in a 'post-Iraq' context (2005–14)

As the wars in Afghanistan and Iraq dragged on, the high political, financial and strategic costs of the War on Terror became increasingly apparent for Washington. Against such a backdrop, the mid-2000s saw a return to a retreat from the unilateralism of the post-11 September years, and led the US to pay greater attention to multilateralism, diplomacy and the non-military elements of crisis management in Washington (Haass, 2005; Work, 2008). Some scholars interpreted this policy shift as symptomatic of a deeper trend and even went as far as speaking of US/Western decline (Cox, 2007; Zakaria, 2008), post-hegemony (Halliday, 2009) or non-polarity (Haass, 2008).

While its shift towards multilateralism led the US to take the views of its European allies more seriously, this did in no way reverse the waning of Washington's strategic attention to European security. If anything, the long and resource-draining engagements in Iraq and Afghanistan pulled Washington's attention away from Europe – at a time when the old continent appeared to enjoy a period of geopolitical stability. Successive developments would seem to compound Washington's geostrategic shift away from Europe. The confluence of the 2008 financial crisis and war fatigue drew President Obama's political attention towards domestic economic reform, and away from foreign policy, during his first three years in power (Haass, 2013). In turn, the economic and strategic rise of China and Asia led Obama to announce in late 2011 a pivot or rebalance of US global priorities towards the Asia–Pacific region (Ratner, 2013). Notwithstanding the various obstacles that might stand in the way of the so-called US rebalance, the increasing strategic importance of the Asia–Pacific threatens to take Washington's mind further and further away from Europe.

The long wars of Iraq and Afghanistan were pulling Washington's mind away from Europe precisely at a time when the eastern enlargement of NATO and the EU (set in motion in the 1990s) was consummated. This coincidence was not free from irony, and would actually see important alterations in Europe's geopolitical landscape. For one thing, the fulcrum of European power was shifting away from Atlantic Europe – where it had been concentrated since the end of World War Two – towards Central Europe, thus underscoring Germany's increasing political centrality in the old continent (Szabo, 2004). For another, the consummation of enlargement took NATO and the EU into Russia's former sphere of influence. Again, the fact that this was occurring precisely at the time when Washington's attention towards Europe reached a historical low is rather paradoxical. Indeed, a sense of vulnerability (produced by NATO's eastwards expansion) and opportunity (as per Washington's absence) would conspire to stimulate a Russian geopolitical comeback from the mid-2000s (Lucas, 2008).

The many changes the international context was undergoing from the mid-2000s left an important mark upon NATO and CSDP debates. As the focus of the Iraq and Afghanistan wars shifted from combat to stabilisation, the question of how to strike the right balance between military and civilian tools became increasingly prominent in NATO and CSDP debates (Gross, 2008; Jakobsen, 2008). Additionally, Washington's retreat to a more multilateral attitude and growing appreciation for the non-military elements of crisis management facilitated a process of Transatlantic rapprochement from the mid-2000s (Zaborowski, 2006). This, in turn, made it politically easier for Europeans to become engaged in NATO's Afghanistan operation, and also resulted in an improvement of EU–NATO relations. However, each of the big European countries had their own perspective about the changes the international context was undergoing and what they meant for NATO and the CSDP.

Keeping the West strong and cohesive remained critical to Britain's preservation of its status as a geostrategic bridge between Europe and America. Therefore, London would continue to place a premium on the need to empathise with Washington's evolving strategic needs in a post-Iraq context. Of particular importance for Britain was the evolution of the situation on the ground in Iraq and Afghanistan from a widely spread military campaign into localised warfare, and towards post-conflict stabilisation and reconstruction (Farrell and Gordon, 2009). In particular, the latter demanded greater attention to non-military means and a more comprehensive or integrated civilian–military approach to crisis management. This would largely explain Britain's own national efforts to develop a more integrated civilian–military approach to crisis management, its attempts to promote the so-called *comprehensive approach* in a NATO and EU context and its efforts to develop civilian CSDP (Korski, 2009).

Through the mid-2000s, Britain supported Washington's calls for improving NATO's access to civilian capabilities and cooperation with other international institutions in the realm of crisis management, including the EU (Interview 12). As far as the CSDP is concerned, London began to move away from its earlier emphasis on expeditionary military capabilities, instead emphasising the need to develop the 'civilian' element of the CSDP and strengthen civilian-military coordination at the EU level (Interview 13). During their 2005 EU Presidency, the British played a leading role in the setting up of the Civilian Planning and Conduct Capability or CPCC (Interview 14). They also promoted a number of civilian CSDP missions, including in Iraq and Afghanistan (in support of the broader US–Western effort in those countries), and overall displayed a rather high level of engagement in civilian CSDP operations (Grevi *et al.*, 2009).

Beyond the question of the comprehensive approach, Britain continued to support the idea of a more globally active NATO, as well as resist successive French calls for EU strategic autonomy (Interview 1). London's contribution to the Alliance's mission in Afghanistan was second only to that of the US, both in terms of numbers and level of military ambition (Farrell and Gordon, 2009). In a CSDP context, Britain would continue to oppose France's plans to create an EU OHQ; it limited the EDA's budget and powers in the realm of armaments and industrial cooperation; and it made a negligible contribution to EU military operations (Interview 4).

For France, the notion of a US in retreat and a weakening West was far more discomforting than that of US overreach. While Paris had always been concerned about US unilateralism, it was well aware that the US-led Western security system guaranteed a balance of power in Europe and beyond that was broadly favourable to its own geopolitical interests and influence (Lellouche, 2009).

From a French perspective, the fact that the waning of Washington's geostrategic attention to Europe overlapped in time with eastern enlargement and with a growing emphasis on the non-military elements of security was perhaps especially distressful. After all, all those factors would seem to underscore Germany's influence and civilian power narrative, and weaken France's own standing within the EU – which was bound to the notion of military modernisation and European strategic autonomy (Simón, 2013). Critically, the prospect of a wavering US commitment to the security of Europe and Europeans' increasing hostility to military force was a recipe for instability in the broader European neighbourhood (French White Paper, 2008, pp. 33–4). Against such a backdrop, the reinvigoration of the Transatlantic relationship became a French foreign policy priority during the post-Iraq years (Bozo and Parmentier, 2007). This resulted in a much more open attitude towards NATO, illustrated by France's re-integration within the Alliance's military structure in 2009, its increasing support to the Afghanistan mission from 2008 onwards and its greater openness to EU–NATO cooperation in crisis management (Interview 15).

France's renewed interest in the Atlantic Alliance did in no way represent an abandonment of its traditional commitment to EU strategic autonomy. If anything, the French saw the weakening of the West and the ongoing shift of US strategic priorities away from Europe as a vindication of their view that Europeans had to take greater responsibility for their own security, particularly in their immediate neighbourhood. In this regard, France's ongoing commitment to European strategic autonomy continued to manifest itself in a strong support of military CSDP and represented a limitation to the country's re-engagement with NATO (see Chapter 9). Through the mid- and late 2000s, the French continued to lobby consistently for an EU OHQ and for greater European armaments and defence industrial cooperation (Interview 16). They were also the main force behind successive CSDP military operations, namely EUFOR DRC (2006), EUFOR Chad (2008), EUNAVFOR Atalanta (2008), EUFOR CAR (2014), and the EU training missions in Somalia (2010) and Mali (2012) (Interview 17). As far as NATO was concerned, France re-integrated within the military structure and accepted the idea of greater cooperation with the EU (Bozo, 2008). However, it insisted that the Alliance should not develop in-house civilian capabilities nor attempt to coordinate other international organisations in crisis management, let alone the EU (Jakobsen, 2008), and that the European pillar of NATO should be strengthened (Védrine, 2012).

As already argued, the post-Iraq context saw a strengthening of Germany's autonomy and influence in Europe. The shift away from expeditionary military capabilities and the revalorisation of multilateralism, diplomacy and the non-military aspects of crisis management seemed to vindicate Germany's civilian power narrative (German White Paper, 2006, pp. 21–2). In turn, the eastern enlargement of NATO and the EU contributed to the stability of Germany's borders, thereby reducing the country's sense of geopolitical vulnerability and security dependence on the West, and creating opportunities for the expansion of its economic and diplomatic influence in Central and Eastern Europe (Szabo, 2004).

Berlin was well aware of the importance of reassuring its allies and partners that a more autonomous and influential Germany would remain strongly anchored within the existing Western and European order (Interview 18). This represented an important incentive for Germany to try to reinvigorate its political links with the US/NATO as well as to seek greater cooperation with France, including in the CSDP framework (Interview 18). Admittedly, there were additional factors that prompted Germany to both re-engage with NATO and lend support to the cause of EU strategic autonomy. For one thing, Russia's increasing assertiveness in Eastern Europe emphasised the indispensability of the Transatlantic link as the ultimate guarantee of European security (Chivis and

Rid, 2009). This would only gain further prominence following Russia's annexation of Crimea and the ensuing crisis in German–Russian relations. For another, the weakening of the West and the possibility of a wavering US commitment to European security made it sensible for Germany to hedge its bets and lend support to the CSDP (Interview 18). Last but not least, its ongoing attachment to civilian power continued to impose limits on Germany's engagement with either NATO or military CSDP.

Throughout 2005–10, Germany's policies towards NATO and the CSDP reflected the need to navigate somewhat contradictory priorities: the country's attachment to civilian power, its commitment to reinvigorating the Transatlantic link, and its renewed interest in reappraising its special relationship with France and furthering the cause of European strategic autonomy.

Germany would seek to capitalise on the broader Western shift towards multilateralism and the non-military aspects of security by actively promoting a more comprehensive approach to crisis management within both NATO and the CSDP. In a NATO context, Berlin supported the idea of greater civilian-military synergies and cooperation with other international organisations (Interview 19). However, it insisted that the Alliance should not develop in-house civilian capabilities or attempt to play a coordinating role in crisis management, but instead should remain an equal partner to other international organisations, including the UN and the EU (Interview 19). As far as the CSDP is concerned, Germany concentrated most of its efforts on promoting the development of civilian CSDP and a more comprehensive approach to crisis management. Berlin was a strong supporter of the creation of the CPCC in 2005, emerged as the greatest advocate and contributor to CSDP civilian missions, and constantly advocated an integrated civilian-military approach to the planning and conduct of all CSDP missions (Interview 19).

Germany's interest in reaffirming its links with France and furthering the cause of EU strategic autonomy led it to lend diplomatic support to the idea of an EU OHQ, engage with the EDA's initiatives in the area of armaments and industrial cooperation, and participate in some of the CSDP military operations launched (Interview 18). However, its ongoing attachment to civilian power would continue to impose clear limits on Germany's engagement with each of those elements of military CSDP. Perhaps most notably, Berlin's support of the idea of an EU OHQ was rather modest, and was in any case focussed on emphasising civilian-military synergies in the realm of planning – the notion of a purely military OHQ being rejected (Interview 20).

Germany's participation in CSDP military operations has been relatively modest (especially if compared to France's), as illustrated by its absence from EUFOR Chad (2008) and EUFOR RCA (2014). Additionally, Germany's contribution to CSDP military operations usually came at the expense of reductions in military ambition (Interview 17). Such was the case EUFOR DRC (2008), EUNAVFOR Atlanta (2008) and EUTM Mali (2012) (Interview 17). A similar contradiction informed Germany's engagement with NATO in a post Iraq context. On the one hand, its commitment to the US and the Transatlantic relationship led Berlin to make an important contribution to the Alliance's mission in Afghanistan

(Interview 19). On the other hand, however, its reservations on the use of military force resulted in important functional caveats and restricted Germany's contribution to reconstruction and development tasks (Meiers, 2007).

Conclusions

By examining the interplay between a dynamic international environment, the strategic priorities of Britain, France and Germany and the evolution of CSDP and NATO, this contribution has sought to unveil the evolving tension between conflict and cooperation in European security. While the Neorealist proposition that geopolitical decline represents a systemic incentive for European security cooperation is broadly accepted, this chapter has set out to unpack and qualify the otherwise vague concepts of *change in the international environment* and *European security cooperation*. More particularly, the emphasis has been placed on how different European countries process a dynamic international environment, and on their different visions to cope with geopolitical decline. Those differences, this chapter contends, account for conflicting priorities over the direction of the CSDP and NATO.

It has been argued here that Classical Realism can help us better understand the mixed picture of European security politics, characterised by patterns of cooperation and conflict. First, its emphasis on nations and their incessant quest for power allows us to explain the CSDP and NATO through the lens of Europe's (most powerful) nation-states. Systemic change does indeed have an impact upon the CSDP and NATO, but primarily by virtue of its impact upon the evolving strategic priorities of Britain, France and Germany. In other words, the relationship between systemic change and European security cooperation is heavily mediated or filtered by Europe's most powerful countries.

Second, and relatedly, Classical Realism's focus on power allows us to transcend the fuzzy notion that cooperation is inherently beneficial to all European countries. The CSDP and NATO can indeed constitute useful resources for European countries. However, in order for a given European country to maximise its power or influence, the CSDP and NATO must develop in a direction that reflects their own specific interests and comparative advantages. And insofar as European countries have different geopolitical interests and feature different strengths and weaknesses, they also hold different visions over the direction the CSDP or NATO ought to take. In other words, European countries are competing with each other over the direction for the CSDP and NATO, and the outcome of such competition will have important repercussions for their international power of influence. This highlights the importance of the regional level of the balance of power and intra-European competition for influence and power.

The link between power maximisation and intra-European competition is critical. A narrow conception of security would seem to feed the notion that cooperation (whether through the CSDP or NATO) is an inherently positive value in Europe, because it contributes to fostering a stable regional environment, and thus enhances the security of all European countries. In turn, an emphasis on influence and power maximisation underscores the idea that European countries must constantly win over CSDP and NATO. Conflicting national priorities over how to arrange the terms of cooperation, it is argued, emphasise the ongoing relevance of intra-European competition and expose the hollowness of the notion of *European security cooperation.*

References

Art, R. J. (1996) Why Western Europe needs the United States and NATO. *Political Science Quarterly.* 111 (1). pp. 1–39.

Baun, M. J. (1995–6) The Treaty of Maastricht as High Politics: Germany, France and European Integration. *Political Science Quarterly.* 110 (4). pp. 605–24.

Baylis, J. (1993) *The Diplomacy of Pragmatism: Britain and the Origins of NATO, 1942–1949.* Kent, OH: The Kent State University Press.

Berensktoetter, F. and Giegerich, B. (2010) From NATO to ESDP: A Social Constructivist Analysis of German Strategic Adjustment after the End of the Cold War. *Security Studies.* 19 (3). pp. 407–52.

Blair, T. (2003) Speech opening the debate on the Iraq crisis in the House of Commons, 18 March.

Bozo, F. (2008) *Alliance atlantique: la fin de l'exception française? La fin de l'exception française.* Document du travail. Paris. Fondation pour l'Innovation Politique.

Bozo, F. and Parmentier, G. (2007) France and the United States: waiting for regime change. *Survival.* 49 (1). pp. 181–98.

Buzan, B. and Waever, O. (2003) *Regions and Powers: The Structure of International Security.* Cambridge: Cambridge University Press.

Calleo, D. (2009) *Follies of Power: America's Unipolar Fantasy.* Cambridge: Cambridge University Press.

Chirac, J. (2003) Discours lors de la XIème Conférence des ambassadeurs. Élysée Palace, Paris, 29 August.

Chivis, C. and Rid, T. (2009) The Roots of Germany's Russia Policy. *Survival.* 51 (2). pp. 105–22.

Cladi, L. and Locatelli, A. (2013) Worth a Shot: On the Explanatory Power of Bandwagoning in Transatlantic Relations. *Contemporary Security Policy.* 34 (2). pp. 374–81.

Cladi, L. and Locatelli, A. (2012) Bandwagoning, Not Balancing: Why Europe Confounds Realism. *Contemporary Security Policy.* 33 (2). pp. 264–88.

Coker, C. (2003) Empires in Conflict: the Growing Rift between Europe and the United States. *Whitehall Paper* 58. London: Royal United Services Institute.

Cox, M. (2007) Is the United States in Decline – Again? An essay. *International Affairs.* 83 (4). pp. 643–53.

Dumont, J. F. (2007) Les capacités opérationelles de l'OTAN: la France et la NRF. *Défense* 128, July–August.

Dumoulin, A. (2006) *France-OTAN: vers un rapprochement doctrinal? Au dela du 40e anniversaire de la crise franco-atlantique.* Brussels: Bruylant.

Durand (de), E. (2007) Quel format d'armée pour la France? *Politique Etrangére.* 4. pp. 729–42.

Dyson, T. (2013) Balancing Threat, not Capabilities: European Defence Cooperation as Reformed Bandwagoning. *Contemporary Security Policy.* 34 (2). pp. 387–91.

Dwan, R. (2001) Jean Monnet and the European Defence Community, 1950–1954. *Cold War History*. 1 (3). pp. 141–60.

Farrell, T. and Gordon, S. (2009) COIN Machine: The British Military in Afghanistan. *RUSI Journal*. 154 (3). pp. 18–25.

Freedman, L. (2003) Prevention, Not Pre-emption. *The Washington Quarterly*. 26 (2). pp. 105–14.

German Ministry of Defence (2006) *White Paper on German Security Policy and the Future of the Bundeswehr*. Berlin, October.

Grevi, G. (2009) *The Interpolar World: A New Scenario*. Occasional Paper 79. Paris. EU Institute for Security Studies.

Grevi, G., Helly, D. and Keohane, D. (2009) (eds) *European Security and Defence Policy: the first 10 years (1999–2009)*. Paris: EU Institute for Security Studies.

Grieco, J. M. (1995) The Maastricht Treaty, Economic and Monetary Union and the Neo-Realist Research Programme. *Review of International Studies*. 21 (1). pp. 21–40.

Grieco, J. M. (1988) Anarchy and the Limits of Co-operation: a Realist Critique of the Newest Liberal Institutionalism. *International Organization*. 42 (3). pp. 485–507.

Gross, E. (2008) *The EU and the Comprehensive Approach*. DIIS Report 13. Copenhagen. Danish Institute for International Studies.

Haass, R. (2013) *Foreign Policy Begins at Home: The Case for Putting America's House in Order*. New York: Basic Books.

Haass, R. (2008) The Age of Nonpolarity – What Will Follow US Dominance. *Foreign Affairs*. 87 (3). pp. 18–43.

Haass, R. (2005) *The Opportunity: America's Moment to Alter History's Course*. New York: Public Affairs.

Halliday, F. (2009) International Relations in a Post-Hegemonic Age. *International Affairs*. 85 (1). pp. 37–53.

Harnisch, S. and Maull, H. W. (ed.) (2001) *Germany as a Civilian Power? The Foreign Policy of the Berlin Republic*. Manchester: Manchester University Press.

Hoffmann, S. (1966) Obstinate or Obsolete? The Fate of the Nation-State and the Case of Western Europe. *Daedalus, Journal of the American Academy of Arts and Sciences*. 95 (3). pp. 862–915.

Howorth, J. (2010) The EU as a Global Actor: Grand Strategy for a Global Grand Bargain? *Journal of Common Market Studies*. 48 (3). pp. 455–74.

Howorth, J. (2003) France, Britain and the Euro-Atlantic Crisis. *Survival*. 45 (4). pp. 173–92.

Hyde-Price, A. (2006) Normative Power Europe: A Realist Critique. *Journal of European Public Policy*. 13 (2). pp. 217–34.

Ikenberry, J. (2002) America's Imperial Ambition. *Foreign Affairs*. 81 (5). pp. 44–60.

Ikenberry, G. J. (1998) Institutions, Strategic Restraint and the Persistence of American Post-War Order. *International Security*. 23 (3). pp. 43–78.

Interview 1. Interviews with multiple UK officials, 2008–9.

Interview 2. Interview with UK official, Foreign and Commonwealth Office, London, 22 April 2008.

Interview 3. Interview with UK official, Ministry of Defence, London, 21 May 2009.

Interview 4. Interviews with multiple EU officials, 2008–9.

Interview 5. Interviews with multiple UK and NATO officials, 2008–9.

Interview 6. Interviews with multiple French officials, 2008–9.

Interview 7. Interview with French official, Ministry of Defence, Brussels, 22 May 2008.

Interview 8. Interview with French official, Ministry of Defence, Paris, 19 May 2009.

Interview 9. Interviews with multiple EU, French and German officials, 2008–9.

Interview 10. Interview with German official, Ministry of Defence, Berlin, 2 April 2008.

Interview 11. Interview with German official, Ministry of Defence, Brussels, 23 May 2008.

Interview 12. Interview with UK official, Foreign and Commonwealth Office, Brussels, 22 May 2008.

Interview 13. Interviews with multiple UK and EU officials, 2008–9.

Interview 14. Interview with UK official, Ministry of Defence, London, 4 June 2008.

Interview 15. Interviews with multiple French officials, 2008–9.

Interview 16. Interview with French official, Ministry of Defence, Paris, 26 May 2009.

Interview 17. Interviews with multiple EU officials, 2008–14.

Interview 18. Interviews with multiple German officials, 2008–14.

Interview 19. Interview with German official, Foreign Ministry, Brussels, 22 May 2008.

Interview 20. Interview with German official, Ministry of Defence, Brussels, 21 May 2008.

Jakobsen, P. V. (2008) *NATO's Comprehensive Approach to Crisis Response Operations: A Work in Slow Progress*. DIIS Report 15. Copenhagen. Danish Institute for International Studies.

Jervis, R. (2003) Understanding the Bush Doctrine. *Political Science Quarterly*. 118 (3). pp. 365–88.

Jones, B. (2011) *Franco-British Military Cooperation: A New Engine for European Defence?*. Occasional Paper 88. Paris: EU Institute for Security Studies.

Jones, S. (2007) *The Rise of European Security Cooperation*. Cambridge: Cambridge University Press.

Kahn, R. and Kupchan, C. (2013) Europe's Make or Break Moment. *Survival*. 55 (6). pp. 29–48.

Korski, D. (2009) British Civil–Military integration. *The RUSI Journal*. 154 (6). pp. 14–24.

Kramer, S. P. (2003) Blair's Britain After Iraq. *Foreign Affairs*. 82 (4). pp. 90–104.

Kupchan, C. (2012) No One's World: The West, the Rising Rest and the Coming Global Turn. Oxford: Oxford University Press.

Lelouche, P. (2009) *L'allié indocile: La France et l'OTAN, de la Guerre froide à l'Afghanistan*. Paris: Editions du Moment.

Lindley-French, J. (2002) Terms of Engagement: The Paradox of American Power and the Transatlantic Dilemma Post-11 September. *Chaillot Paper 52*, EU Institute for Security Studies.

Lindstrom, G. (2007) Enter the EU Battlegroups. *Chaillot Paper 97*. Paris: EU Institute for Security Studies.

Londsdale, D. J. (2003) The Strategy of Pre-emption: Dealing with the Post-9/11 Security Environment. *Defence Studies*. 3 (2). pp. 102–107.

Lucas, E. (2008) *The New Cold War: How the Kremlin Menaces both Russia and the West*. Palgrave Macmillan: New York.

McInnes, C. (2003) A Different Kind of War? September 11 and the United States' Afghan War. *Review of International Studies*. 29 (2). pp. 165–84.

Mearsheimer, J. J. (1990) Back to the Future: Instability in Europe After the Cold War. *International Security*. 15 (1). pp. 5–56.

Mearsheimer, J. J. (2001) The Future of the American Pacifier. *Foreign Affairs*. 80 (5). pp. 46–61.

Meiers, F. J. (2007) The German Predicament: The Red Lines of the Security and Defence Policy of the Berlin Republic. *International Politics*. 44 (5). pp. 623–44.

Menon, A. (2011) European Defence From Lisbon to Libya. *Survival*. 53 (3). pp. 75–90.

Morel, J. F. (2004) Les relations UE-OTAN: une vision européenne. *Défense Nationale*, May.

Morgenthau, H. J. (1948/1985) *Politics Among Nations: The Struggle for Power and Peace*. New York: Knopf.

Nuttall, S. J. (1992) *European Political Co-operation*. Oxford: Oxford University Press.

Overhaus, M. (2007) Germany's Security and Defence Policy from the Schroeder to the Merkel Government. *Policy Brief* WSI Brussels. 1. February.

Posen, B. R. (2006) European Union Security and Defence Policy: response to unipolarity? *Security Studies*. 15 (2). pp. 149–86.

Posen, B. (2004) ESDP and the Structure of World Power. *The International Spectator*. 39 (1). pp. 5–17.

Press-Barnathan, G. (2006) Managing the Hegemon: Nato under Unipolarity, *Security Studies*. 15 (2). pp. 271–309.

Ratner, E. (2013) Rebalancing to Asia with an Insecure China. *The Washington Quarterly*. 36 (2). pp. 21–38.

Ringsmose, J. (2013) Balancing or Bandwagoning? Europe's Many Relations with the United States. *Contemporary Security Policy*. 34 (2). pp. 409–12.

Rosato, S. (2011) Europe's Troubles: Power Politics and the State of the European Project. *International Security*. 35 (4). pp. 45–86.

Rynning, S. (2011) Realism and the Common Security and Defence Policy. *Journal of Common Market Studies*. 49 (1). pp. 23–42.

Schelling, T. (1958) The Strategy of Conflict. Prospectus for a Reorientation of Game Theory. *The Journal of Conflict Resolution*. 2 (3). pp. 203–64.

Simón, L. (2014) *Geopolitical Change, Grand Strategy and European Security: The EU-NATO Conundrum in Perspective*. New York: Palgrave Macmillan.

Simón, L. (2013) The Spider in Europe's Web? French Grand Strategy from Iraq to Libya. *Geopolitics*. 18 (2). pp. 403–34.

Simón, L. (2010) Command and Control? Planning for EU Military Operations. *Occasional Paper* 81. Paris: EU Institute for Security Studies.

Simón, L. and Fiott, D. (2014) Europe After the US Pivot. *Orbis: A Journal of World Affairs*. 58 (3). pp. 413–28.

Szabo, S. F. (2004) *Parting Ways: The Crisis in German-American Relations*. Washington DC: The Brookings Institution.

Treacher, A. (2001) Europe as a Power Multiplier for French Security Policy: Strategic Consistency, Tactical Adaptation. *European Security*. 10 (1). pp. 22–44.

UK Ministry of Defence (2003) *Delivering Security in a Changing World: Defence White Paper* London, December.

Ulriksen, S., Gourlay, C. and Mace, C. (2004) Operation Artemis: The Shape of Things to Come? *International Peacekeeping*. 11 (3). pp. 508–25.

Vedrine, H. (2012) *Report for the President of the French Republic on the Consequences of France's Return to NATO's Integrated Military Command, on the Future of Transatlantic Relations, and the Outlook for the Europe of Defence*. 14 November. Available from: www.diplomatie.gouv.fr/en/IMG/pdf/12-2226-Rapport_H_VEDRINE_VEN.pdf [accessed: 20 February 2015].

Walt, S. M. (2001) Beyond bin Laden: Reshaping US Foreign Policy. *International Security*. 26 (3). pp. 56–78.

Walt, S. M. (1987) *The Origins of Alliances*. Ithaca, NY: Cornell University Press.

Waltz, K. (1993) The Emerging Structure of International Politics. *International Security*. 18 (2). pp. 44–79.

Waltz, K. (1979) *Theory of International Politics*. New York: Columbia University Press.

Wither, J. (2007) An Endangered Partnership: The Anglo-American Defence Relatinship in the Early Twenty-first Century. *European Security*. 15 (1). pp. 47–65.

Work, R. O. (2008) *The Future Security Environment: Multidimensional Challenges in a Multi-Player World*. Centre for Strategic and Budgetary Assessments. 21 August. Available from: www.csbaonline.org/4Publications/PubLibrary/S.20080820.Future_Security_En/S.20080820.Future_Security_En.pdf [accessed: 20 February 2015].

Zaborowski, M. (ed.) (2006) *Friends Again? EU–US Relations After the Crisis*. Paris: EU Institute for Security Studies.

Zakaria, F. (2008) *The Post-American World*. New York: W. W. Norton & Company.

9 France, America and the issue of balancing (soft or otherwise)

A tale of two cycles

David G. Haglund

Introduction

Charles Dickens's *A Tale of Two Cities*, from which I draw inspiration for my chapter's subtitle as well as its theme, is remembered for many reasons, not the least being its evocative opening line regarding the French Revolution: 'It was the best of times, it was the worst of times' (1950, p. 1). We may not be living through any revolutionary moments in Transatlantic relations, but we have probably entered a period to which this Dickensian depiction applies. In some ways, and certainly compared to the period of intra-alliance rancour associated with the Iraq war of a dozen years ago, we are experiencing (hard as it may be to believe) the best of times for NATO.

This is especially true if we concentrate solely upon the important sea-change that has occurred in respect of relations between the US and France, the two countries most immediately implicated in the debate over whether alliance dynamics might be captured more accurately by images of *balancing* rather than of *bandwagoning* – the debate covered so well in this volume's Chapter 1. Consider that, only eleven years ago, many observers were on the verge of pronouncing that an irremediable strategic breach had taken place between the West's *two oldest allies* (Serfaty, 2002; Miller and Molesky, 2004; Timmerman, 2004; Chesnoff, 2005) – a breach, moreover, that threatened to suck in several other members of the Western alliance, forcing them to choose whose gang to join in this brewing Transoceanic rumble, France's, or America's. In this stark thesis, France was clearly *balancing* against the US, with the only question being whether its balancing could be kept merely to the *soft* variant of the phenomenon.

For reasons I discuss in the following section of this chapter, the tensions between France and the US had been mounting ever since the early 1990s, and truth to tell, prior to that time relations had been pretty sour between the two countries for about as long as anyone could remember, taking a decided turn from bad to worse in the early stages of the Fifth Republic, and not improving very much during the next three decades (Furniss, 1960; Harrison, 1981; Costigliola, 1992; Cogan, 1994). But with the ending of the Cold War and the concomitant demise of bipolarity, Franco-American *froideur* appeared to hit a new low, and, even more than in the past, the quality of bilateral relations was being negatively affected by calculations of relative capability (i.e. of *power*, especially the *hard* sort associated with military and economic prowess). Specifically, many in France thought the US possessed too much power for its own good, and certainly for France's good. It needed, in a word, to be *balanced*.

No one better illustrated the French power-based neuralgia prevalent a decade or so ago than Robert Kagan, author of a widely discussed book entitled *Of Paradise and Power*, most remembered today for some planetary imagery that evidently spoke volumes about the West's predicament, the result of Europe (including, to Kagan, France) living in a Kantian post-historical *paradise* at a time when the US remained stuck in a decidedly Hobbesian history, very determined to wield its enormous power in defence of its interests. 'Americans' wrote Kagan (2003, pp. 3–4), 'are from Mars and Europeans are from Venus: They agree on little and understand one another less and less'. Now fast forward a decade and witness this same Robert Kagan, in the wake of the French decision to intervene in Mali in January 2013, lavishing praise upon the country that had so recently been the target of his and so many other Americans' wrath. To Steven Erlanger, Paris bureau chief of the *New York Times*, Kagan gushed in admiration of his quondam French adversaries, 'I have a new philosophy: If the French are ready to go, we should go'. (quoted in Erlanger, 2013a; see also Cohen, 2013). Exemplifying this newly (re)discovered source of guidance and even legitimacy for American strategic choice was Secretary of State John Kerry's reminder on 30 August 2013 that France is America's *oldest ally* – a comment made in gratitude for support shown by President François Hollande, and one that has been interpreted as a not so subtle dig at the British, for refusing to endorse a military strike against Syria in retaliation for Damascus's use of poison gas on 21 August (Mazzetti and Gordon, 2013; Erlanger, 2013b).

If nothing else, the remarks of the policy pundit and the policy maker certainly provide a reason to imagine that we are living in the *best of times* for Transatlantic relations, a cycle of strategic bonhomie the likes of which has only inconsistently been glimpsed within the West over the past several decades – bonhomie that not even the recent spatting over electronic snooping by American intelligence agencies (which seems in Europe to have upset the Germans more than anyone else) has been able to dispel (Kietz and Thimm, 2013; Bittner, 2013; Thimm, 2014). Nor has it been dispelled by the even more recent tiff over France's desire to sell two amphibious assault ships to a suddenly not-so-grata Putinesque Russia, in the wake of Moscow's annexation of Crimea in early 2014 (Gordon, 2014; *The Economist*, 2014).

At the same time, though, there is a second cycle in operation, one that reflects recurring debates within the field of US foreign policy, and this more sobering phase provides some guidance as to why, when we contemplate Robert Kagan's new-found appreciation of French strategic virtue, we might want to curb our enthusiasm; his adulation of Paris is intended to stand as a rebuke of Washington. In particular, he worries that the current American administration shows itself too diffident when it comes to contemplating how America might best utilise its power on behalf of its own interests as well as those of its allies. Nor is his a lonely voice these days among those who follow American foreign policy (Joffe *et al.*, 2014). Quite to the contrary, the chorus of critics of the Obama administration has been increasing in size of late, and the nub of their critique is that the US is willingly turning itself into what one of those critics Vali Nasr calls, with more than a touch of sarcasm, the *dispensable nation* (Nasr, 2013).[1] Again, as was the case a decade or so ago, at the epicentre of the controversy is American *hard* power. In 2003, it was thought to be worrying because an administration sought to wield it too easily, and with too little regard for the preferences of allies. A decade later, it was almost the reverse: American power was posing a problem because it was considered unavailable for uses to which certain allies might otherwise like to see it put.

The argument I will make in this chapter is that something really has changed doctrinally; that it surely does concern hard power; and that it carries significant implications for the manner in which the Western allies will relate to each other in the years ahead. The Transatlantic cycle, notwithstanding its reasonably (though not wildly) optimistic implications at present, remains dependent upon developments in the American cycle, and it is these latter that are beginning to arouse apprehension on the part of certain allies, starting with the discontent that had been expressed by states in Central and Eastern Europe (the *new Europe* of Donald Rumsfeld's imagination a dozen years ago), but not stopping with them. At the same time, the doctrinal shift in Washington has been responsible for the recent elevation of *smart power* to a central conceptual place in Brussels, as well as in other alliance capitals, all of whom will do well to contemplate what it means for their strategic interests that America has, for the moment at least, embraced a new grand strategy, under the label of the *Obama Doctrine*. In this respect, the pivot of greatest interest to the allies should not be the mooted geographical one, to the Asia–Pacific region, but rather the conceptual one, from an alloyed version of *Wilsonianism* to a similarly melded version of *Jeffersonianism*, to use paradigms creatively employed by Mead (2001).

I develop my argument about Dickensian cycles in two steps. On the upbeat side of the ledger, I start by analysing the important alteration in the Franco-American strategic relationship. On a perhaps less optimistic note, I underscore what it means when we invoke the *Obama Doctrine*, and how this relates to the broader traditions of American foreign policy. I conclude with some observations about the likely implications of the doctrinal pivot for America's allies, including France.

John Heywood revisited: France's recent rapprochement with the United States

It would be easy to claim that the current period of relatively good strategic relations between France and the US owes exclusively to the decision made by President Nicolas Sarkozy to rejoin the alliance's integrated military apparatus, announced definitively at NATO's Strasbourg–Kehl summit in April 2009 but clearly prefigured in the previous summer's French white paper on defence (Erlanger, 2009; Pesme, 2010). It would, however, also be wrong to make such a claim. While there is no question that France's re-integration has been a positive move from the standpoint of Transatlantic relations, it alone did not bring about the aforementioned sea change in bilateral ties. Other developments of note in respect of the improving tenor of relations between Paris and Washington include personalities, especially what the late Kenneth Waltz would have called *first-image* variables associated with the respective countries' leaders. When he took office in early 2009, Barack Obama reaped great benefit simply from not being George W. Bush, in the estimation of French and other European observers.[2] *Mutatis mutandis*, much the same could be said of Americans' assessments of the impact of France being led by someone who was not named Jacques Chirac (lampooned in certain quarters in the US prior to the unseating of Saddam Hussein as *Jacques Iraq*). So happy were American officials with Chirac's successor that when Sarkozy delivered an address in the House of Representatives in early November 2007, the new president received no fewer than 25 rounds of applause, ten of which were standing ovations, in the Democratic-controlled chamber (Nougayrède, 2007).

Still, it would be unwise to accord too much prominence to matters of personality, and not simply because the attractiveness of President Obama to Europeans has waned a bit in the past few years, or that Nicolas Sarkozy vacated the Elysée palace three years ago. More importantly, there is a structural (what Waltz would term a *third-image*) basis to the rapprochement, one that comes tinged with irony. This is because much of the improvement in relations between France and the US has been the result of trouble on other fronts. Not for the first time, and certainly not for the last, we witness gain being extracted from adversity, testimony to an observation that the sixteenth-century English proverbialist, John Heywood, expressed in the well-known phrase about 'an ill wind that bloweth no man to good' (quoted in Bartlett, 1968, p. 185).[3]

In this case, the ill wind has risen from both inside and outside Europe, and no matter its provenance, its cause has been the same: the deterioration in one category of Europe's *hard power*, namely its economic competitiveness (Nye, 1990).[4]

The external challenge we can associate with a phenomenon currently said by all and sundry to be occurring – structural change in the international system, suggesting that we are either entering into, or already firmly ensconced within, a *post-American* age (Zakaria, 2009). The world, at least in economic terms, is argued to have become a *multipolar* place, yet, curiously, this transition has not constituted for Europe or France the balm that, not so very long ago, multipolarity was widely expected to be. Mostly, this is because Europeans have not figured among the leading dramatis personae on a political-economy stage whose limelight has been monopolised by the so-called BRICs (Brazil, Russia, India, and China – with a few observers even tossing into the mix South Africa).

Related to this is the internal source of the adversity that is blowing some good in the direction of the France–US relationship: the current downturn in intra-European integrative fortunes, associated in great (though not exclusive) measure with the European economic and fiscal crises of the past several years, and the stalling of enthusiasm for the European *dream*, as symbolised by the May 2014 European parliamentary elections, in which anti-EU populist parties did so well in France, the UK, and some other European countries (Higgins, 2014). Hard as it is to believe today, a decade or so ago some observers of international politics imagined that, with the EU going from strength to strength, it was only a matter of time before Europe supplanted the US as *leader* of the West, if not of the international system writ large (Kupchan, 2003; Rifkin, 2004; Leonard, 2005). Over the past few years, a different question has surfaced, asking not whether (or when) Europe will replace the US at the top of the global heap, but whether Europe can itself be saved from sinking into economic and geopolitical irrelevance, or worse (Krugman, 2011). *Pari passu*, a great deal of air has gone out of the quondam *balancing* balloon.

Not only this, but the combination of the external and internal challenges has resulted in the disappearance (possibly only temporarily) of America as Europe's *significant oppositional other*, the necessary foil for gauging Europeans' own self-worth, as well as for energizing their self-promotion. It may not be that the current travails of the Old Continent are so severe as to remind Europeans of the ongoing need for what Uwe Nerlich once memorably termed their American *pacifier*, as French International Relations scholar Erwan Lagadec claims they are, when he tells us that

> the US security guarantee remains indispensable to Europeans, even while it has ceased to be so in American eyes ... Europe does not look to Washington out of foolishness or short-sightedness. It does so because contrary to America itself, Europe cannot comfortably live in a post-American world.
>
> (2012, p. 18)

Nevertheless, it cannot be denied that Europeans' current, and real, challenges have been accompanied by a decrescendo in what had been developing into a zero-sum *ontological* shouting-match with Americans.

With far bigger fish to fry at home, the Europeans necessarily spend much less time these days agonising over what it means for them if America possesses *too much* power. That agonising was, in any event, fuelled more by identity concerns than by anything else (see Chapter 5), as it is far from clear (at least, to me) how America being the sole superpower constituted a threat to any tangible European interests – unless *amour propre* is considered a tangible interest. Figuring as the central Transatlantic player in that long-running ontological contestation had been France, the country that in many ways earned for itself the title of ring-leader of the non-American (some even held anti-American) camp within the Western alliance (Revel, 2002; Roger, 2002; Rigoulot, 2004). As Marisol Touraine (1993, p. 808) explains, this has been so because French policy was guided more by 'the concern for affirming what France "is" or should be', than by a focused emphasis upon its security and other tangible interests. In other

8

words, France had conceived of its problems not in terms of challenges to its physical security, but rather to threats to its international stature and its *national identity* – quite different matters. The net result had been prickliness with regard to American power and above all to American claims to lead the Western alliance. In this struggle, it was easy, and for a time nearly obligatory, for French leaders to imagine that the EU could serve as a *force multiplier* for France (Boniface, 1998).

All of this is a far cry from today's European, and Transatlantic, realities. To understand the full dimensions of the transformation that has led to the first of this chapter's Dickensian cycles, let us revisit the debate over *balancing* that was touched off by the ending of bipolarity nearly a quarter-century ago. What the surprise ending of the Cold War did, for reasons that we now can discern to be structural in nature, was to alter gravely the tone, as well as the substance, of France-as-ally discussions, as these had been emanating from both sides of the Atlantic ever since the 1960s. It was as if Pogo was not just remarking on life in the Okefenokee Swamp but rather uttering a more universally valid truth about alliance dynamics in announcing, *we have met the enemy and he is us*. Flush with their victory over the Cold War foe, the US and France quickly discovered in each other a surrogate menace, albeit of a different sort. To more than a few observers in Washington (and elsewhere), France appeared to have gone on a footing of permanent opposition to America, as reflected in the assertion of President François Mitterrand that 'we are at war against America'. ('Nous sommes en guerre contre l'Amérique', quoted in Melandri and Vaïsse, 2001, p. 455). In this increasingly poisonous atmosphere, it should have shocked no one that an American secretary of state could, in 1992, bluntly put to his French counterpart the extremely undiplomatic question, 'Is France for us or against us?' (Bölte, 1992, p. 2).

Paris, suspect in Washington's (and several other NATO capitals') thinking for so many years, now grew even more worrying, to the point that Thierry de Montbrial was exaggerating only slightly when he suggested in that same year that his country was apparently emerging as America's new 'public enemy number one' (de Montbrial, 1992, p. 3). Quite so, for to many American policymakers and even theorists of international relations who canvassed the prospects of the West hanging together in the absence of its erstwhile Soviet foe, it was never a difficult task in those pre-9/11 years to see trouble ahead, or to round up the usual suspects among the miscreants and pick out France as their organiser. And if it might still have been possible to maintain during the 1990s that France and America were on amicable terms, it was only in the Pickwickian sense captured so well in the title of one French writer's book about the *world's worst friends* (Durandin, 1994; Guisnel, 1999).

There were many sources of Franco-American discord, but power differentials were at the centre of the difficulty. Admittedly, this was not the first time that considerations of relative capability were known to play a prominent part in assessments of the policy relevance of the Transatlantic *other* that France had been for the US, and vice versa. But it was new to discover allies expressing discontent with one of their set being thought *too* powerful. In the early days of NATO, for instance, American analysts who turned their attention to France and its relative capability had been known, paradoxically perhaps, to highlight the country's strategic relevance precisely because it was deemed not powerful *enough*. This was the gist of the thesis advanced in the closing days of the Fourth Republic by American political journalist David Schoenbrun, who proclaimed France to be *the* Western European country of greatest geopolitical import to the US, as well as the keystone to the arch of European, and by extension global, security. There was a sound strategic rationale, said Schoenbrun (1957, pp. 9, 15–16), in America having selected the country to host NATO's headquarters, 'because geographically, politically and strategically France is the linchpin of any Continental coalition'. For sure, France was 'sick' beyond dispute, but that is what made it so important. Failure to keep it from falling into a totalitarian embrace would signify nothing less than a failure to safeguard America's own political and civil liberties, because combating a Soviet empire that included France would require the establishment in America of a virtual garrison state for as far into the future as anyone dared to glimpse. Thus, concluded Schoenbrun, 'as France goes, so go the plans and hopes of many other nations, for the case of France is a case of world concern'.

By the early 1990s, many in Paris were returning the backhanded compliment, and imagining the case of America being one of world concern, but for the opposite reason. Now, France began to stir up disquiet in some Transatlantic quarters because it was propounding a desire (rhetorical if nothing else) to cut America down a peg or two, and this so as to attain the nirvana of multipolarity, helped along by a phenomenon termed *soft balancing* (Pape, 2005; Paul, 2005; Schreer, 2009). NATO had managed to ride out the tensions between Paris and Washington during the Cold War, and that conflict's fortuitous outcome might have led to the conclusion that Franco-American strife was rather irrelevant to the functioning of the Transatlantic alliance and to the broader community known as the West. This, however, is not how observers of the bilateral relationship tended to regard the issue once the Soviet Union disappeared, and new challenges to security began to crop up. Surprisingly perhaps, in this altered global security environment the consequences of France–US tension were said by many to be even more profound than they had been during the era of superpower rivalry, if for no other reason than that the Cold War had constituted such a credible basis for holding the allies together. That rivalry having ended, the other allies would presumably be tempted to go their separate ways, and France looked only too eager to shepherd them on their pilgrimage.

Particularly bothersome, for those who continued to take inspiration from a common set of Atlanticist values held to incarnate liberal-democracy's creedal and normative foundations, was the suspicion, solidifying during the 1990s, that France had defected from the universalistic Western undertakings it had once espoused and henceforth was going to throw itself wholly into the project of building an exclusionary Europe, primarily for reasons related to ontological, rather than physical, security (Coker, 1998; Mitzen, 2006). This Europe, once constructed, would be bound to widen the distance separating France from America. One word best summed up this new, French-conceived Europe: *autonomy*. It was hardly necessary in France (at times, to British dismay) to identify the significant oppositional other for the newly autonomous Europe: it was, and *had* to be, the US (Howorth and Keeler, 2003; Ash, 2004). Nor were French analysts hesitant about making explicit the referent, should the occasion call for it (Biarnès, 1998).

By the close of the 1990s, this prospect of Transatlantic rupture was troubling Samuel Huntington, who, only a few years earlier, had been arguing that the West, as a civilisational grouping distinct from the world's other major such groupings, could and did constitute a fairly coherent ideational entity, one even capable of *civilisation rallying* in moments of crisis. To those who, midway through the 1990s, believed the West to be in terminal decline, Huntington had even offered the hopeful rebuttal that 'if North America and Europe renew their moral life, build on their cultural commonality, and develop close forms of economic and political integration to supplement their security collaboration in NATO, they could generate a third Euroamerican phase of Western economic affluence and political influence' (Huntington, 1996, p. 308). Yet, just a few years later, Pollyanna would turn into Cassandra, as Huntington himself recanted his recently expressed faith in civilisation rallying. Now, the solidity of Western civilisation itself was under dire threat, only not from the *rest* beyond the pale, but worse, from *within* its very own ranks. And who was undermining this unity? None other than the French, bent as they were upon forging an antihegemonic coalition to balance American power.

In this undertaking, success could only depend upon Paris's ability to entice Germany to slip from its traditional pro-NATO, pro-Washington, moorings. The future of world order depended upon Europe, which could make or break the dispensation known as America's *hegemony*, since the latter, to function, required others to want to follow US leadership – exactly what France was contesting. Thus to Huntington the way to preserve hegemony and stave off the loneliness of America's *superpowerdom* was obvious: prevent France from winning over Germany, for 'given the pro- and anti-American outlooks of Britain and France, respectively, America's relations with Germany are central to its relations with Europe' (Huntington, 1999, p. 48).

The stakes were being ratcheted up in a way they could not have been as long as there still was a Soviet Union. France, which at the outset of the Cold War owed its importance to its weakness, had become relevant to America after the Cold War because of a disposition known to be rebarbative, and as a result bilateral relations were at the point of rupture, as judged by some students of the relationship (Davis, 2003). On its own, France might continue to count for little in the global balance of power, but if it could organise Europe according to its own lights, then the consequences could be momentous, enabling Paris to utilise the collective strength of its European partners for its own objectives. What those objectives might be, no one could say for sure; but, for more than a few observers of Transatlantic affairs, developments in the transformation of Western

European power were much more likely to result in a systemic change – i.e. an alteration of the distribution of power *within* the international state system – than was any mooted rise of an Asiatic state (read: China) as a potential peer competitor of the US (Gilpin, 1981).[5]

Charles Kupchan, shortly before the onset of the Iraq war, sounded a decidedly Huntingtonian note in announcing the impending demise of the West and proclaiming that 'the coming clash of civilisation will not be between the West and the rest but within a West divided against itself' (Kupchan, 2002, p. 44; Glucksmann, 2003). Nor was it hard to ignore, in the incredibly strained atmosphere of late 2002 and early 2003, the possibility that Iraq would prove to be the decisive, and therefore final, crisis of the West. Yet, though the war hardly constituted a tonic for the Western alliance, it did not turn out to be the mother of all crises many thought it was going to be. Far from representing NATO's 'near-death' (Pond, 2004) experience, the war gave the appearance of nearly sounding the death knell for Europe itself. It did so because the EU, America's ostensible peer challenger in the opinion of Kupchan and so many others, witnessed its many Member States, to say nothing of the numerous aspirants to membership, falling out over whether to back the Anglo-American coalition or the Franco-German *axis* (de Grossouvre, 2002). Not surprisingly, except to those who still believed in the willingness of Europeans to follow a French lead, the overwhelming majority of the EU's members and would-be members (though not their publics) opted for the Anglo-American picture of the Transatlantic future, warts and all.

Thus was set in motion a pattern of relative disintegration in Europe, which has been ongoing, and some say accelerating, for a decade now. Provocative as it might be to some to have it said, it bears repeating that the downturn in the European ontological project has had positive implications for the France–US relationship. But the Transatlantic cycle, improving as it has been, will in future be dependent upon that *other* cycle introduced above: the internal, endless debate that goes in the US about the country's preferred *grand strategy*. How Americans themselves choose to conceive and implement that strategy will have major bearing on the course of Transatlantic relations over the coming years – and this will be irrespective of the improvements wrought by the structural shift described and analysed in the preceding pages.

The Obama doctrine and American diplomatic tradition

Since no one can say anything sensible about the strategic choices effected by the administration that will come to power as a result of the November 2016 presidential election, the best that can be done in this section is to attempt to capture the sense and significance of what has been termed the *Obama doctrine*. Ever since Barack Obama declared his candidacy for president, more than eight years ago,[6] essayists have been taking turns speculating as to the kind of *doctrine* he would or should develop, or might already *have* developed. Their speculations have fallen into two, temporal, categories: those that started to make the rounds during the course of Obama's successful campaign for the presidency prior to the November 2008 election; and those that were expressed subsequent to his entering the White House in January 2009. Thus it did not take his inauguration as the 44th president to trigger discussion about an *Obama Doctrine*, for, as early as 26 August 2007, the term appeared in an article published in the *Providence Journal*, even before the official start of the caucus/primary season. Author James Kirchik did not intend to praise the candidate in the way he chose to brand Obama's opposition to America undertaking unilateral military intervention in Darfur – a position he feared was going to presage an Obama Doctrine that would be synonymous with America's 'remain[ing] impassive in the face of genocide (quoted in Sullivan, 2007). That interpretation, while harsh, constitutes one of the two prominent understandings of the Obama Doctrine, as a guide more for strategic *inaction* than strategic action. The alternative interpretation construes the Obama Doctrine more idealistically, as a call for principled intervention on behalf of humanitarian and liberal-democratic norms – a call that made appeal to the more altruistic side of American diplomacy.

In view of recent events, and notwithstanding the fulminations of right-wing commentators on AM radio and elsewhere – fulminations that generally depict the president as some kind of woolly idealist when he is not painted as an out-and-out Muslim/Marxist radical – it is clear that the Obama Doctrine is firmly nested within the major paradigms of the American diplomatic tradition, where it is much closer to the Realist pole of the continuum than it is to the Idealist side. Just as is the case for IR theory in general, so too is it the case for theories of US foreign policy: each has had a first *great debate* whose polar antagonists have been labelled Realists and Idealists. One name has figured prominently in both debates, that of Hans Morgenthau, sometimes argued to have been the *founding father* of the IR and American schools of Realism, because of his emphasis upon the implications for international and national security possessed by human nature, which he saw as both defective and as the root cause of conflict. For Morgenthau (1952, p. 961), 'modern political thought is the story of a contest between two schools which differ fundamentally in their conception of the nature of man, society, and politics' – the schools, of course, being Realism and Idealism.

As a first cut at trying to situate the Obama Doctrine, we could do worse than to ask where on the Morgenthau continuum we are most likely to find the President. It might be thought that Barack Obama, who, after all, was the *change* candidate championing a progressive domestic agenda – *Change We Can Believe In* as the 2008 campaign mantra went – and who also was the first of the major presidential aspirants to oppose the Iraq war, would be a staunch idealist committed to what Reinhold Niebuhr so memorably called an 'ethic of progressive justice' (Niebuhr, 1957, p. 9; Holder and Josephson, 2012). There *is* more than a bit of this idealism in Obama – but, significantly, it is an idealism whose first and by far most important referent objects are domestic not international in nature. When this president disparages *nation building* abroad, it does not mean that he has abandoned his earlier progressivism, for he remains very much committed to a domestic agenda that truly can be styled as social-democratic more than anything else (what in the American usage, is used almost synonymously with *liberalism*, quite unlike the practice in France and elsewhere in Europe).

Does his privileging of domestic over foreign populations mean, then, that a second dichotomy requires to be invoked if we are to gain some appreciation of the Obama Doctrine – a dichotomy whose polar opposites are not Realism and Idealism, but rather *isolationism* and *internationalism*? Many think it does, but it would be grossly inaccurate to imagine that either of these latter orientations (assuming we even knew their connotations) adequately captures the essence of the Obama Doctrine. So let us look elsewhere for guidance on the latter's paradigmatic root(s). There is one source that turns out to be indispensable for understanding American strategic choices within a doctrinal framework. It is a book cited earlier in this chapter, Walter Russell Mead's *Special Providence.*

Mead divides the American foreign policy tradition into schools eponymously titled the Hamiltonians, Jeffersonians, Jacksonians, and Wilsonians. He does this not to establish a strict adherence to the namesake of each school, but simply to signify the general orientation of the policies articulated by Alexander Hamilton, Thomas Jefferson, Andrew Jackson, and Woodrow Wilson (only the last three of whom, be it recalled, were actually presidents). Thus, Hamiltonians believe the first order of foreign policy is to strengthen the national economy as well as foster an international climate favourable to trade, but they also advocate that America try to work constructively with powers espousing similar values; adherents to this school, which Mead likens to America's own brand of *Realpolitik*, have included Dean Acheson, George H. W. Bush, and Theodore Roosevelt. Jeffersonians have usually (though not always) opposed Hamiltonians and have put the priority on building democracy at home, refraining from imposing US values on others, and employing military force only when vital security interests were threatened; George Kennan would be a prime example of this tradition. Jacksonians and Wilsonians are both willing to exercise military might, although the former are far more populist and nationalistic in their focus upon American *interests*, while the latter tend to be more ideationally driven, seeking to export such *values* as democracy and liberty (Mead, 2001, pp. 80–93).

Barack Obama straddles two of these schools, namely the Hamiltonian and the Jeffersonian ones, with one foot and several toes from the other in the Jeffersonian camp. His administration's foreign policy has sought to expand America's economic influence by reorienting national security away from the militaristic democracy promotion – one could even term it a *Jacksonian-Wilsonian* hybrid – of the George W. Bush administration (Haglund and Kertzer 2008). Instead, the thrust has been on promoting core US interests even as it furthers the very important strategic pivot towards the Asia–Pacific, and away from what had once been the cynosure of American strategy, the Transatlantic world (not that this administration is either *anti-European*, or *abandoning* Europe, as is sometimes argued) (quoted in Cohen, 2010, p. 6). Moreover, much of this administration's foreign policy has been conducted behind the scenes, a tactical preference that indeed warrants, both literally and metaphorically, being labelled as *leading from behind* (LFB), as oxymoronic as that might seem.

For some commentators, LFB is not only an oxymoron, it is an outrage. They mistake it at times for isolationism, and at other times for cowardice (Krauthammer, 2011). But it is neither. It was first coined by an anonymous administration official who employed it, in a conversation with Ryan Lizza of the *New Yorker*, as a means of denoting the Obama policy toward Libya (Lizza, 2011). Although Republican commentators saw cravenness in the imagery, there is another way of looking at LFB, as a piece of sage advice borrowed verbatim from a figure greatly admired by Barack Obama, South Africa's Nelson Mandela, who in his autobiography reflected upon the best means for getting one's way. 'I always remember', Mandela wrote, 'the regent's axiom: a leader, he said, is like a shepherd. He stays behind the flock, letting the most nimble go out ahead, whereupon the others follow, not realising that all along they are being directed from behind' (Mandela, 1994, p. 19).

The deliberate insertion of LFB in the Libyan context during early 2011 reflected the administration's keen understanding that the US had a credibility gap in the Middle East, and that sloganeering about *democracy* and *freedom* would find little support among Arabs who, themselves, were genuinely discomfited by the Gaddafi regime. Therefore, it was determined that only by aggressive diplomacy behind the scenes would the US be able to mobilise, or at least facilitate, a coalition in support of its objectives. Importantly (and here the Hamiltonian side of Obama showed clearly), it was necessary for America to work closely with like-minded powers, the two most relevant of such, naturally, being the UK and France.

Nor was that all. *Leading from Behind* has a further connotation, bespeaking an increasingly unified approach to security that combines spies and soldiers, and operates behind the lines of combat. Operationally, LFB finds its most direct translation not in refraining from the use of force, as many Obama critics mistakenly complain, but in using force from a distance, where the *shepherd* may be thousands of miles away from the *flock* (in this case of drones) that is being directed to its targets. There has, of course, been developing lately an intense debate, even in the US, about the merits of long-distance killing (Byman, 2013). That debate can be left for others to agonise over, but one thing needs correcting here, namely the claim that in respect of the drones, strategy has been subordinated to tactics (Cronin, 2013). This is not true. To the contrary, the stepped-up reliance on drone strikes can be taken as a military consequence of a grand strategy predicated upon Jeffersonianism; it is a choice *driven* by strategy. Everyone agrees that one cannot do *nation building* with drones (or for that matter, with aerial warfare of a more conventional nature). But Jeffersonians, unlike Wilsonians, really are not in favour of building any nation but their own. When they *are* moved to embrace intervention, their preference will be strongly in favour of aerial, not ground, combat – as we continue to witness in the case of American air strikes against Islamic State (IS) militants in Iraq, Syria, and elsewhere

Notwithstanding the controversial, and to some even pejorative, implications of LFB, the concept itself does enjoy a rather respectable scholarly cachet, albeit usually only when it gets expressed in different words (Harries and Switzer, 2013). For what is implied by LFB is nothing other than the logic contained in the familiar notion of *offshore balancing*. As Christopher Layne (1997), one of the leading exponents of this logic, puts it, offshore balancing seeks to transfer as much responsibility as possible to America's partners, if necessary by prodding them into assuming a greater share of the collective-defence burden even if that implies American *by-standing* and *buck-passing* behaviour. Stephen Walt (2005, p. 223) continues this thought by suggesting that offshore balancing 'husbands the power on which US primacy depends and minimises the fear that US power provokes'. For some time, offshore balancing had been getting bruited as a replacement grand strategy for America. Under Obama, it has become *the* grand strategy, testifying to the relative distribution of the current administration's Jeffersonian and Hamiltonian proclivities, in favour of the former. The full application of this strategy would radically recast US security and defence policy, inter alia by employing a lighter footprint, closing some bases overseas and opening new ones, and refocussing priorities. The latest Defense Strategic Guidance, from January 2012, spells out the contours of the strategic shift: '*Whenever possible, we will develop innovative, low-cost, and small-footprint approaches to achieve our security objectives*, relying on exercises, rotational presence, and advisory capabilities' (United States. Department of Defense, 2012, p. 3; emphasis original).

Conclusions

From the analysis above, three concluding observations suggest themselves regarding this volume's *problématique*, which is to assess various theoretical claims regarding the logic and consequence(s) of EU foreign policy, in light of the role played therein by whatever the US chooses to do or, as the case may be, *not* to do. I have sought to argue two major points, enshrouding them within a Dickensian motif that insists upon the *cyclical* nature of alliance dynamics. The first point is that the restoration of strategic comity between the US and France has been an inestimable asset to both countries, and it has brought back a welcome dose of realism to the discussion of Transatlantic relations. This point is actually a *highpoint*, and deserves to be underscored, especially because it contradicts the chronic mood of pessimism that permeates so much of what passes for debate within the alliance. It is an instance of an alliance dynamic that owes a very great deal to perceived (or real) shifts in structural power, primarily of Europe – shifts brought about, as I have tried to show, by developments extrinsic and intrinsic to the Old Continent. For a volume such as ours, this comes as a reminder that more important than the debate surrounding America's apprehended decline is the reality of the EU's relative loss of hard power (with all that this must imply for Europe's *soft* power). In other words, if we really are entering a *post-American* age, then a fortiori we are also entering a *post-European* age – and this has profound implications for so-called *soft balancing* in particular.

And this gets us to the second point, suggestive as it is of a pessimistic reading of the current state and future prospects of Transatlantic relations. Specifically, there is the implication that, as alliance doctrine very much reflects American doctrine, then it might follow that a very current rubric of choice in Transatlantic security discussions (smart power) is simply a rhetorical device through which is masquerading the longstanding, and contentious, *burden-sharing* problem in Transatlantic relations (Foucault and Mérand, 2012). Given that this issue has sown such controversy and discord between allies in the past, can it really be expected that its smart-power doppelgänger will have a different impact upon relations between the allies in the future? Moreover, if America's recent doctrinal adjustments are such as to put a premium on harbouring and not squandering the country's hard-power assets (and this is the only logical implication of Jeffersonianism), will not some in Europe be quick to conclude that an Obama Doctrine made manifest in the grand strategy of *leading from behind* (otherwise known as offshore balancing) must be bad for them, as it leaves them unprotected against the Russians (see Chapter 10) – and, as some see it, even unprotected against themselves?

To be sure, such a pessimistic reading might turn out to be accurate, and for the reasons above. But there is one final observation worth making here, and it derives from the marriage between the two dominant paradigms within which the Obama Doctrine is encased. While Jeffersonian instincts and assumptions, as argued above, do provide the lion's share of this administration's strategic preferences, the Hamiltonian component of the Obama Doctrine is also of importance. And to the extent that, within Europe, the UK continues to have a relationship with the US that is qualitatively different from other bilateral relationships elsewhere in Europe – no matter whether we call it a *special* or an *essential* relationship – then the Hamiltonian influence on American foreign policy can be expected to set in motion a new Transatlantic dynamic, one that sees the UK and France becoming increasingly influential in Transatlantic security matters, and this notwithstanding the mooted pivot of the US from Europe (and the Middle East) to the Asia–Pacific region. This is due to two recent trends in Transatlantic security: (1) France's growing security and defence cooperation with Britain within Europe; and (2) the more important rapprochement between France and the US.

This leads to the speculation that the dwindling band of Gaullists within French security and defence circles, who might otherwise be tempted to lament that General de Gaulle must be spinning in his grave as a result of this new trilateralism in Transatlantic security, would do well to remember that the General himself initially proposed the idea of a tripartite directorate of the alliance in the very earliest days of the Fifth Republic. Ironically, it is an idea whose time may finally have come, even if not exactly as imagined, or intended.

Notes

1   The sarcasm inheres in Nasr's paraphrase of Madeleine Albright's well-known assertion about American exceptionalism, made while the secretary of state was being interviewed

on NBC's *Today show* in February 1998, some ten months before Operation Desert Fox was unleashed against Saddam Hussein's Iraq:

> [I]f we have to use force, it is because we are America; we are the indispensable nation. We stand tall and we see further than other countries into the future, and we see the danger here to all of us.

In fact, Albright was merely repeating a phrase used by President Bill Clinton the year before, in his second inaugural address in January 1997: 'America stands alone as the world's indispensable nation' (Quoted in Lieber, 2012, p. 67).

2   Surveys conducted in the first year of the Obama administration routinely found the new president to be more popular in Europe than he was in America itself.

3   Heywood did not coin this and the numerous other pithy sayings by which he is remembered today, but he collected and published them in his 1546 edition of Proverbs.

4   For reasons I have never understood, European analysts frequently miscategorise economic prowess as falling outside the ambit of hard power, and this notwithstanding that none other than the guru of *soft power* himself, Joseph Nye, was explicit in writing that this latter, stemming from such power resources as 'culture, ideology, and institutions', stood in contrast with the 'hard power usually associated with tangible resources like military and economic strength' (Nye, 1990, p. 32).

5   There is a difference between *systemic* and *systems* change in the international system. The former entails changes in the way power is distributed, and reflects the implicit logic glimpsed in the theme of this volume. The latter suggests a major alteration in the very organising principle of the system, as for instance when the modern states system supplanted the medieval European system.

6   In a speech delivered in the Illinois capital, Springfield, on 10 February 2007.

References

Ash, T. G. (2004) *Free World: America, Europe, and the Surprising Future of the West.* New York: Random House.

Bartlett, J. (1968) *Familiar Quotations: A Collection of Passages, Phrases and Proverbs Traced to Their Sources in Ancient and Modern Literature.* 14th edn, rev. and enl. edn. Emily Morison Beck. Boston: Little Brown.

Biarnès, P. (1998) *Le XXIe siècle ne sera pas américain.* Paris: Éd. du Rocher.

Bittner, J. (2013) Between Paranoia and Naïveté. *New York Times.* 29 August. p. A21.

Bölte, E. (1992) *Zwischen Paris und Washington geht zur Zeit kaum etwas.* General-Anzeiger (Bonn), 30 May.

Boniface, P. (1998) *La France est-elle encore une grande puissance?* Paris: Presses de la Fondation Nationale des Sciences Politiques.

Byman, D. (2013) Why Drones Work: The Case for Washington's Weapon of Choice. *Foreign Affairs.* 92. pp. 32–43.

Chesnoff, R. Z. (2005) *The Arrogance of the French: Why They Can't Stand Us – and Why the Feeling Is Mutual.* New York: Sentinel.

Cogan, C. G. (1994) *Oldest Allies, Guarded Friends: The United States and France Since 1940.* Westport, CT: Praeger.

Cohen, R. (2010) Europe and Benign Neglect. *International Herald Tribune.* 7 September. p. 6.

Cohen, R. (2013) French Muscle, American Cheese. *New York Times,* 15 November. p. A25.

Coker, C. (1998) *Twilight of the West.* Boulder, CO: Westview.

Costigliola, F. (1992) *France and the United States: The Cold Alliance Since World War II*. New York: Twayne.

Cronin, A. K. (2013) Why Drones Fail: When Tactics Drive Strategy. *Foreign Affairs*. 92. pp. 44–54.

Davis, J. K. (2003) *Reluctant Allies and Competitive Partners: US–French Relations at the Breaking Point?* Dulles, VA: Institute for Foreign Policy Analysis/Brassey's.

De Grossouvre, H. (2002) *Paris–Berlin–Moscou: La voie de l'indépendance et de la paix*. Lausanne: L'Age d'Homme.

De Montbrial, T. (1992) La France est-elle 'l'ennemie numéro 1' des États-Unis? *Le Figaro*. 16 June. p. 3.

Department of Defense (2012) *Sustaining US Global Leadership: Priorities for 21st Century Defense*. Washington, DC: Department of Defense, January.

Dickens, C. (1950, orig. pub. 1859) *A Tale of Two Cities*. New York: Modern Library.

Durandin, C. (1994) *La France contre l'Amérique*. Paris: Presses Universitaires de France.

Erlanger, S. (2009) French Return to NATO Heals an Atlantic Rift. *International Herald Tribune*. 6 March. p. 3.

Erlanger, S. (2013a) The French Way of War. *New York Times*. 20 January. p. 5.

Erlanger, S. (2013b) In Turnaround, It's France Backing Arms While Britain Sits on Syria Sidelines. *New York Times*. 30 August. p. A6.

Foucault, M. and Mérand, F. (2012) The Challenge of Burden-Sharing. *International Journal*. 67. pp. 423–9.

Furniss, E. S. (1960) *France, Troubled Ally*. New York: Praeger.

Gilpin, R. (1981)*War and Change in World Politics* Cambridge: Cambridge University Press.

Glucksmann, A. (2003) *Ouest contre Ouest*. Paris: Plon.

Gordon, M. R. (2014) 2 Ships' Sale to Russians Worries US. *New York Times*. 15 May.

Guisnel, J. (1999) *Les Pires Amis du monde: Les relations franco-américaines à la fin du XXe siècle*. Paris: Stock.

Haglund, D. G. and Kertzer, J. D. (2008) From Geo to Neo: The Unusual 'Geo-Ethnic' Roots of Neoconservatism in US Foreign Policy. *Geopolitics*. 13. pp. 519–44.

Harries, O. and Switzer, T. (2013) Leading from Behind: Third Time a Charm? *American Interest*. 8. pp. 7–15.

Harrison, M. M. (1981) *The Reluctant Ally: France and Atlantic Security*. Baltimore: Johns Hopkins University Press.

Higgins, A. (2014) Populists' Rise in Europe Shakes Leaders. *New York Times*. 27 May. pp. A1–A8.

Holder, R. W. and Josephson, P. B. (2012) *The Irony of Barack Obama: Barack Obama, Reinhold Niebuhr and the Problem of Christian Statecraft*. Farnham, UK: Ashgate.

Howorth, J. and Keeler, J. T. S. (eds) (2003) *Defending Europe: The EU, NATO and the Quest for European Autonomy*. New York: Palgrave Macmillan.

Huntington, S. P. (1996) *The Clash of Civilizations and the Remaking of World Order*. New York: Simon & Schuster.

Huntington, S. P. (1999) The Lonely Superpower. *Foreign Affairs*. 78. pp. 35–49.

Joffe, J., Eliot, A., Cohen, G., Ikenberry, J., Shevtsova, L. and Aida, H. *et al.* (2014) America Self-Contained? *The American Interest*. 9. May/June. pp. 7–49.

Kagan, R. (2003) *Of Paradise and Power: America and the New World Order*. New York: Alfred A. Knopf.

Kietz, D. and Thimm, J. (2013) Zwischen Überwachung und Aufklärung: Die amerikanische Debatte und die europäische Reaktion auf die Praxis der NSA. *SWP-Aktuelle*, no. 51.

Krauthammer, C. (2011) The Obama Doctrine: Leading from Behind. *Washington Post*. 28 April.

Krugman, P. (2011) Eurotrashed. *New York Times Magazine*, 18 January. pp. 26–33.

Kupchan, C. A. (2002) The End of the West. *Atlantic Monthly*. 290. November. pp. 42–4.

Kupchan, C. A. (2003) *The End of the American Era: US Foreign Policy and the Geopolitics of the Twenty-First Century*. New York: Knopf.

Lagadec, E. (2012) *Transatlantic Relations in the 21st Century: Europe, America and the Rise of the Rest*. London: Routledge.

Layne, C. (1997) From Preponderance to Offshore Balancing: America's Future Grand Strategy. *International Security*. 22 (1). pp. 86–124.

Leonard, M. (2005) *Why Europe Will Run the 21st Century*. London: Fourth Estate.

Lieber, R. J. (2012) *Power and Willpower in the American Future: Why the United States Is Not Destined to Decline*. Cambridge: Cambridge University Press.

Lizza, R. (2011) The Consequentialist. *New Yorker*. 2 May. p. 44.

Mandela, N. (1994) *Long Walk to Freedom: The Autobiography of Nelson Mandela*. Boston: Little Brown.

Mazzetti, M. and Gordon, M. R. (2013) Support Slipping, US Defends Plan for Syria Attack. *New York Times*. 31 August. pp. A1, A7.

Mead, W. R. (2001) *Special Providence: American Foreign Policy and How It Changed the World*. New York: Knopf.

Melandri, P. and Vaïsse, J. (2001) *L'Empire du mileu: Les États-Unis et le monde depuis la fin de la Guerre Froide*. Paris: Odile Jacob.

Miller, J. J. and Molesky, M. (2004) *Our Oldest Enemy: A History of America's Disastrous Relationship with France.* New York: Doubleday.

Mitzen, J. (2006) Ontological Security in World Politics: State Identity and the Security Dilemma. *European Journal of International Relations*. 12 (3). pp. 341–70.

Morgenthau, H. J. (1952) Another 'Great Debate': The National Interest of the United States. *American Political Science Review*. 46. pp. 961–88.

Nasr, V. (2013) The Dispensable Nation: American Foreign Policy in Retreat. New York: Doubleday.

Niebuhr, R. (1957) *Love and Justice*. Philadelphia: Westminster.

Nougayrède, N. (2007) Sarkozy célèbre à Washington la réconciliation avec l'Amérique. *Le Monde*, 9 November. pp. 1–4.

Nye, J. (1990) *Bound to Lead: The Changing Nature of American Power.* New York: Basic Books.

Pape, R. A. (2005) Soft Balancing Against the United States. *International Security*. 30 (1). pp. 7–45.

Paul, T. V. (2005) Soft Balancing in the Age of US Primacy. *International Security*. 30 (1). pp. 46–71.

Pesme, F. (2010) France's 'Return' to NATO: Implications for Its Defence Policy. *European Security*. 19 (1). pp. 45–60.

Pond, E. (2004) *Friendly Fire: The Near-Death of the Transatlantic Alliance*. Washington: Brookings Institution Press.

Revel, J. F. (2002) *L'Obsession anti-américaine: Son fonctionnement, ses causes, ses inconséquences*. Paris: Plon.

Rifkin, J. (2004) *The European Dream: How Europe's Vision of the Future Is Quietly Eclipsing the American Dream*. New York: Penguin.

Rigoulot, P. (2004) *L'Antiaméricanisme: Critique d'un prêt-à-penser rétrograde et Chauvin*. Paris: Robert Laffont.

Roger, P. (2002) *L'Ennemi américain: Généalogie de l'antiaméricanisme français*. Paris: Seuil.

Schoenbrun, D. (1957) *As France Goes*. New York: Harper.

Schreer, B. (2009) A New 'Pragmatism': Germany's NATO Policy. *International Journal*. 64 (2). pp. 383–98.

Serfaty, S. (2002) La France vue par les États-Unis: Réflexions sur la francophobie à Washington. Paris: Centre français sur les États-Unis/Institut français des relations internationals, November.

Sullivan, A. (2007) The Obama Doctrine: Take Two. *The Atlantic*. 26 August.

The Economist (2014) Mistral Blows. 17 May. pp. 51–2.

Thimm, J. (2014) Inseparable, but Not Equal: Assessing US–EU Relations in the Wake of the NSA Surveillance Affair. *SWP Comments*. 4 January.

Timmerman, K. R. (2004) *The French Betrayal of America*. New York: Crown Forum.

Touraine, M. (1993) La Représentation de l'adversaire dans la politique extérieure française depuis 1981. *Revue française de science politique*. 43 (5). pp. 807–22.

Walt, S. M. (2005) *Taming American Power: The Global Response to US Primacy*. New York: W. W. Norton.

Zakaria, F. (2009) *The Post-American World*. New York: W. W. Norton.

10 The EU's policy towards Russia

National interests and path dependency

Serena Giusti

Introduction

This chapter explores the EU's policy towards Russia from a diachronic perspective, from the dissolution of the Soviet Union in 1991 until the upsurge of
the Ukrainian crisis at the end of 2013 that marks the lowest point in the relationship. The main features of this policy are traced back to the International
Relations mainstream theoretical paradigms discussed in the book. From this
perspective, the proposed analysis can be considered as a case study. So far,
neither the EU nor Russia has developed a strategic conception for the relationship. While initially the EU embraced a path dependency pattern, later on, as
Russia turned to being an assertive player, it has been simply reactive. The EU
has typically countered Russian actions or provocations in an extemporary
manner without any clear-cut strategy agreed beforehand. We, therefore, believe
that this study is particularly suitable for a *mirror technique* (i.e. observing actor
A's (Russia) behaviour and analysing how this is reflected in actor B's (EU)
response).

Considering the very different *genetic make-up* of the actors and the ups and
downs that have characterised their relationship over time, our initial hypothesis
is that no single theoretical paradigm can alone capture its multifaceted evolution. Some of the paradigms debated elsewhere in the volume might, however,
contribute to enlightening specific phases of the relationship's progression. In
particular, the EU's approach towards Russia has been influenced by geopolitical concerns coupled with calculations of interests. Conflict of values has not
dissipated, hindering the deepening of the relationship that has dramatically and
quite unexpectedly deteriorated as a consequence of the annexation of Crimea
and the continuous meddling of the Kremlin in the eastern regions of Ukraine.

The relationship has also constantly suffered from a lack of trust and misun-
derstandings. On the one hand, the Kremlin is reluctant to deal with such a cross-
breed organisation whose postmodern nature is not clearly understood
(Caporaso, 1996, pp. 29–52; European Commission, 2005). Russia prefers
dealing directly with EU Member States or even companies, rather than negotiating on collective positions agreed beforehand. The Russian political élite
thinks that Europe is losing attractiveness since it is no longer at the centre of the

international system due to the rapid shift of global influence towards other regions such as the Asia–Pacific. In addition, the global financial crisis has, from a Russian standpoint, discredited the Western model of capitalism and the EU has failed to become 'the most competitive and dynamic knowledge-based economy in the world by 2010' as foreseen in the Lisbon strategy (2000). On the other hand, the EU has not fully understood the complex process of transformation and redefinition of identity that Russia experienced after losing its superpower status (Mankoff, 2012, p. 11).

In the first stage of the relationship, while both actors were reforging their foreign policy (the EU had to respond to the end of the bipolar system, while the Russian Federation was absorbed by a complex process of state building), the European institutions settled the pattern of cooperation on the basis of already experienced instruments. The EU offered Russia the usual cooperation agreement that entails a sectorial involvement, leaving aside high politics issues. The first clash of values was soon recorded when Russia intervened militarily in Chechnya in 1994. This caused a delay in the ratification of the Partnership and Cooperation Agreement (PCA), which finally entered into force in 1997 and was complemented in 2003 by adding the four *common spaces*. The most innovative form of cooperation that the EU offered to Russia was the Partnership for Modernisation (PfM) in 2010, which was mainly economically focused.

Like the US, the European institutions also believed that pragmatism could in the long run be a rewarding approach towards Russia. This seemed to work until the normative incongruity brutally re-emerged in the five-day war with Georgia (2008) and a few years later in Ukraine (2013). Any time tensions with Russia arise, the EU Member States tend to react unilaterally, following their individual national interests and less tangible fears. This confirms that Intergovernmentalism generally prevails. Once the EU started to use its powers (disguised as a process of norms diffusion) on the so-called post-Soviet space, what was a conflict of values turned into geopolitical competition.

Intergovernmentalism: a key to interpretation

An accurate analysis of the EU's posture towards Russia evidences that Intergovernmentalism still predominates in the organisation's external projection. The EU Member States have repeatedly displayed colliding positions when confronting Russia. This inconsistency depends on the EU Member States' different interests, in particular on the economy and energy (see, for instance, Chapter 2),[1] and on perceptions that might vary in relation to the countries' past experience with Russia (e.g. of being ex-satellites and former Soviet Republics).

The predominance of national interests in the EU's foreign policy is primarily related to its intergovernmental nature. Although we are not tackling here the delicate question of the Union's polity (federal/confederal), we maintain that pointing out the differences between the EU's and a traditional state's foreign policy is an important corollary to further the debate on the theoretical approaches hereafter considered. Despite the efforts of the Treaty of Lisbon, national foreign policies have not yet been subsumed by a new common foreign policy, so that they continue to exist alongside a progressively enhanced Common Foreign and Security Policy (CFSP).

The *nationalisation* of foreign policy does not exclude the fact that a certain degree of Europeanisation may occur in such an intergovernmental field as foreign policy, but the dynamics of Europeanisation take place on a more 'voluntary and non-hierarchical basis' (Bulmer and Radaelli, 2004, p. 7).[2]

As far as Russia is concerned, two approaches have surfaced: some of the EU member States (e.g. France, Germany and Italy) consider Russia as a potential partner that can be drawn into the EU's orbit through a process of Europeanisation that might end in more integration without, however, contemplating any possibility of membership. They favour involving Russia in as many institutions as possible and encouraging Russian investment in some EU strategic sectors such as energy (Leonard and Popescu, 2007).

Other members (whose perception is influenced by the burden of the common memories and experience during the Cold War, such as Poland and the Baltic States) still see Russia as a threat because of its recently rising power, growing control over the post-Soviet space and its 'managed democracy', which does not entirely match Western values and principles. These countries support a harder EU approach towards Russia, based on the respect for democracy, rule of law and human rights. They endorse NATO's further eastward expansion and promote a policy of progressive co-optation of the EU's Eastern neighbours in the EU's institutional architecture (Leonard and Popescu, 2007). This line of orientation is also shared by countries such as Great Britain and Sweden.

These two mainstream factions do not tend to be steady. In some specific issues, other subgroups are likely to emerge in a variable geometry fashion, with states shifting from one group to another according to interests, perceptions and political culture. Recently, a divide was evident among the twenty-eight Member States over the extent, or sometimes even the very idea, of sanctions against Russia. The EU states divided along an unprecedented north/south line, with the former Soviet satellites (especially the Baltics and Poland) embracing a harder line and the Mediterranean EU members (though also Hungary and Bulgaria) being unenthusiastic (Pridham, 2014, pp. 58–9). To complicate the picture, some differences might emerge even within countries.

Since foreign policy is a traditionally intergovernmental policy and the EU Member States' interests vis-à-vis Russia are particularly heterogeneous, the EU's interaction with Moscow has been generally divisive and unpredictable. Although some other perspectives may contribute to explaining the EU–Russia relationship, we believe that Intergovernmentalism is an inescapable interpretational key.

From the Cold War to post-bipolarism

Russia, in its various manifestations (Russian Empire, Soviet Union, Russian Federation), has greatly impacted on Europe's evolution. The bipolar configuration of the international system has been regarded as an extraordinary prompt for the amalgamation of European states through the process of European integration. As has been argued by, among others, Rosato (2011), the presence of the Soviet superpower on the continent persuaded Western European countries to go beyond simple power aggregation, as an alliance or coalition would allow. Well aware of their weakness even in combination, the Western European states opted for gradual integration.

Contrary to what some Realists had assumed (Mearsheimer, 1990; Layne, 2006), once the Soviet Union disintegrated, putting de facto an end to the bipolar system, the process of European integration did not collapse. That systemic change unexpectedly generated 'pressures for further development of the European Communities' (Armstrong et al., 1996, p. 200) rather than causing its breakdown. After that, the EEC/EU finally took an international stance and started to elaborate on its external dimension as pressures from Eastern European countries to reconnect to the Western mainstream were mounting. However, the EU was not so audacious as to exploit the US willingness to disengage from Europe by putting forward a Common Defence Policy and eventually a common army.

Nevertheless, the Treaty on the European Union that came into force in 1993 comprised a pillar entirely devoted to the CFSP. While maintaining the intergovernmental character of the policy,[3] the new pillar introduced instruments of action – joint actions and common positions – and opened possibilities for the creation of a common defence policy.[4] The Treaty was meant to pave the way for the EU's biggest and most complex enlargement to include, between 2004 and 2007, twelve new Member States (including eight satellites and three former Soviet Republics). The eastward enlargement became the most successful story of the EU's foreign policy (European Commission, 2009; Hillion, 2010; LSE, 2013).

The accession of these countries to the EU institutional setting triggered a process of policy export that was unprecedented in terms of both its width and its formulation. The EU became a potent regulator (rule maker), a normative power (Manners, 2002), while the acceding countries transformed into regime takers. The *Europeanisation* (Featherstone and Radaelli, 2003) of the new members and soon of those countries close to the borders of the enlarged Union was considered the best way to stabilise the post-Soviet space and perhaps Russia too.

The hypothesis of a progressive democratisation through a gradual familiarisation with the EU (although without a membership perspective) proved wrong. The instability, intrinsic in the process of democratisation, and the uncertainty that remains in an *incomplete Kantian world*, where the Hobbesian state of anarchy has not yet entirely disappeared from the international system, persisted (Mearsheimer, 1990). Transition processes proved very difficult and not necessarily conducive to consolidating democratic regimes. There has been, on the contrary, a growing number of illiberal democracies or hybrid regimes (Zakaria, 1997).

This was certainly the case in Russia, where the relevance of domestic variables was underestimated, assuming that the country would have smoothly adapted to the systemic change of the international system. On the contrary, domestic specificities have reinforced differentiation at the structural level, showing the deep interconnection between domestic and international politics. The demise of the Soviet Union, on the one hand, opened new windows of opportunity for the EU (e.g. crafting a reasonable foreign policy, widening its leverage on the Eastern countries, gaining new economic markets); but on the other hand, it confronted the organisation with new security challenges (minorities question, frozen conflicts, secessionism, organised crime) and finally with Russia itself. As a result of the 2004 enlargement, Russia is an EU neighbouring country keen on playing a prominent role in the area *in between*.

Formalising relations

The beginning of the Russian Federation was marked by instability and disorientation. As Prizel underlined,

> Within the short space of three years the Russian people have seen the ideology that dominated their polity for seven decades de-legitimised. Worse still, they have lost the vast territories that for centuries [they] considered their own and have witnessed the disappearance of an imperial status that has been part and parcel to Russia's national being since at least the sixteenth century.
>
> (1998, pp. 239–40)

In the first years of its existence, Russia not only risked a political destabilisation, but also an economic default. The anchorage to the West was seen by President Boris Yeltsin (1991–9) and his foreign minister, Andrei Kozyrev (1992), as a means of survival for Russia.

They advocated a new system of values (the supremacy of democracy, human rights, freedom, and legal and moral standards) on which Western societies were based. They supported the gradual participation of Russia in Western organisations (not as a partner, but as a full member enjoying all the benefits of membership) and its integration into the world economy, hoping that, with the assistance of international financial institutions, they could recover from a disastrous economy. Russia's leadership also looked to the West as a security provider, because conflicts along the country's new borders could easily threaten the domestic reform process. All this created a favourable climate for the formalisation of EU–Russia relations.

The EU did not come out with any special plan for Russia. It simply extended to it the traditional pattern of agreements available for third countries. In 1994, Brussels and Moscow signed the PCA,[5] which only came into force in 1997; the EU in fact suspended the ratification process as a way of exerting conditionality for Russia's military in the Second Chechen War.[6]

The agreement was established for an initial period of ten years, with a clause stating that it is automatically extended on an annual basis unless either side withdraws from it. The PCA can be classified as an entry-level agreement that does not envisage membership but endorses the interest of both parties in developing further mutual cooperation. It is a mixed agreement that goes beyond the EC framework and has a clear EU cross-pillar dimension involving the CFSP and Justice and Home Affairs (Hillion, 2000).

In this phase, the EU and its Member States privileged an institutional approach – formalising relations within a set of instruments already experienced in other contexts – that entails a path dependency approach. This occurs precisely because it is often easier or more cost-effective to simply continue along a path already set than to create an entirely new one. Levi's definition:

> Path dependence has to mean, if it is to mean anything, that once a country or region has started down a track, the costs of reversal are very high. There will be other choice points, but the entrenchments of certain institutional arrangements obstruct an easy reversal of the initial choice
>
> (1997, p. 28)

is particularly suitable for interpreting Brussels' offer to Moscow.

The EU hoped that the PCA could pave the way for a further deepening of the relationship. Instead, relations remained stagnant and the potential of the PCA was rather unexploited. Nevertheless, at the St. Petersburg Summit in May 2003, Brussels and Moscow agreed on the creation of four *common spaces* (the Common Economic Space; the Common Space of Freedom, Security and Justice; the Common Space of External Security, including crisis management and non-proliferation; and the Common Space of Research and Education). The Moscow Summit in May 2005 developed the instruments to put these common spaces into effect by setting *road maps* with specific objectives and actions required. Despite the apparent will of the parts to strengthen their partnership, the *four spaces* did not become a platform for deeper and more comprehensive cooperation. The EU was absorbed by the integration of the new Eastern European members and confronting the setback caused by the rejection of the European Constitution (Butorina, 2013). Meanwhile, Russia's economic recovery made the leadership more confident and less disposed to conform to the EU's requests.

Realigning the relationship

As Vladimir Putin consolidated his power, the relationship worsened, as the balance of power between the two entities had been modified. Drawing on the immense new wealth generated by oil and gas exports, as well as on his ability to recentralise political power, Putin explicitly committed his government to regaining Russia's status as a Great Power. Putin's foreign policy has gone through various sequential phases: strengthening the state politically and economically; restoring the country's international status; acting assertively on the international scene (Giusti and Penkova, 2008).

Putin's Russia claimed it should be treated in the same way by the EU as NATO was doing by establishing in May 2002 the NATO–Russia Council (NRC), a mechanism for consultation, consensus building, cooperation, joint decision and joint action. Under the NRC, Russia and NATO Member States meet as equals *at 29* – instead of in the bilateral *NATO + 1* format under the previous Permanent Joint Council.[7]

Over a few years (roughly from 2003 to 2008), Russia's relations with the West deteriorated dramatically. The alleged Western support for the so-called Colour Revolutions (Georgia, 2003; Ukraine, 2004; Kyrgyzstan, 2005), the EU engagement in the post-Soviet space through its 2004 Neighbourhood Policy (ENP), the Bush administration's project for a missile defence system to be established in Poland and the Czech Republic,[8] the recognition of Kosovo's independence in 2008 by two-thirds of the EU members and, finally, Bush's proposal (blocked by France and Germany) to extend NATO Membership Action Plans (MAP) to Georgia and Ukraine at the April 2008 NATO summit were the causes of an increasing tension.

Meanwhile, the EU and Russia started to renegotiate a new PCA after a two-year delay, as Poland and Lithuania withdrew their veto (DeBardeleben, 2009, p. 95). The negotiations were then interrupted because of the Russian military intervention in Georgia. Thanks to the firm diplomatic action of then French President Nicholas Sarkozy, in charge of the EU presidency, Moscow and Tbilisi agreed to sign a ceasefire and the issue of sanctions against Russia, raised by some Eastern EU members, was avoided. The negotiations for the renovation of the PCA still suffer from some hindrances such as the question of energy supplies, Russian reticence to ratify the EU Energy Charter Treaty and the European opposition to liberalisation of the visa regime for Russian people.[9] Until visa facilitation/liberalisation is introduced, socialisation will remain modest, thereby thwarting better understanding between Europe and Russia.

Russia's desire to play a greater role in regional security induced President Dmitry Medvedev to propose a new European security architecture *from Vancouver to Vladivostok*. During a speech made in Berlin on 5 June, 2008 before an audience of 500 politicians and business leaders, Medvedev recalled that

> Our predecessors during the Cold War years managed to draw up the Helsinki Final Act …, and so why should we not be able to take the next step today? Namely, drafting and signing a legally binding treaty on European security in which the organisations currently working in the Euro-Atlantic area could become parties.
>
> (Medvedev, 2008b)

This new pact would be, according to him, 'a regional pact based, naturally, on the principles of the UN Charter and clearly defining the importance of force as a factor in relations within the Euro-Atlantic community.' In contrast to Mikhail Gorbachev's idea (1989) of a 'Europe from the Atlantic to the Urals', entailing the survival of the Soviet Union, which would have simply cooperated with both the US and the EU, Medvedev's proposal presented a post-bipolar view in which Russia was considered one of the key players and shapers. Although Medvedev (2008a) provided some more details in a speech a few months later, on 8 October at the World Policy Conference in Evian (France) his proposal was perceived by the Western public as too vague and it did not have any serious follow-up (Van Herpen, 2008).

EU–Russia relations improved, after the tension of the five-day war in Georgia, thanks to the *reset the button* policy inaugurated by the Russian Foreign Minister Sergey Lavrov and US Secretary of State Hillary Clinton in March 2009. The policy consisted of a new approach to dealing with Russia (achieving top political targets like Iran, Afghanistan, international terrorism, energy and non-proliferation), while courting its sensitivity with compensation for previous neglect of its interests, rather than offering a long-term strategy. Warmer relations with Washington have detoxified relations with Poland and the Baltics, and public lecturing about human rights and democracy has largely stopped (e.g. the issue of human rights is being discussed in special rounds of human rights consultations). The EU moved from the assumption that Russia cannot be equated to a country in transition toward the Western mainstream, but has to be treated as a *sui generis* entity. Implicitly, the EU renounced playing its normative role and acquiesced to a functional and selective cooperation.

This new trend was confirmed by the PfM, launched during the Rostov-on-Don summit (31 May–1 June 2010), an innovative form of cooperation responding to Russia's priorities. The issue of modernisation had already been raised during Vladimir Putin's presidencies (2000–8), but it was with President Medvedev (2008–12) that it became central to the national political agenda. In his vision, modernisation should cover all spheres of the country's life, bringing about the diversification of Russia's economy from dependence on natural resources to an economy based on innovations (Medvedev, 2009). Although the President admitted that there is a correlation between democracy and modernisation, he nevertheless did not establish any causal link between the two. Modernisation is not conceived as a holistic process but as a conservative project (Trenin, 2010). While the state's polity is to remain almost unaffected, changes will take place selectively and will gradually become compatible with the stability of the country.[10]

Foreign Minister Lavrov advocated the creation of 'modernising alliances with the US and Europe' in order to secure technology transfers and attract Western investors to overcome Russia's secular technological backwardness and economic isolation.[11] The PfM has therefore been presented as a common modernisation agenda to advance the EU and Russian economies and to bring their citizens closer, while contributing to global recovery and stronger international economic governance. The PfM is primarily a flexible framework for prompting reforms, enhancing growth and raising competitiveness (among its priority areas: innovation, medium-sized enterprises, the alignment of technical regulations and standards, intellectual property rights). The implementation of the activities entails the involvement of various actors – institutional and private – with both an economic-financial craft and a political mission. In comparison with other programmes of cooperation put forward by the EU, the PfM is more open to the involvement of informal actors and better suited to blurring the boundaries between the public and private spheres. The EU expected that cooperation would have produced spillover effects and called for a more political approach. Moreover, frequent interaction in a dense *organisational field* can set in motion processes of *institutional isomorphism*, making organisations increasingly homogeneous and inclined to adopt growing similarities of regulatory practice.

Within the PfM, Russia is less constrained, because the usual stress over values is more relaxed and the principle of conditionality is not contemplated. The PfM is based on a process of learning, persuasion and co-ownership inspired by a lesson-drawing model. Such a model does not include direct rewards from the EU, but only expected benefits deriving from the adoption of a set of rules. This is considered to be more efficient and beneficial (Schimmelfennig and Sedelmeier, 2002).

The soft tools of the PfM have the merit of engaging Russia formally (institutional actors) and informally (non-institutional actors), so that Russia does not fear external interference in its domestic politics. The PfM's procedures make it possible to speed up negotiations that might otherwise stall if legally binding commitments were sought.

The pact matches both sides' interests: on the one hand, Russia's desire for external investment and partnerships in order to accomplish its modernisation mission, and, on the other hand, the EU's hope of improving economic relations and creating better opportunities for European companies and, as a *non-deliberate* outcome, of upgrading the quality of democracy in the country (Giusti, 2011).

The PfM shows that the EU, like other prominent actors such as the US, has found that lecturing Russia on the need to reform is not fruitful. It is therefore better to address Russia's own interest by offering help with what has become a national priority. The PfM's codes of practice vary a lot, but they are not all legally binding and are generally subject to revision and recontracting.[12] These measures work better in a context of cooperation rather than integration, and they are particularly suited to improving governance.

Competing for the post-Soviet space

Despite the PfM's attempt to depoliticise and de-escalate tensions with Russia, a new phase of conflict started in 2009, when the EU launched the Eastern Partnership (EaP). It was a joint Polish–Swedish proposal in June 2008 to boost the Eastern dimension of the ENP – the sequel to the grand 2004 enlargement, designed to bolster relations with the nearest countries of Eastern Europe, the southern shore of the Mediterranean and the South Caucasus (Wiśniewski, 2013). Even during the negotiation phase to join the EU, Poland proposed acting as Brussels' special interlocutor for bridge-building with countries in Eastern Europe and Russia itself. Once it had secured its purpose, Poland was at pains to focus Europe's foreign and security policy on the precarious state of the countries squeezed in between the enlarged Union and a resurgent Russia. However, what began as a conciliatory attitude on Poland's part has turned into Moscow baiting, and in doing so the Poles have been egged on by other countries of the so-called *new Europe*. The other promoter of the scheme, Sweden, is one of the EU members with least tolerance for Russia's hybrid brand of democracy (Giusti and Ceccorulli, 2015).

Although in its genesis the EaP got off to a weak start – the EU Member States divided over involving Russia and Turkey or the political expediency of making overtures to Belarus's president Alexander Lukashenka – it was more ambitious in its targets than the initial draft of the ENP. Cooperation over immigration through rapid introduction of a more elastic visa system (with a view to eventually getting visas abolished) was accompanied by plans to create a free exchange area and the possibility of drawing up Association Agreements (AA). Furthermore, the EaP extends from bilateral to multilateral cooperation, encouraging dialogue between partner countries and the EU over issues of common interest,[13] on a *best practice* basis.

An opening was also to be left for collaboration with third-party states (especially Russia) that in principle could have taken part, case by case, in concrete EaP projects. Initially, the policy was seen as elastic to the point that eligible countries did not have to plump clearly for one side or the other: many of them were still receptive to overtures from Russia, which had more cultural affinity than the EU and an increasing influence in the area.

Although the European Commission had stated that the EaP was to develop in parallel with the strategic partnership with Moscow, the posture of those promoting it immediately made Russia suspect that the EaP was a less-than-neutral stabilisation policy. Moreover, the official launch of the EaP coincided with an announcement that Brussels would be supporting modernisation of the gas lines crossing Ukraine, and with the *south corridor* declaration whereby the EU, Georgia, Turkey, Azerbaijan and Egypt committed themselves to strengthening their ties in the energy sector (Council of the EU, 2009).

Russian political elites considered the EaP as an attempt by Brussels to develop its own sphere of influence in the post-Soviet space. Russia's Foreign Minister Sergei Lavrov also pointed out that pressures were put on Belarus (notably governed by an autocratic regime close to Moscow) to induce the country not to recognise the independence of the Georgian breakaway regions South Ossetia and Abkhazia in exchange for EU rewards. According to Lavrov, this strategy was not about promoting democracy, but was rather a form of blackmailing countries. Russia also rejected the formula of more EU, less NATO for the post-Soviet countries. Therefore, the Russians would not have been less lenient towards deeper integration within the EU just because a MAP with NATO was not a feasible option any more. Russia simply considered the EaP as a zero-sum game.[14] To support this claim, the Kremlin mentioned the alleged EU opposition to the compatibility between the EaP and the integration processes within the Eurasian Economic Union promoted by the Kremlin. Actually, Russia has presented its project of regional integration as a normative one, inspired by a neo-functionalist approach borrowed from the EU's successful experience.[15]

Both the EU and Russia have therefore promoted an increasing institutionalisation of the post-Soviet space, using a similar rhetoric, though they differ in their basic values and intentions. They are both employing strategies that reflect their own interests and are based on an acceptable degree of rationality. The EU's aim is to repeat the positive experience of the eastward enlargement, though if there are no prospects of membership its influence is rather limited. By contrast, Russia considers the ex-Soviet area as not only embodying a sizeable part of its Euro-Asian identity, but also as a pillar of its international projection. Russia sees the international system as a polyarchy where each pole power is defined by the ability to dominate its regional area (Lavrov, 2007). Therefore, the control of the near abroad (conceived as a special extension of the state) is, for Russia, a premise for regaining its status.[16]

Such control has been exerted through a wide array of instruments. The Kremlin has reinforced cultural links with former Soviet republics by financing educational, linguistic and social programmes, and it has supported their economies. It has often relied on the political use of energy, based on the gradual reduction of subsidies for oil and gas exports to its neighbours, accompanied by implicit foreign policy requests (not accepting the EU's offers) and promoting the process of institutionalisation of different kinds of regional organisations (e.g. the Collective Security Treaty Organisation and the Customs Union). The Customs Union is being upgraded to a single economic area with the goal of an economic union by 2015, and might later constitute a bridge between Europe and the Asia–Pacific region.

As a result of a double pressure, the national leaders of the EaP countries have been encouraged (most markedly in Ukraine) to draw tactically on support sometimes from Brussels, sometimes from Moscow, for domestic and often personal reasons. Such oscillation by national elites has hardly been conducive to consolidating democracy. The *two-way periphery* has been torn between what still seems too abstract an attraction to the EU and the more concrete promises/ retaliations being made by Russia.

Even if independent and formally fully sovereign, some of the EaP countries enjoy de facto a limited freedom – which might be addressed as a *negative liberty* – that makes their condition extremely delicate. Although politically entitled to project influence toward its neighbourhood, the EU is posing a clear geopolitical challenge to Russia's influence in the region. The fact that the EU is using civilian means and, in particular, its normative capabilities does not dismiss its power politics goal: extending its leverage towards the East to the detriment of Russia.

Fighting for Ukraine

It was in this climate of mounting competition between Brussels and Moscow for the *control* of the post-Soviet space that protests in Maidan Square in Kiev erupted violently in November 2013 as the Ukrainian President Viktor Yanukovych curtly suspended preparations for the signing of the AA. The sudden switch by Yanukovych, following weeks of brinkmanship, left European policy towards the post-Soviet states in tatters. Demonstrations rapidly led to a regime change. Unexpectedly, Russia reacted by annexing Crimea, violating Ukrainian sovereignty and territorial integrity through acts of aggression by its armed forces.

Although there had been a problematic process of negotiation, the Ukraine's AA was considered by Brussels as evidence of its successful transformative power to have 'spillover' effects on other partners (Penkova, 2014, p. 3). Ukraine's unpredicted decision to abandon the AA left the EU with no regional source of influence. Once again, the reaction of the EU was not consistent since its members disagreed on a common strategy to confront Russia's use of force. A clash between political values over the threat to European security and economic interests, due especially to some EU members' deep dependence on energy supply, surfaced clearly (Pridham, 2014, p. 59). The EU's initial response was, therefore, timid and formal rather than substantive: the EU cancelled the summit with Russia and decided not to hold regular bilateral summits. Some restrictive measures were adopted, and only after pressure from the US did the EU take the decision to apply economic sanctions targeting state-owned banks and forbidding the export of technologies needed by Russia's oil and defence industries.[17] The restrictions, however, left the gas industry largely unaffected, a clear concession to the EU's dependence on Russian gas. In addition, the EU barred future defence deals only, so that France's €1.2 billion sale of Mistral class warships will not be touched. All this obviously fractures the EU's credibility. The renewal of Russian sanctions is already stirring a debate within the EU, with Moscow lobbying what it sees as sympathetic EU capitals – supposedly Budapest, Nicosia and Rome (Eurobserver, 2014).[18]

President Putin (2014) immediately reacted by signing a decree 'On the use of specific economic measures', which mandated an effective embargo for a one-year period on imports of most of the agricultural products whose country of origin had either 'adopted the decision on introduction of economic sanctions in respect of Russian legal and (or) physical entities, or joined same'.

The EU sanctions against Russia, as well as the country's economic countermeasures, are causing grave economic losses for the EU countries, showing the high interdependency reached over time.[19] Russia has become the third trading partner of the EU and the EU is the first trading partner of Russia, as Moscow is the EU's most important single supplier of energy products, accounting for over 25 per cent of the EU consumption of oil and gas. In turn, Russia's economy remains highly dependent on the export of energy raw materials, with the EU as its most important destination. The EU has so far been the most important investor in Russia. It is estimated that up to 75 per cent of Foreign Direct Investment stocks in Russia come from EU Member States including Cyprus (European Commission Directorate-General for Trade, 2014).

Despite the hard line undertaken by the EU with the sanctions, a compromise approach was agreed for the signature of the AA with Ukraine. This in fact occurred in two different phases: the political provisions of the Treaty were signed on 21 March 2014, after the ousting of the then incumbent President Yanukovych, while the section dedicated to trade integration was put on hold (awaiting the results of the 25 May 2014 Ukrainian presidential elections). The EU realised too late that it was in the middle of a geopolitical game. As Techau (2014) pointed out, 'The EU brought a low-politics toolbox to a high-politics construction site'. Only when the pro-EU President Petro Poroshenko took office (27 June 2014) did the EU and Ukraine sign the economic part of the AA (a Deep and Comprehensive Free Trade Agreement (DCFTA), together with Moldova and Georgia. On 12 September, however, EU Trade Commissioner De Gucht announced that an agreement had been reached between the EU, Russia and Ukraine to delay the implementation of the DCFTA. The postponement of the DCFTA was meant to give Moscow an additional incentive to stick to a ceasefire that Russia, Russian-supported rebels and the Ukrainian government had agreed to on 5 September, 2014.

On the one hand, the delay of the DCFTA lessens the EU's economic leverage on the country (the European institutions will find it more difficult to hold the Ukrainian government accountable for its promises, unless there is a realistic plan of reforms agreed); on the other hand, some have argued that, from an economic standpoint, the deal is relatively positive for Ukraine, because it relieves the pressure to adapt to EU norms immediately and maintains free trade with Russia intact. In terms of power politics, the break-up and postponement of the AA marks the success of Russia's behaviour. It seems that Ukraine was forced by Russia to delay the full implementation of its AA as Moscow threatened the renewal of military action and a complete economic blockade if Ukraine did not postpone implementation. The EU also wanted to address the diffuse criticism that it had ignored Russian geopolitical concerns regarding the EaP and the AA. So, the compromise on the postponement of the DCFTA was considered a quite affordable solution, both economically and politically. The EU would not have renounced its EaP policy, while Russia would not have adopted retaliation measures while continuing to negotiate a solution for the Ukraine's secessionist regions.

Besides the compromise reached by the parties on the AA, the West and the EU perceived Russia's behaviour in Ukraine as a break with the country's previous international commitments and a disruption of the existing international order (Makarychev and Yatsyk, 2014, p. 63). As McFaul (2014) put it, 'Since the late Gorbachev–Reagan years, the era was defined by zigzags of cooperation and disputes between Russia and the West, but always with an underlying sense that Russia was gradually joining the international order. No more.'

Conclusion

The analysis of EU–Russia relations confirms that the very hybrid nature of the EU has prevented it from crafting a sound and credible policy. The EU approach towards Russia is mostly of an intergovernmental nature and lacks a long-term strategy on how to restructure the pan-European space after the end of the Cold War. These two elements have made the EU policy vis-à-vis the Kremlin essentially reactive and not proactive. Systematically reassessing the strategy in response to the Russian moves has also reduced the European room for manoeuvre while diminishing its leverage.

The EU's position in the relationship has suffered from the mutable divisions within the organisation. Any time the EU is dealing with contentious issues affecting sensitive EU members' interests, these members promptly either try to dictate the EU's CFSP direction, or just outstrip it. This has also regularly happened in the case of Russia.

A number of EU states have been circumspect and cautious towards Russia, while some others have been more inclined to strengthen cooperation. Different attitudes are explainable partly in terms of economic interdependence (often energy supplies dependency), partly in terms of what Constructivists would call identity items, and finally also in terms of values. Italy, Germany and France's benevolence reflects these countries' economic interests (e.g. pipeline projects, energy dependency and military sales); Poland and the Baltic States' firmness is due to their experience of the Soviet legacy and consequent fears of a Russian revanchism; while Sweden and the UK find the Kremlin's domestic verticalisation of power and the external mounting aggressiveness incompatible with the European values implicit in the broad definition of a democratic state. The different factors behind EU Member States' various stances on Russia show that no single theoretical approach alone is explanatory. While for some countries Realism is a valuable account, for others more intangible factors come into play. Actually, each stage of the relationship might fit a different theoretical approach.

In general, the EU has opted for a path dependency approach, giving prominence to the traditional tools for dealing with third countries. The progressive institutionalisation of the relationship through a well-experienced sequence has sometimes been obstructed by those members who in the past suffered from the Soviet legacy. Energy dependency and economic interdependency account for some other members pressing for an improvement of the relationship. The most innovative and potentially fruitful policy – the PfM – put forward by the EU responds to a more cooperative climate. It is also an attempt to depoliticise the partnership and lessen tensions. The underpinning idea is that a more neutral cooperation might in the long run contribute to Russia's transformation into a more democratic country. In this case, the EU has preferred to favour a pragmatic selective cooperation rather than binding it to the respecting of certain conditions (norms-based) on the part of the Kremlin. This formula, however, has not prevented a dramatic deterioration of the relationship as in the case of Ukraine. The management of the post-Soviet space has become the most conflictual topic between Brussels and Moscow.

While claiming to exert its normative/transformative power in the neighbourhood, the EU has de facto put forward a plan that has solid geopolitical implications and that clashes with an alternative project sponsored by Moscow. Russia, on the other hand, has been so clever in portraying its strategy for controlling the near abroad as a *normative* project that in fact is trying to reproduce the successful path of European integration. The EU has produced a policy that might have been conceived as normative, but whose impact has not been positive, as demonstrated by Russia's hard reaction in Ukraine. Already, when the Russia military intervened in Georgia, the EU was split over its response. That happened again as Russia annexed Crimea. This time, though, also under US pressure, the EU Member States finally agreed on economic sanctions as a coercive measure. This manifestation of hard power has nevertheless gone along with a lack of strategy on how to manage the overall situation. In the wake of politics, the institutions have reacted by adapting the usual tools to unexpected events (e.g. the reproposal of the AA to Ukraine despite the country's instability).

To conclude, the EU's policy towards Russia is very puzzling due to its being a unique political entity which acts in multiform ways that cannot be ascribed to a clear-cut theoretical framework. On the contrary, an eclectic approach combining different contributions appears the most appropriate.

Notes

1 There are significant differences among EU members in terms of trade: Germany (with €27.4 billion or 30 per cent of EU exports) was by far the largest exporter to Russia in the first nine months of 2013, followed by Italy (€8.0 billion, 9 per cent), the Netherlands and Poland (both €6.1 billion or 7 per cent). Germany (with imports worth €28.8 billion, 19 per cent of EU imports) was also the largest importer, followed by the Netherlands (€22.4 billion, 14 per cent), Italy (€14.9 billion, 10 per cent) and Poland (€13.9 billion, 9 per cent). Twenty Member States recorded deficits in trade with Russia in the first nine months of 2013, the largest being observed in the Netherlands (€–16.3 billion), Poland (€–7.8 billion), Italy (€–6.8 billion) and Greece (€–4.8 billion). Surpluses were modest, the highest being recorded in Austria (€+1.2 billion). Just over 85 per cent of EU28 exports to Russia in the first nine months of 2013 were manufactured goods, while energy accounted for nearly 80 per cent of imports (Eurostat, 2014).
2 Also Bulmer and Radaelli (2013, p. 359) claim that 'virtually every policy area is now affected to a greater or lesser extent by the EU'.
3 The fact that it was part of the intergovernmental pillar is particularly significant for the decision-making procedure: indeed, in contrast to areas belonging to the Community pillar, in order to make decisions in intergovernmental domains a consensus, and not a majority, was needed. Moreover, the role of European institutions in the intergovernmental pillar is much more limited.
4 Article 2 of the Common Provisions stated that one of the objectives of the Union is 'to assert its identity on the international scene, in particular through the implementation of a common foreign and security policy, including the eventual framing of a common defence policy, which might in time lead to a common defence'.
5 Since the end of the 1990s, the EU has concluded similar Partnership and Cooperation Agreements with Armenia, Azerbaijan, Georgia, Kazakhstan, Kyrgyzstan, Moldova, Ukraine, Uzbekistan and Tajikistan. These agreements seek to provide a suitable framework for political dialogue; support the efforts made by the countries to strengthen their democracies and develop their economies; accompany their transition to a market economy; and encourage trade and investment. The partnerships also aim to provide a basis for cooperation in the legislative, economic, social, financial, scientific, civil, technological and cultural fields. The PCA with Russia also provides for

the creation of the necessary conditions for the future establishment of a free trade area.

6 The EU conditionality – setting rules as conditions that the recipients have to fulfil in order to receive rewards – has, for instance, shaped the Central and Eastern European countries, which were obliged to develop their administrative capacities in complete convergence with the *acquis communautaire* in order to join the Union. The ENP still conceptually relies on conditionality as the main tool to promote legislative approximation.

7 See NATO's website: www.nato.int/cps/en/natohq/topics_50091.htm.

8 Russia strongly opposed the system and proposed as an alternative the Qabala Radar in Azerbaijan, which Russia leased, but Washington refused the offer. The Kremlin threatened to place short-range nuclear missiles on its borders with NATO if the US went ahead with the project. In April 2007, then President Putin warned of a new Cold War if Washington deployed the shield in Central Europe. Putin also affirmed that Russia was ready to relinquish its obligations under the Nuclear Forces Treaty of 1987 with the US. The Obama administration stopped the project in 2009.

9 At the EU–Russia Summit in Brussels (15 December 2011) the parties agreed on the implementation of common steps towards visa-free short-term travel for Russian and European citizens. This consists of a list of actions for both the EU and Russia to implement in preparation for visa-free travel for short-term stays. These concern document security, for example the introduction of biometric passports; combating illegal immigration and border management; and public order, security and judicial cooperation, including the fight against transnational organised crime, terrorism and corruption.

10 Similarly to perestroika, the plan for modernisation sought to make the system survive, not to replace it. President Medvedev clearly explained that modernisation does not entail radical and revolutionary changes:

> Hasty and ill-considered political reforms have led to tragic consequences more than once in our history. They have pushed Russia to the brink of collapse. We cannot risk our social stability and endanger the safety of our citizens for the sake of abstract theories. We are not entitled to sacrifice stable life, even for the highest goals.
>
> (Medvedev, 2009)

11 See Program for Effective Utilization of Foreign Political Factors on a Systematic Basis for Purposes of Long-Term Development of the Russian Federation published by *The Russian Newsweek Magazine* (10 February 2010).

12 The PCA is more constraining, compared to the PfM. Article 55 of the PCA asserts that an important condition for strengthening the economic links between the two parties is the approximation of legislation and that, to this purpose, 'Russia shall endeavour to ensure that its legislation will be gradually made compatible with that of the Community'. The PCA, however, did not provide the basis for obligatory, but rather for voluntary, harmonisation; the only compulsory obligation was to 'endeavour to ensure' compatibility, but if an endeavour is not successful Russia cannot be accused of not having complied with the PCA.

13 Four platforms have been selected: democracy; good government and stability; economic integration and convergence with EU policy; and securing energy and contacts between peoples.

14 Interview reported by Euobserver, http://euobserver.com/foreign/27827, 21 March, 2009.

15 In his speech to the Federal Assembly on the occasion of the Crimean annexation, Putin (2014) affirmed:

> The Eurasian Union is a project for maintaining the identity of nations in the historical Eurasian space in a new century and in a new world. Eurasian integration is a

chance for the entire post-Soviet space to become an independent centre for global development, rather than remaining on the outskirts of Europe and Asia.

(Putin, 2014)

16 According to Putin's doctrine, as Aron (2013) explains,

> the pursuit of regional hegemony has acquired a new dimension: an attempt at the 'Finlandisation' of the post-Soviet states, harkening back to the Soviet Union's control over Finland's foreign policy during the Cold War. In such an arrangement, Moscow would allow its neighbours to choose their own domestic political and economic systems but maintain final say over their external orientation.

(Aron, 2013)

17 The West's fitful response to Russian tactics has most likely been the product of a disagreement between hardliners in the US state department and a more reticent Germany supported by Italy. Like their German counterparts, which have publicly lobbied against more broad-based economic sanctions, Italian companies have deep and long-standing ties to Russia. Diplomats from governments who wanted to get tough on the Kremlin have accused Rome of sapping momentum from the sanctions drive to placate Italian industry (The *Financial Times*, 2014).

18 Cyprus and Hungary are allegedly already pushing for a broad sanctions review and Greece, Italy and Slovakia would support a partial rollback. Diplomatic sources say the Czech Republic is also wobbly. The UK, the Baltic States, Poland and Sweden are the most hawkish. France and Germany are not siding for now (Euobserver, 2014).

19 The flow of trade between Russia and the EU showed steep growth rates until mid-2008, when the trend was interrupted by the economic crisis, only to resume again in 2010 and reach record levels in 2012. In the first nine months of 2013, compared with the first nine months of 2012, EU28 exports to Russia fell slightly and imports decreased.

References

Armstrong, D., Lloyd, L. and Redmond, J. (1996) *From Versailles to Maastricht: International Organisation in the Twentieth Century*. London: MacMillan Press.

Aron, L. (2013) The Putin Doctrine. *Foreign Affairs*. 8 March. [Online]. Available from: www.foreignaffairs.com/articles/139049/leon-aron/the-putin-doctrine [accessed: 10 February 2015].

Bulmer, S. and Radaelli, R. (2013) The Europeanization of Member States Policy. In Bulmer, S. and Lequesne, C. (eds) *The Member States of the European Union*. 2nd ed. Oxford: Oxford University Press. pp. 357–83.

Bulmer, S. J. and Radaelli, C. M. (2004) The Europeanisation of national policy? *Queen's Papers on Europeanisation* No. 1/2004.

Butorina, O. (2013) *European Union and Russian Partnership Without Strategy*. Russian Council, 26 April. [Online]. Available from: http://russiancouncil.ru/en/inner/?id_4 =1766#top [accessed: 11 February 2015].

Caporaso, J. (1996) The European Union and Forms of State: Westphalian, Regulatory or Post-modern? *Journal of Common Market Studies*. 34 (1). pp. 29–52.

Council of the European Union (2009) *Joint Declaration of the Prague Eastern Partnership Summit*. Prague May 7. [Online]. Available from: www.consilium.europa.eu/ uedocs/cms_data/docs/pressdata/en/er/107589.pdf [accessed: 11 February 2015].

DeBardeleben, J. (2009) The impact of EU Enlargement on the EU–Russian Relationship. In Kanet R. E. (ed.) *A Resurgent Russia and the West. The European Union, NATO and Beyond*. Dordrecht: Republic of Letters Publishing, pp. 93–112.

Eurobserver (2014) *Russia Targets Cyprus, Hungary, and Italy for Sanctions Veto*. 11 December. [Online]. Available from: https://euobserver.com/foreign/126879 [accessed: 11 February 2015].

European Commission (2009) *Report: Five Years of an Enlarged EU. Economic Achievements and Challenges*. [Online]. Available from: http://ec.europa.eu/news/economy/090220_1_en.htm [accessed: 11 February 2015].

European Commission (2005) *Values Define Europe, Not Borders*. [Online]. Available from: www.ec.europa.eu/commission_barroso/rehn/pdf/statements/rehn_ft_european_values_en.pdf [accessed: 11 February 2015].

European Commission (2000) *Social Policy Agenda 2000–2005*, Brussels, COM (2000) 379 final. Eurostat (2014).

European Commission Directorate-General for Trade (2014) *Russia – Trade Statistics*. [Online]. Available from: http://ec.europa.eu/trade/policy/countries-and-regions/countries/russia/ [accessed: 11 February 2015].

Eurostat, European Commission, European Union Trade in goods with Russia, Directoral General for Trade, http://trade.ec.europa.eu/doclib/docs/2006/september/tradoc_113440.pdf

Featherstone, K. and Radaelli, C. M. (eds) (2003) *The Politics of Europeanization*. Oxford: Oxford University Press.

Financial Times (2014) *Italy accused of blocking tougher sanctions on Russia*. July 13.

Giusti, S. (2011) *Russia's Modernizing Alliance with the EU*. ISPI Studies. September. [Online]. Available from: www.ispionline.it/it/documents/Pages%20from%20MAE_RUSSIA%20June%202011-%20Serena%20Giusti.pdf [accessed: 11 February 2015].

Giusti, S. and Ceccorulli, M. (2015) *From Soviet Satellite to Regional Power: Poland after 1989*. Washington, DC: The Brookings Institute. forthcoming.

Giusti, S. and Penkova, T. (2008) *Russia: Just a Normal Great Power?* ISPI Working Paper 34. October. [Online]. Available from: www.ispionline.it/sites/default/files/pubblicazioni/wp_34_2008_0.pdf [accessed: 11 February 2015].

Gorbachev, M. (1989) *Council of Europe, Official Report, Forty-first Ordinary Session*. 8–12 May and 3–7 July. Vol. I. Sittings 1 to 9. 1990. pp. 197–205.

Hadfield, A. (2012) Energy and Foreign Policy: EU–Russia Energy Dynamics. In Smith, S., Hadfield, A. and Dunne, T. (eds) *Foreign Policy: Theories, Actors, Cases*. Oxford: Oxford University Press.

Hillion, C. (2010) The Creeping Nationalism of the EU Enlargement Process. Sieps n.6. Available from: www.sieps.se/sites/default/files/2010_6_.pdf [accessed: 11 February 2015].

Hillion, C. (2000) Common Strategies and the Interface between EC External Relations and CFSP in Dashwood, A. and Hillion, C. (eds) *The General Law of EC External Relations* London: Sweet & Maxwell, pp. 287–301

Lavrov, S. (2007) *Speech by Minister of Foreign Affairs of the Russian Federation Sergey Lavrov at the XV Assembly of the Council on Foreign and Defense Policy*, 17 March. [Online]. Available from: www.mid.ru/brp_4.nsf/e78a48070f128a7b43256999005b-cbb3/b31681458d90c7b8c32572a3004992f5?OpenDocument [accessed: 11 February 2015].

Layne, C. (2006) The Unipolar Illusion Revisited: The Coming End of the United States Unipolar Moment. *International Security*. 31 (2). pp. 7–41.

Leonard, M. and Popescu, N. (2007) *A Power Audit of EU–Russia Relations*. London: ECFR.

Levi, M. (1997) A Model, a Method, and a Map: Rational Choice in Comparative and Historical Analysis. In Lichbach, M. and Zuckerman, A. (eds) *Comparative Politics:*

Rationality, Culture, and Structure. Cambridge: Cambridge University Press, pp. 19–41.

London School of Economics (2013) *The Crisis of EU Enlargement.* Special Report, LSE Ideas [Online]. Available from: www.lse.ac.uk/IDEAS/publications/reports/SR018. aspx [accessed: 11 February 2015].

McFaul, M. A. (2014) Confronting Putin's Russia. *New York Times*, March 2014.

Makarychev, A. and Yatsyk, A. (2014) The Four Pillars of Russia's Power Narrative. *The International Spectator.* 49 (4). pp. 62–75.

Mankoff, J. (2012) *Russian Foreign Policy.* Lanham, MD: Rowman and Littlefield Publishers.

Manners, I. (2002) Normative Power Europe: A Contradiction in Terms? *Journal of Common Market Studies.* 40 (2). pp. 235–58.

Mearsheimer, J. (1990) Back to the Future. *International Security.* 15 (1). pp. 5–56.

Medvedev, D. (2009) Rossiyavperëd. Stat'ya Prezidenta Dmitriya Medvedeva, 9 September [Online]. Available from: www.kremlin.ru/news/5413 [accessed: 11 February 2015].

Medvedev, D. (2008a) Speech at Evian. [Online]. Available from: www.kremlin.ru/eng/speeches/2008/10/08/2159_type82912type82914_207457.shtm [accessed: 11 February 2015].

Medvedev, D. (2008b) President of Russia Dmitry Medvedev's Speech at Meeting with German Political, Parliamentary and Civic Leaders., Berlin, 5 June, 2008, Ministry of Foreign Affairs of the Russian Federation, Information and Press Department. [Online]. Available from: www.ln.mid.ru/brp_4.nsf/e78a48070f128a7b43256999005bcbb3/c080 dc2ff8d93629c3257460003496c4? [accessed: 11 February 2015].

Penkova T. (2014) The Vilnius Summit and Ukraine's Revolution as a Benchmark for EU Eastern Partnership Policy. *ISPI Analysis No. 240*, March. [Online]. Available from: www.ispionline.it/sites/default/files/pubblicazioni/analysis_240__2014.pdf [accessed: 11 February 2015].

Pridham, G. (2014) EU/Ukraine Relations and the Crisis with Russia, 2013–14: A Turning Point. *The International Spectator.* 49. (December). pp. 53–61.

Prizel, I. (1998) *National Identity and Foreign Policy.* Cambridge: Cambridge University Press, pp. 239–40.

Putin, V. (2014) Address by President of the Russian Federation. Moscow, 18 March. [Online]. Available from: http://eng.kremlin.ru/news/6889 [accessed: 11 February 2015].

Rosato, S. (2011) *Europe United: Power Politics and the Making of the European Community.* Ithaca, NY, Cornell University Press.

Schimmelfennig, F. and Sedelmeier, U. (2002) The Europeanisation of Eastern Europe. Evaluating the Conditionality Model. *Paper for the ECFR Workshop on European Governance on Enlargement*, Turin.

Techau, J. (2014) Europe's Five Deadly Sins on Ukraine. Euractiv.com, 27 August. [Online]. Available from: www.euractiv.com/europes-east [accessed: 11 February 2015].

Trenin, D. (2010) Russia's Conservative Modernisation: A Mission Impossible? *SAIS Review.* 30 (1). Winter–Spring, pp. 27–37.

Van Herpen, M. H. (2008) Medvedev's Proposal for a Pan European Security Pact. Cicero Working Paper. [Online]. Available from: www.cicerofoundation.org/lectures/Marcel_H_Van_Herpen_Medvedevs_Proposal_for_a_Pan-European_Security_Pact. pdf [accessed: 11 February 2015].

Wiśniewski, P. D. (2013) The Eastern Partnership – It is High Time to Start a Real Partnership, Carnegie Moscow, November [Online]. Available from: http://carnegieendowment.org/files/CP_Wisniewski_Eng_web.pdf [accessed: 11 February 2015].

Zakaria, F. (1997) The Rise of Illiberal Democracy. *Foreign Affairs*. 76 (6). November/December, pp. 22–43.

11 The EU's foreign policy towards the Israeli–Palestinian conflict

A story of underachievement?

Lorenzo Cladi

Introduction

After almost five decades of European involvement in the Israeli–Palestinian (I–P) conflict, only one truthful statement seems to hold: the European Union (EU) Member States agree on the two-state solution but there remain significant divisions as to how to achieve this objective. The chapter argues that the dominance of the United States (US) as a third party mediator throughout the period under consideration has both enabled as well as hindered European involvement. On top of that, the European approach towards the I–P conflict has not appeared credible in several instances due to the internal divisions among the Member States of the European Community (EC)/EU. The degree of involvement of the EC/EU in the I–P has gradually risen, but this has gone hand in hand with the EC/EU's ability to tie its preferences to the US. The more the EU distances itself from the US, the less influential it is. At the same time, however, by tying its preferences to the US, the EU has compromised over its normative values, thus giving less credibility to its approach.

In terms of involvement, the EC/EU has made substantial progress concerning the I–P conflict. In the early days of the Cold War, the EC was a mere declaratory actor. In the post-Cold War period it was recognised as an economic actor by the US and in the post 9/11 period it was also recognised as a diplomatic actor. While the EU has become more involved, its influence has been limited by external factors such as the US dominance as a third party and internal divisions among its Member States.

The chapter proceeds as follows: the first section reviews the formation of a European stance during the Cold War. This is important as it highlights a number of themes that would set the European foreign policy towards the I–P conflict in the years to come. First, the EC's commitment to the principle of Palestinian self-determination, the commitment to Palestinian state-building and the need to work towards a two-state solution. In other words, the EC set the normative tone of its engagement during the Cold War, but at the time it was not recognised as a player by any of the parties involved. The second section is about the European foreign policy towards the I–P conflict during the 1990s. The most important change that occurred in the post-Cold War period was that the US welcomed the

EU's new approach to the I–P conflict, based on economic but not diplomatic involvement. The third section is about the post 9/11 period and it focuses, in particular, on the work of the Quartet for Peace. In the post 9/11 period there was another important change, as the EU had the chance to work in conflict resolution, it was welcomed by the US into the Quartet and there was a significant level of diplomatic convergence between the US and the EU for the first time. In the post 9/11 period, the EU had the chance to become more influential as its diplomatic involvement appeared to be desired by the US. However, during this period, the EU took some important decisions that contradicted its normative power. The last section reviews developments in recent years and it focuses, in particular, on the UN vote in September 2011 to upgrade Palestine to non-member observer state. The evidence shows that the EU lost another important opportunity to be more influential as it showed significant divisions among its members.

The formation of a European stance on the I–P conflict during the Cold War

Europe has sought to assert its influence in the I–P conflict since the creation of the state of Israel in 1948 and the consequent problem regarding the issue of the Palestinian refugees. In the decades from the creation of the state of Israel and the launch of the European Political Cooperation (EPC) in 1970 no single European position emerged.

At first, Israel was suspicious of German involvement because of the all too clear memory of the Holocaust; it was also against British involvement because of the UK's previous attempts to stop the entry of refugees and immigrants prior to 1948 (Newman and Yacobi, 2004). France was instead Israel's most important European ally and arms supplier from 1948 up until the 1967 Arab–Israeli conflict (Lewis, 1999). In 1965, Germany and Israel established formal diplomatic relations and the former gradually became Israel's closest ally (Lavy, 1996). Nevertheless, Israel would always be able to play the guilt card every time the statements of German politicians looked closer to the Palestinians (Wolffsohn, 1993).

The 1967 Arab–Israeli War was a watershed event in terms of future European involvement in the I–P conflict, as it brought France's cooperation with Israel to a halt and it changed future European and American approaches to it. Charles De Gaulle banned all arms deliveries to frontline states in the 1967 conflict, a move that clearly undermined Israel in light of the arms sales of the preceding years (McDowall, 1990). The conflict was also perceived in different ways in Washington and the European capitals: whereas Americans saw the 1967 war as an unavoidable historical event, as it put the survival of Israel at stake, Europeans viewed the war as the forerunner of the 'illegal Israeli occupation of Palestinian land' (Kaye, 2003, p. 186). Furthermore, Republican and Democratic administrations alike started to see Israel as the state that had defeated two Soviet client states in the 1967 war (Quandt, 2006). The break-up of French–Israeli strategic relationship paved the way for the beginning of the US–Israeli strategic relationship and France's rapprochement with Arab states. The formation of the EPC in 1970 provided the French with an opportunity to highlight the Middle East dispute as a European issue (Gfeller, 2012). Notwithstanding this, the French concern with the Arab situation was not shared by all the EC Member States. For instance, whereas the Italian position was in line with the French one, other countries such as Germany and the Netherlands were supportive of Israel, and Belgium remained neutral (Dosenrode and Stubkjaer, 2002). While initial agreement among the six members of the EC was not easy to achieve, the 1971 Schuman document was consistent with UN Resolution 242, in which the issue of Palestinian refugees was raised for the first time (Nuttall, 1992). In 1971, the EC also began to assist the Palestinians economically, as the first contribution was made to the regular budget of the United Nations Relief and Works Agency for Palestine refugees in the Near East (Ginsberg, 2001).

The October 1973 Arab–Israeli War was another important external factor influencing the EC to push the Middle East agenda forward. In late October 1973, the Europeans were not included in the negotiations for a ceasefire between the parties of the Yom Kippur War. As noted above, despite the apparent unity showed by the Schuman Declaration, the Europeans remained too divided to be considered as a credible party for the negotiations: France took the side of the Arabs, whereas the Netherlands held Egypt and Syria responsible for the outbreak of the conflict (Mueller, 2013).

While agreement was harder to reach among the nine before the 1973 Arab–Israeli war, the Arab oil embargo by OPEC countries in response to US military aid to Israel prompted the EC to reassess its policy towards the Middle Eastern conflict (Hamilton, 2006). The EC reacted to the Arab oil embargo with the Brussels Declaration on 6 November 1973, where the nine agreed on the following points:

I   the inadmissibility of the acquisition of territory by force;
II the need for Israel to end the territorial occupation which it has maintained since the conflict of 1967;
III respect for the sovereignty, territorial integrity and independence of every State in the area and their right to live in peace within secure and recognised boundaries;
IV recognition that in the establishment of a just and lasting peace account must be taken of the legitimate rights of the Palestinians.

(Brussels Declaration, 1973)

Nevertheless, the apparent unity manifested by the nine with the Brussels Declaration masked notable differences in their national approaches, which arguably prevented the Europeans from taking any concrete steps beyond the declaration, leaving the resolution of the problem in the hands of the superpowers. There was a significant division between France and the UK over whether the EC should take the lead in conflict resolution in the Middle East. Whereas France ideally wanted the EC to engage in conflict resolution without relying on the US, the UK preferred to keep the US involved. The UK subscribed to the Brussels Declaration as it had just joined the EC, but it urged the French not to include reference to the UN Security Council playing a greater role in the negotiations (Hamilton, 2006). As the Europeans faced the oil embargo posed by OPEC countries, 'the declaration agreed by EC ministers on 6 November was in part intended to shield those Member States, such as the Netherlands, whose position the Arabs considered too sympathetic to Israel, against the rigors of a reinforced oil embargo' (Hamilton, 2006, p. 885). As noted by Ilan Greilsammer and Joseph Weiler (1984, p. 135), the EPC allowed the Member States to 'shift the forum of foreign policymaking outside the national capitals' and to use Europe's common foreign policy 'as a justification for a posture which might not have been possible for a government to adopt independently at home'.

The EC reiterated its position on 29 June 1977, as the nine proclaimed that any negotiation should include Palestinian representation and that any settlement must acknowledge the right to a Palestinian homeland (Aoun, 2003). Subsequently, with the Venice Declaration of June 1980, the EC outlined its clearest vision for the solution of the I–P conflict (Altunisk, 2008). With the Venice Declaration, the Europeans did not only reaffirm their support for the Palestinian right to self-determination and the importance of ending the occupation of lands that had taken place since 1967, but also laid out a vision for the negotiation and settlement process itself through a negotiation with the two sides and a rejection of unilateral action (Venice Declaration, 1980). As David Allen and Michael Smith (1984, p. 187) argue, the Venice Declaration 'can be seen as a direct reaction to the American sponsored Camp David process'. The Venice Declaration 'constituted an absolute success for the system of European political cooperation and contributed to the upgrading of the European role as a diplomatic actor in the international scene' (Gianniou, 2006, p. 5).

Yet, the upgrading of the EC as a diplomatic actor occurred without external recognition by the US and Israel (Altunisk, 2008). The influence of the EC upon the I–P conflict remained scarcely significant during the Cold War. Deep divisions among the nine also prevented the EC from being as influential as planned and the tone of the Venice Declaration was lowered. In fact, as Rory Miller notes,

> it played safe by calling for PLO association rather than participation in future peace negotiations. In these terms the Venice Declaration failed to provide a real alternative to Camp David because it refused to give formal recognition to the PLO or to express explicit support for the establishment of a Palestinian State. This left the Community with no more influence over the PLO after the document had been published than before.
>
> (2013, p. 171)

The EC was able to act normatively in international politics by virtue of its common declarations. It also achieved the important result of bringing the

Palestinian issue to international attention. Following the Venice Declaration the EC did not have chances to become involved again in the I–P conflict and it took nearly two decades before the EU brought the Palestinian issue to attention. The EC's willingness to get involved was remarkable, as with EPC the Europeans for the first time showed unity of intent in a region where they had traditionally maintained diverging foreign policy preferences. Nevertheless, the divisions between single European governments remained and the EC's approach was therefore not influential. Furthermore, the EC's approach was not endorsed by the US, thus limiting the extent to which the EC's normative approach could prove of any benefit beyond declaratory politics.

The EU's position from Madrid to Camp David: economically active, diplomatically marginalised

The post-Cold War period opened up space for a renewed European involvement in the I–P conflict. In light of the demise of the Soviet Union, the US could now exert unprecedented influence in the I–P conflict and the extent to which the European allies could carve out a space to act in the conflict was dependent upon the US's willingness to allow European involvement.

The EC had the opportunity to become involved with the I–P conflict again as the Madrid conference was launched by the US and the Soviet Union. President George H. W. Bush, in his opening remarks, stated that

> the objective must be clear and straightforward. It is not simply to end the state of war in the Middle East and replace it with non-belligerency. This is not enough. This would not last. Rather, we seek peace, real peace. And by real peace, I mean treaties, security, and diplomatic relations.
>
> (Bush, 1991)

The EC was invited as an observer to the Madrid conference and the principles it had advocated during the Cold War, such as the importance of including a Palestinian delegation in the negotiations, were endorsed by the superpowers (Susser, 2012). Yet, the EC would not be able to take credit for it: the tone set by the US President meant that, while other actors such as the EC would be invited to attend the conference, US leadership in conflict resolution would not be under discussion.

The EC did not seek to counter the US as it had done with the Venice Declaration by responding to the US-sponsored Camp David agreement, but welcomed the US initiative as it was able to participate as an observer and to contribute financially to the peace process (Robin, 1997; Musu, 2011). In fact, the EC was awarded responsibility for the Regional Economic Development Working Group (REDWG) which, as Newman and Yacobi (2008, p. 182) remind us, 'brought together Palestinians, Israelis, Jordanians and Egyptians who jointly developed ideas for several economic cooperation projects in the region'. The EC could now back its 1980 Venice Declaration with practical means (Altunisik, 2008). Through the REDWG, the EC would be able to provide funds for initiatives such as the set-up of the Palestinian Authority (PA) that took place in 1994 (Persson, 2014). The US acknowledged that the EC had a comparative advantage in the sphere of financial aid, and the Europeans were able to be more involved in the peace process. At the same time, however, the US had awarded the EC an economic, not political role, in the conflict. In fact, as Persson (2014, p. 117) argues, the EC only had the role of 'observer', this being a sign of its marginalisation from a diplomatic point of view. Moreover, the conference defied several cardinal points of European foreign policy towards the I–P conflict: the conference was sponsored by the superpowers, not by the United Nations (UN), the Palestine Liberation Organisation (PLO) had not been associated, the Palestinians had no separate delegation and Palestinians residents of Jerusalem could not take part at the request of Israel (Pardo and Peters, 2010).

In 1993, the EU supported the Oslo Accords, the first direct agreement between Israel and representatives of the Palestinians (Bouris, 2010; Pressman, 2007; Cordesman, 2005). The inclusion of the Palestinians as legitimate partners in the peace process was the realisation of what the EC had in fact wished for in the 1970s. In 1995, the EU then sought to *regionalise* the I–P conflict, which was seen as an obstacle to the implementation of broader aims of good governance, stability and wealth in the region as stated by the European Mediterranean Policy programme (Asseburg, 2002). The programme would give the EU more visibility in the region and allowed the EU to assert the view that any peace agreement would be sustainable if backed up by cooperation among civil societies, economic integration and cultural links (Asseburg, 2002).

On the diplomatic front, the US continued to maintain the lead and 'expected the Europeans to be supportive but in the background' (Hollis, 2013, p. 340). The EU went along with this but it became concerned as it observed lack of progress after Oslo as far as peace was concerned. The return to power of the Likud party under the leadership of Benjamin Netanyahu in 1996 meant that Israel would be firmly opposed to a 'Palestinian state, to the Palestinian right of return and to the dismantling of Jewish settlements' (Shlaim, 2005, p. 246). Netanyahu was critical of the EU's support for the PLO and in 1997 he urged the EU to adopt a 'balanced, factual and responsible position' on the relationship between the Israelis and the Palestinians (Inbar, 2007, p. 31). The EU, however, was unwilling to witness the collapse of the Oslo process, as this would have contributed to its further marginalisation.

The EU confirmed its support for Palestinian statehood with the important Berlin Declaration in 1999. As stated in the declaration,

> The European Union reaffirms the continuing and unqualified right to self-determination including the option of a state and looks forward to the early fulfilment of this right. It appeals to the parties to strive in good faith for a negotiated solution on the basis of existing agreements, without prejudice to this right, which is not subject to any veto. The European Union is

convinced that the creation of a democratic, viable and peaceful sovereign Palestinian State on the basis of existing agreements and through negotiations would be the best guarantee of Israel's security and Israel's acceptance as an equal partner in the region. The European Union declares its readiness to consider the recognition of a Palestinian State in due course in accordance with the basic principles outlined above.

(European Council, 1999)

With the election of the more moderate Labor party in Israel in 1999, the EU was hopeful that the peace talks would resume (Rynhold and Steinberg, 2004). Nevertheless, the Berlin Declaration did not serve any purpose from a diplomatic point of view, since the US maintained a firm grip on the peace process, as a summit took place in July 2000 between Clinton, Arafat and Barack. The summit failed, and the EU could do nothing but observe the deterioration of the situation. The outcome of the summit was negative, particularly for the issue of Palestinian refugees and the status of Jerusalem (Hanieh, 2001). At Camp David, the Israeli and the Palestinian delegations manifested opposing views over the 1948 Palestinian Nakba.[1] The failure of the summit at Camp David was not, arguably, completely unexpected. On a number of occasions during Clinton's presidencies, American actions particularly antagonised the Palestinians, leading to a growth of Anti-Americanism in the wider Arab world (Salt, 2008). For instance, the Palestinians did not favour change in US policy to one of support for the construction of settlements in east Jerusalem and the Congress' decision to move the US embassy to Jerusalem by 1999 (Pundak, 2001).

The EU could only stand on the side as the Camp David meeting failed. The principles it had affirmed in the Berlin Declaration were not taken into account and its efforts to promote economic growth through its financial instruments did not achieve significant results, as the second Intifada broke out in September 2000. As David Allen and Michael Smith (2001, p. 107) explain, '2000 was not a good year for the EU in the Middle East, despite the fact that a number of Arab States expressed a preference for a much stronger EU involvement in the peace process'.

Looking back over the 1990s, the EU was recognised as an economic actor by the US, and its financial aid did not achieve much in terms of conflict resolution, as evidenced by the eruption of violence with the second Intifada in 2000. The EU improved its status and took its financial commitments to the I–P conflict very seriously, and its efforts were accorded sympathy among the Palestinians. However, the EU gained hardly anything in terms of conflict resolution, as they only seemed to delay the eruption of violence as the second Intifada broke out (Meital, 2006). Furthermore, the exclusion of the EU from the peace process at Camp David shows that the EU's diplomatic involvement in the peace process was not yet endorsed by the US. What changed, compared to the Cold War years, was that the US welcomed European involvement, albeit from a financial point of view. As economic instruments turned out to be of secondary importance as the conflict escalated, European foreign policy towards the I–P conflict proved less influential (Keukeleire, 2003).

The Quartet for Peace and diplomatic convergence: more influence for the EU?

With the formation of the Quartet for Peace in Madrid in 2002, the US seemed to abandon its tendency to be the only third party between the Israelis and the Palestinians, as it committed itself to a multilateral framework alongside the EU, the UN and Russia (Bouris, 2010; Tocci, 2011). This was a major turning point for the aspirations of the EU to be considered as equal to the US in having political, not just economic, relevance to solve the conflict (Gianniou, 2006). Again, more European involvement came as a result of a US initiative.

Within the Quartet, the EU and the US showed a remarkable level of diplomatic convergence. In fact, for the first time the US demonstrated agreement with the two-state solution. In a speech delivered on 24 June 2002, US President George W. Bush stated 'We are working for the day when two states – Israel and Palestine – live peacefully together within secure and recognised boundaries' (quoted in Freedman, 2007, p. 287).

The work of the Quartet continued for half a year as a draft document of the Roadmap was completed in October 2002 and began to be circulated (Meital, 2006). The Roadmap was the first concerted effort by the EU and the US to solve the conflict and it 'endorsed many European positions' (Möckli, 2010, p. 67). The Roadmap foresaw three phases of implementation aimed at establishing a Palestinian state in three years: the first phase would be characterised by cessation of violence, Palestinian reform, including security sector reform, settlement freezes, Israeli withdrawal to the pre-intifada lines as the security situation improved, and Palestinian elections. Second, the creation of a Palestinian state with provisional borders would follow. Third, Israeli–Palestinian negotiations would take place with the view of them leading to a permanent status solution (Tocci, 2011).

The test for the Roadmap would be, however, the extent to which the EU and the US would be able to enforce the terms of the agreement on the parties involved. Israeli Prime Minister Ariel Sharon manifested his discontent with the document in January 2003, as he began downgrading the EU's role with statements such as 'To the European side I said ... your attitude towards Israel and the Arabs and the Palestinians should be balanced ... when it will be balanced you are mostly welcome to participate' (Bennett, 2003). In July 2003, Israel took the decision to build the so-called security fence, a wall intended to be 580 kilometres long at an estimated cost of $1.5 billion (Elizur, 2003). As Quandt (2006, p. 501) stresses, 'the barrier would follow the 1967 lines in some areas, while in others it would intrude into the West Bank in very disruptive ways for Palestinians'. To borrow from Salt (2008, p. 341), Israel sought 'to fragment the territories, to enclose and disarm the Palestinians, to stifle their economic and social development, to break them psychologically, and to prevent them from establishing anything that could be realistically called a state'.

At first, the EU and the US responded to Sharon's move in a similar way by expressing their concern. The US position, however, would soon be influenced by Bush's concern regarding the strongly pro-Israel conservative Christian supporters, as he urged Israel to 'consider the consequences of its actions on the peace process' (Cornwell, 2003). As Sharon insisted on the necessity of the fence to contain Palestinian terrorism, Bush later agreed on the fact that the latter was a fundamental obstacle to peace (Stout, 2003). At this point, the EU should have had to put pressure on Sharon in order for the Roadmap to survive. In 2004, the UN General Assembly (UNGA)

> approved a resolution overwhelmingly ... demanding that Israel obey a World Court ruling to abandon and dismantle its separation barrier on the West Bank and pay compensation to Palestinians affected by its construction. 150 members (including the entire EU) voted in favour and 6 against – including the United States, Australia and three small Pacific island countries – with 10 abstentions.
>
> (McGreal, 2004)

The EU showed exceptional unity in the UN vote and Israel significantly accused the EU of 'encouraging Palestinian terrorism' for backing the UN resolution. With the EU's stance rejected by Israel and with the US now having subscribed to Sharon's view, the EU preferred not to call for sanctions on Israel and not take the matter further (McGreal, 2004). This allowed the EU to remain within the Quartet but it significantly undermined the credibility of its normative approach. In particular, the EU came to compromise over its long-term strategy of state building by not further challenging Sharon's decision to build the fence.

The EU's long-term strategy of institution building and support for the PA was also challenged when Hamas won the Palestinian legislative election in the Gaza Strip in 2006. The coalition government of Fatah and Hamas had been a cornerstone of the EU's efforts and it broke down following the victory of Hamas. The credibility of the EU's approach was questioned as the EU sanctioned the party that had won elections that were classified as relatively 'free and fair' (Mueller, 2013, p. 20). It was not consistent with the EU's normative projection of democratic values and it undermined the credibility of the EU in the eyes of the Arabs. As Muriel Asseburg (2009, p. 38) reminds us, the EU's sanction of Hamas was 'an extremely dubious signal, both to authoritarian Arab regimes and to the Arab street'.

Again, the EU sided with the US, but doing so contradicted its approach. The Quartet developed three principles that demanded from Hamas a denunciation of violence, the recognition of Israel and the acceptance of previous agreements (Möckli, 2010, p. 67). When Hamas failed to comply, the EU followed the US and stopped all financial aid to Hamas, using its policy instrument of sanctions. In combination with Israel's blockade of the Gaza Strip, a humanitarian crisis ensued. By adopting the so-called *West Bank First* approach, the EU aimed at strengthening the government of Fayyad in the West Bank while cutting all ties to Hamas (Malley and Miller, 2007).

Nevertheless, *West Bank First* proved counterproductive: the EU's boycott of Hamas led to further radicalisation in the Gaza Strip and increased the polarisation between Hamas and Fatah (Mueller, 2011, p. 1). Even when Hamas and Fatah reconciled in 2007, the EU followed a strategy of isolating Hamas (Asseburg, 2009, p. 34). The boycott of Hamas can be seen as the only situation in which the EU exerted influence and imposed sanctions (Altunişik, 2008, p. 114). In doing so it sided with the US and Israel but it undermined its own strategy of Palestinian reconciliation and institution building. The EU's help with humanitarian assistance to alleviate the consequences for the Palestinians in the Gaza Strip was remarkable, but it was a proposed solution to a situation indirectly provoked by the EU.

With the EU and the US now having given in to Israel's pressure, the EU also sought to advance its role by focussing on security. To this end, it launched two important European Security and Defence Policy missions which are still ongoing: EUBAM Rafah and EUPOL COPPS. EUBAM Rafah started in November 2005 and four EU Member States are contributing. The object of the mission was for the EU to 'undertake the role of third party at the Rafah Crossing Point, on the border between the Gaza Strip and Egypt, to inter alia monitor and verify the performance of the PA border and customs authorities' (European Union External Action, 2013). The mission suffered a temporary setback on 13 June 2007, following Hamas's takeover of the Gaza Strip, but on July 2013 the Council extended its mandate until 30 June 2014 (Bulut, 2009; European Union External Action 2013). EUPOL COPPS was deployed in November 2005 in the West Bank following the Palestinian request for support in taking responsibility for law and order and, in particular, to help improve 'its civil police and law enforcement capacity' (European Council, 2012).

At the Quartet's inception, the EU's position could be summarised, as Youngs (2006, p. 162) has stressed, as 'we help build the Palestinian state first, then we aim to perfect democracy'. Bush's commitment to the Roadmap got weaker and weaker as the White House brought its position closer and closer to Israel, and the EU took important decisions to side with the US. The EU's foreign policy decision to impose sanctions on Hamas proved influential, but at the cost of a compromise over its normative values.

The post-Lisbon Treaty years: the choice for the EU

After the Lisbon Treaty, the EU moved from single to triple representation in the Quartet with the newly established office of the High Representative of the Union for Foreign Affairs and Security Policy (HR) and the appointment of Catherine Ashton, but the unanimity-based decision-making procedure of the CSFP remained in place.

The immediate post-Lisbon years were characterised by diplomatic convergence between the EU and the US. US President Obama, in a keynote speech delivered in Cairo in 2009, asserted that the only resolution is for the aspirations of both sides to be met through two states, where Israelis and Palestinians each live in peace and security [and] Israelis must acknowledge that just as Israel's right to exist cannot be denied, neither can Palestine's.

(Obama, 2009)

In 2010, Catherine Ashton also gave a speech in Cairo in which she highlighted that

Our aim is a viable State of Palestine in the West Bank including East Jerusalem and the Gaza Strip, on the basis of the 1967 lines ... the EU position on settlements is clear ... settlements are illegal, constitute an obstacle to peace and threaten to make a two-state solution impossible. A solution that the Israeli Prime Minister says he supports. He is right, and these talks are urgent.

(European Council, 2010)

While Obama was not influenced by the EU in his approach, he certainly was committed to working in partnership with the EU (Möckli, 2010). Obama did not label the settlements as illegal like Ashton did, but his proposals to 'freeze all settlement activity' as well as the fact that the pre-1967 borders should be the basis for a peace agreement upset Israeli Prime Minister Benjamin Netanyahu (Carter, 2011). The occasion for the EU was timely, as Obama seemed to recognise the value of a common stance (Yossef and Fabbrini, 2011). Was there the chance for a common and influential EU–US stance on the conflict that would move beyond declaratory politics and exert influence upon Israel?

The timely occasion for the EU to prove its influence in the Israeli–Palestinian peace process came with the UNGA Vote to upgrade the PA to a non-member observer state in September 2012. A year before, in September 2011, Palestinian President Mahmoud Abbas submitted a letter to the UN asking for Palestine to be admitted to the UN, but this was immediately rejected by the US (Abu Toameh, 2011). The US also exerted pressure before the vote, warning the Europeans that 'Palestinian statehood can only be achieved via direct negotiations with the Israelis and that European governments should support American efforts to block the bid' (Sherwood, 2012). What was at stake, again, was the EU's credibility, first because the UN arena was the much-desired possibility for the EU to assert its influence within a multilateral setting. Second, openly defying the US position could potentially cause a rift in the relationship. In the run up to the vote, PA President Abbas sought to understand how the EU would vote in light of the US effort to block the bid. As Usher reminds us,

Abbas turned to Catherine Ashton.... If the PA were to see the status of nonmember observer state at the UNGA, he asked, how would the twenty-seven member EU vote? Ashton replied that while individual Member

States may vote positively, the position of the EU as a bloc was to support a return to negotiations – like the US.

(Usher, 2011, p. 62)

As Daniel Levy and Nick Witney (2011, p. 6) have argued, a collective yes vote from the EU would have been consistent with decades of diplomatic efforts to achieve a two state solution. In the worst scenario, a collective abstention would still be better than a split vote, since the latter would further undermine the EU's credibility (Alcaro and Dessi, 2011). In the end, the vote highlighted that the EU was decisively split on the issue. On 29 November 2012, the UNGA voted in favour of Palestine gaining non-member observer status with an overwhelming majority of 138 against nine (UN General Assembly, 2012). The outcome of the vote itself was satisfactory if we consider the principles that the EU had been advancing since the early 1970s. However, once again the EU lost an occasion to move beyond declaratory politics. The EU has recognised Palestine since the 1970s, but, as of 2012, it still showed a lack of unity of intent in the vote. Key Member States such as Germany, the UK, Poland and the Netherlands abstained, other Member States such as France, Italy and Spain voted in favour and the Czech Republic voted against. The Member States were divided; however, the position of the EU as a bloc, as specified by Ashton, was already in line with the US one.

Conclusion

Back in 1974, US Secretary of State Henry Kissinger firmly asserted that the Europeans would be 'unable to achieve anything in the Middle East in a million years' (quoted in Gomez 2003, p. 123). Looking back at more than four decades of European involvement in the I–P conflict, it is possible to evaluate Kissinger's statement by discussing what the EC/EU has been able to achieve and why it has not been able to do more or as much as it would have liked.

The European states had the opportunity to become involved during the Cold War with common declarations that had an important impact upon the US's perception of the European position as adversarial towards Israel and somewhat more sympathetic to the Palestinian cause. The important achievement of the Cold War, in terms of European foreign policy towards the I–P conflict, was the framing of a consensus among the nine which was outlined through the Brussels Declaration in 1973 and, more notably, with the Venice Declaration in 1980. The apparent consensus at a declaratory level did not translate into an influential approach because of the real diverging interests of the EC Member States and of the influence of the superpowers in the conflict.

In the post-Cold War period, the notable change was the US's acceptance of a European involvement from a financial point of view, as decided at the Madrid conference in 1991. PLO participation in the peace process and the Palestinian right to a homeland (cornerstones of the EC's declarations during the Cold War) became the backbone of the guiding principles of the Oslo Declaration in 1993.

In this sense, it is safe to argue that the EC has had a *pioneering role* in the I–P conflict (Aoun, 2003; Mueller, 2013). However, the EU remained subordinate to the US from a diplomatic point of view and it did not have any real influence on the conflict, as exemplified by the fact that it was significantly excluded from the Camp David Summit in 2000. Before the summit, however, in 1999 the EU manifested its commitment to the two-state solution with the Berlin Declaration.

In the post 9/11 period, the EU had the chance to be more influential than ever before in the I–P conflict. This opportunity came with the formation of the Quartet for Peace in 2002, with the US welcoming the EU's involvement from a diplomatic point of view and subscribing to the two-state solution that the EU had outlined with the Berlin Declaration. Again, it is important to note the pioneering role of the EU in this sense. In order to be influential within the Quartet, however, the EU compromised over its normative values on a number of occasions. It did not sanction Israel for the construction of the fence but it imposed sanctions on Hamas following the 2006 Palestinian legislative elections. At the Annapolis peace process in 2007, the US, not the Quartet, was given the task of monitoring progress (Migdalowitz, 2007). At the beginning of the Quartet for Peace, the EU's preference was for the creation of a Palestinian State but by the time Hamas won the elections, the EU had come to subscribe to the altered US view of *democracy first, then Palestinian State*.

In recent years, the diplomatic convergence between the EU and the US on the two-state solution has remained unaltered but, as exemplified by the September 2012 vote on Palestinian non-observer status at the UN, significant European divisions remain evident over how to take the issue forward. The EC/EU has achieved greater involvement in the I–P conflict since the 1970s and this chapter has showed that the US has played an important role in progressively allowing it. Yet, the extent to which the EU can achieve greater influence remains to be seen. The role of the EU's HR, a post created by the Lisbon Treaty, will prove important in providing the necessary leadership to bring the positions of the single EU Member States together. As the 2012 vote showed, this is not an easy task. The HR has to mediate between the diverging foreign policy preferences of the Member States, the preferences of the other members of the Quartet and of the parties involved in the conflict.

Note

1 The Palestinian Nakba is the Palestinian exodus which occurred in 1948 as 700,000 Palestinian Arabs fled or were expelled from their homes as a result of the 1948 Palestinian war which led to the establishment of the State of Israel.

References

Abu Toameh, K. (2011) US Rejects Palestinian Bid to Seek UN Approval for State. *The Jerusalem Post*. 20 April.

Alcaro, R. and Dessi, A. (2011) *The September UN Vote on Palestine: Will the EU Be up to the Challenge?*. IAI Working Papers 11. 27 September.

Allen, D., and Smith, M. H. (1984) Europe, the United States, and the Arab–Israeli Conflict. In Allen, D. and Pijpers, A. (eds) *European Foreign Policy-Making and the Arab-Israeli Conflict*. Lancaster: Martinus Nijhoff Publishers.

Allen, D. and Smith, M. (2001) External Policy Developments. *Journal of Common Market Studies*. 39 Annual Review. pp. 97–114.

Altunisik, M. B. (2008) EU Foreign Policy and the Israeli-Palestinian Conflict: How Much of an Actor? *European Security*. 17 (1). pp. 105–121.

Aoun, E. (2003) European Foreign Policy and the Arab–Israeli Dispute: Much Ado About Nothing? *European Foreign Affairs Review*. 8 (3). pp. 289–312.

Asseburg, M. (2009) *European Conflict Management in the Middle East. Toward a More Effective Approach*. SWP Research Paper. Berlin: German Institute for International and Security Affairs (SWP).

Asseburg, M. (2002) The EU and the Middle East Conflict: Tackling the Main Obstacle to Euro-Mediterranean Partnership. *Mediterranean Politics*. 8 (2). pp. 174–93.

Bennett, J. (2003) Sharon Says Europe Is Biased In Favour of the Palestinians. *New York Times*. 20 January.

Bouris, D. (2010) The European Union's Role in the Palestinian Territory after the Oslo Accords: Stillborn State-building. *Journal of Contemporary European Research*. 6 (3). pp. 376–94.

Brussels Declaration (1973), 6 November. Available from: www.fransamaltingvongeu-sau.com/documents/cw/CH5/12.pdf [accessed: 10 June 2013].

Bulut, E. (2009) EUPOL COPPS (Palestinian territories). In Grevi, G., Helly, D. and Keohane, D. (eds) *European Security and Defence Policy: The First 10 Years (1999–2009)*. Paris: European Union Institute for Security Studies.

Bush, G. H. (1991) *Remarks at the Opening Session of the Middle East Peace Conference in Madrid*. October 30. Public Papers. George Bush Presidential Library. Available from: http://bushlibrary.tamu.edu/research/public_papers.php?id=3566&year=&month [accessed: 25 February 2014].

Carter, J. (2011) After the UN Vote on Palestine. *New York Times*. 13 September.

Cordesman, A. H. (2005) *The Israeli–Palestinian War: Escalating to Nowhere*. London: Praeger.

Cornwell, R. (2003) Sharon Rejects Bush's Call to Take Down 'Security' Fence'. *Independent*. 30 July.

Dosenrode, S. and Stubkjaer, S. (2002) *The European Union and the Middle East*. London: Sheffield Academic Press.

Elizur, Y. (2003) Israel Banks on a Fence. *Foreign Affairs*. 82 (2). pp. 106–19.

European Council (2012) Council decision 2012/324/CSFP of June 2012 amending and extending Decision 2010/784/CSFP of the European Union Police Mission for the Palestinian Territories (EUPOL COPPS). *Official Journal of the European Union*, 26.6.12. Available from: http://eur-lex.europa.eu/LexUriServ/LexUriServ.do?uri=OJ:L:2012:16 5:0048:0048:EN:PDF. [accessed: 24 January 14].

European Council (2010) *Speech by Catherine Ashton, at the League of Arab States. A Commitment to Peace – the European Union and the Middle East*. Cairo. 15 March. Available from: www.consilium.europa.eu/uedocs/cms_data/docs/pressdata/EN/foraff/ 113352.pdf. [accessed: 24 January 14].

European Council (1999) *Presidency Conclusions*. Berlin European Council. 24 and 25 March. Available from: www.consilium.europa.eu/uedocs/cms_data/docs/pressdata/en/ ec/ACFB2.html [accessed: 5 December 2014].

European Union External Action (2013), *EU Border Assistance Mission at Rafah Crossing*

Point (EUBAM RAFAH). Available from: www.eeas.europa.eu/csdp/missions-and-operations/eubam-rafah/pdf/factsheet_eubam_rafah_en.pdf [accessed: 24 January 2014].

Freedman, R. O. (2007) The Bush Administration and the Arab–Israeli Conflict. In Lesch, D. (ed.) *The Middle East and the United States A Historical and Political Reassessment*. Boulder, CO: Westview Press. pp. 275–311.

Gfeller, A. E. (2012) *Building a European Identity: France, the United States, and the Oil Shock, 1973–74*. New York: Berghan Books.

Gianniou, M. (2006) *The European Union's Involvement in the Israeli–Palestinian conflict: an active paradigm of European foreign policy?*. Paper presented at the European Consortium for Political Research. 3rd Pan-European Conference on EU Politics. Bilgi University. Istanbul. 21–23 September. Available from: www.jhubc.it/ecpr-istanbul/virtualpaperroom/045.pdf [accessed: 13 January 2014].

Ginsberg, R. H. (2001) *The European Union in International Politics: Baptism by Fire*. Lanham, MD: Rowman and Littlefield.

Gomez, R. (2003) *Negotiating the Euro-Mediterranean Partnership. Strategic Action in EU Foreign Policy?* Aldershot, UK: Ashgate.

Greilsammer, I. and Weiler, J. (1984) European Political Cooperation and the Palestinian–Israeli Conflict: An Israeli Perspective. In Allen, D. and Pijpers, A. (eds) *European Foreign Policy-Making and the Arab–Israeli Conflict*. The Hague: Martinus Nijhoff. pp. 121–60.

Hamilton, K. (2006) Britain, France, and America's Year of Europe, 1973. *Diplomacy and Statecraft*. 17 (4). pp. 871–95.

Hanieh, A. (2001) The Camp David Papers. *Journal of Palestine Studies*. 30 (2). pp. 75–97.

Hollis, R. (2013) Europe. In Peters, J. and Newman, D. (eds) *The Routledge Handbook on the Israeli–Palestinian conflict*. New York: Routledge. pp. 336–45.

Inbar, E. (2007) *Israel's Strategic Agenda*. Abingdon, UK: Routledge.

Kaye, D. D. (2003) Bound to Cooperate? Transatlantic Policy in the Middle East. *The Washington Quarterly*. 27 (1). pp. 179–85.

Keukeleire, S. (2003) The European Union as a Diplomatic Actor: Internal, Traditional and Structural Diplomacy. *Diplomacy and Statecraft*. 14 (3). pp. 31–56.

Lavy, G. (1996) *Germany and Israel: Moral Debt and National Interest*, London: Frank Cass.

Levy, D. and Witney, N. (2011) *Palestinian Statehood at the UN: Why Europeans Should Vote Yes*. European Council on Foreign Relations Paper 38. Available from: www.ecfr.eu/page/-/ECFR_IsrPal_memo.pdf, [accessed: 29 January 2015].

Lewis, S. W. (1999) The United States and Israel: Evolution of an Unwritten Alliance. *Middle East Journal*. 53 (3). pp. 364–78.

Malley, R. and Miller, A. D. (2007) 'West Bank First': It Won't Work, *Washington Post*. 19 June.

McDowall, D. (1990) *Palestine and Israel: The Uprising and Beyond*. London: I. B. Tauris.

McGreal, C. (2004) Israel Lashes out at EU for Backing UN Vote on Wall. *Guardian*. 22 July.

Meital, Y. (2006) *Peace in Tatters: Israel, Palestine, and the Middle East*. London: Lynne Rienner Publishers.

Migdalovitz, C. (2007) *Israeli–Palestinian Peace Process: The Annapolis Conference*, CRS Report for Congress. 7 December. Available from: http://fpc.state.gov/documents/organization/98093.pdf [accessed: 8 February 2014].

Miller, R. (2013) Faraway Causes, Immediate Effects: The War and European Consequences. In Siniver, A. (ed.) *The Yom Kippur War: Politics, Legacy, Diplomacy.* Oxford: Oxford University Press.

Möckli, D. (2010) The Middle East Conflict, Transatlantic Ties and the Quartet. In Aymat, E. B. (ed.) *European Involvement in the Arab–Israeli Conflict.* Chaillot Papers 124. Brussels: European Union Institute for Security Studies.

Mueller, P. (2013) Europe's Foreign Policy and the Middle East Peace Process. The Construction of EU Actorness in Conflict Resolution. *Perspectives on European Politics and Society.* 14 (1). pp. 20–35.

Musu, C. (2011) European Security and the Middle East Peace Process. In Mérand, F., Foucault, M. and Irondelle, B. (eds) *European Security since the Fall of the Berlin Wall.* Toronto: University of Toronto Press.

Newman, D. and Yacobi, H. (2004) *The Role of the EU in the Israel–Palestine Conflict. Working Papers Series in EU Border Conflicts Studies.* Department of Politics and Government, Ben Gurion University. Beer Sheva, Israel.

Newman, D. and Yacobi, H. (2008) The EU and the Israel–Palestine conflict. In Diez, T., Albert, M. and Stetter, S. (eds) *The European Union and Border Conflict: The Power of Integration and Association.* Cambridge: Cambridge University Press.

Nuttal, S. J. (1992) *European Political Co-operation.* Oxford: Clarendon Press.

Obama, B. (2009) *A New Beginning. Speech at Cairo University.* Cairo. June 4. Available from: www.whitehouse.gov/the_press_office/Remarks-by-the-President-at-Cairo-University-6-04-09/ [accessed: 23 January 2014].

Pardo, S. and Peters, J. (2010) *Uneasy Neighbours: Israel and the European Union.* New York: Rowman and Littlefield Publishers.

Persson, A. (2014) *The EU and the IsraeliPalestinian Conflict, 1981–2013: In Pursuit of Just Peace.* London: Lexington Books.

Pressman, J. (2007) From Madrid and Oslo to Camp David. The United States and the ArabIsraeli Conflict, 1991–2001. In Lesch, D. (ed.) *The Middle East and the United States: A Historical and Political Reassessment.* Boulder, CO: Westview Press.

Pundak, R. (2001) From Oslo to Taba: What Went Wrong? *Survival.* 43 (3). pp. 31–45.

Quandt, W. B. (2006) American Policy in the Post-Cold War Middle East. In Rüland, J., Hanf, T. and Manske, E. (eds) *US Foreign Policy Toward the Third World. A Post Cold War Assessment.* London: M. E. Sharpe, pp. 105–22.

Quandt, W. B. (2007) New US Policies for a New Middle East? In Lesch, D. W. (ed.) *The Middle East and the United States: a Historical and Political Reassessment.* Boulder, CO: Westview Press.

Robin, P. (1997) Always the Bridesmaid: Europe and the Middle East Peace Process. *Cambridge Review of International Affairs.* 10 (2). pp. 69–83.

Rynold, J. and Steinberg, G. (2004) The Peace Process and Israeli Elections. *Israel Affairs.* 10 (4). pp. 181–204.

Salt, J. (2008) *The Unmaking of the Middle East: A History of Western Disorder in Arab Lands.* Berkeley, CA: University of California Press.

Schlaim, A. (2005) The Rise and Fall of the Oslo Process. In Fawcett, L. (ed.) *International Relations of the Middle East,* Oxford: Oxford University Press.

Sherwood, H. (2012) US Warns European Governments Against Supporting Palestinians at UN. *Guardian.* 1 October.

Stout, D. (2003) Israel to Continue Building Security Fence Criticised by Bush. *New York Times.* 29 July.

Susser, A. (2012) *Israel, Jordan and Palestine: The Two-State Imperative*, Boston: Brandeis University Press.

Tocci, N. (2011) *The EU, the Middle East Quartet and (In) Effective Multilateralism*, Mercury E-Paper No. 9. pp. 1–28.

Venice Declaration, 12–13 June 1980. Available from: http://eeas.europa.eu/mepp/docs/venice_declaration_1980_en.pdf [accessed: 19 May 2012].

UN General Assembly (2012) *General Assembly Votes Overwhelmingly to Accord Palestine 'Non-member Observer State' Status in United Nations.* Available from: www.un.org/News/Press/docs/2012/ga11317.doc.htm [accessed: 29 January 2014].

Usher, G. (2011) Letter from the UN: The Palestinian Bid for Membership. *Journal of Palestine Studies.* 41 (1). pp. 57–66.

Wolfssohn, M. (1993) *Eternal Guilt? Forty Years of German–Jewish–Israeli Relations*, New York: Columbia University Press.

Yossef, A. and Fabbrini, S. (2011) Obama in the Middle East: Why He Needs European Support. *European Political Science.* 10 (1). pp. 36–43.

Youngs, R. (2006) *Europe and the Middle East in the Shadow of September 11*. London: Lynne Rienner Publishers.

Conclusion

We thought we knew

Lorenzo Cladi and Andrea Locatelli

European security continues to capture the attention of International Relations (IR) scholars. At the end of the Cold War, we seemed to know that NATO would be destined for the scrapheap of history, but it was not. We seemed to know that the EU would become an important security actor but it did not quite do so. We seemed to know that France would hedge its bet to create an autonomous European pole, independent of the US, but it ended up reintegrating with NATO instead. European security has undergone deep changes in recent years, with the Eurozone crisis of 2008 and the recent Russia–Ukraine dispute being the clearest examples. The need to enhance dialogue among the various theoretical approaches seems greater now than ever.

Starting from these considerations, we opened this volume with a methodological premise: rather than pushing the case for a single paradigm as a catch-all explanation, analytic eclecticism (Sil and Katzenstein, 2010; 2010a) is a more fruitful avenue of research. Analytical eclecticism advocates a problem-driven approach to research through which scholars seek to gain an understanding that stems from an analysis of apparently conflicting theoretical paradigms (Sil and Katzenstein, 2008). In adopting analytical eclecticism, we did not try to hide the complexity of the CSDP process, nor did we try to ascertain whether one paradigm is better than others. On the contrary, starting from the assumption that parsimony is hardly an asset when it comes to explaining complex phenomena, we moved on to consider that the presence of alternative paradigms is not an obstacle to understanding the real world but rather an opportunity to advance dialogue among conflicting views.

Consistent with this approach, the book was divided into two parts. The first part presented a detailed account of four competing research traditions: Realism, Liberalism, Constructivism and Sociology of Bureaucracy. The second part focussed instead on empirical analysis, in order to assess the limits and potential of these paradigms.

Inter-paradigmatic dialogue remains challenging and this book arguably shows that. The different IR theories presented differ in their very basic ontological and epistemological foundations. We can point to three dimensions which form the disputed ground among theories: these are all interrelated, and underline more or less explicitly the theoretical approaches discussed in Chapters 1 to 6. These concern the ontological as well as the methodological approach of IR paradigms: (1) material vs ideational factors; (2) second- vs third-level variables; (3) national vs societal interests.

First, paradigms disagree on the relative role of material and ideational variables. This debate traces its origins to the Constructivist critique of the Neo(realism)–Neo(liberal) approach. As forcefully argued by Michael Brecher (1999), however, this is a flawed dichotomy, as both material and ideational variables concur in shaping actors' behaviour. Throughout the volume, this point is touched upon in various chapters. While Tom Dyson downplays the role of culture, norms and values as an explanatory variable (focussing instead on security concerns and executive autonomy), Carla Monteleone discusses the relevance of ideational factors such as common identity, strategic culture and especially elite socialisation as drivers of voting cohesion among EU Member States in the United Nations General Assembly. From a different perspective, Kamil Zwolski also stresses how the Chemical, Biological, Radiological and Nuclear Risk Mitigation Centres of Excellence initiative helps forge norms and identities and, equally important, how values permeate the moral authority of international bureaucracies. On the other hand, in their assessment of the EU's behaviour towards Russia and the Israeli–Palestinian (I–P) conflict, Serena Giusti and Lorenzo Cladi show that realpolitik considerations hindered the European potential to act as a civilian/normative power.

It is then plausible to argue that both material and ideational factors play a role (albeit different) in shaping the EU's action abroad, as well as European states' attitudes towards the EU. In this context, Kamil Zwolski's approach in treating the EU as an International Bureaucracy transcends the debate on the relative role of material and ideational variables. The Transnational Security Governance approach can thus be helpful to explain *how* the EU is able to shape its internal as well as external environment and how formal and informal networks are created. In order to critically assess *why* the EU acts in a certain way, however, the debate between material and ideational factors remains important. In particular, our book shows that when looking at CSDP, when *high politics* issues are considered (dealing with a resurgent Russia, mediating between the Israelis and the Palestinians), material factors tend to prevail.

Second, a long-standing debate in IR theory revolves around the proper level of analysis. In short, mostly after Waltz's (1979) bold distinction between systemic and reductionist theories, at least in the Realist camp, prominence has been given to third-level variables, to the detriment of domestic politics – a concern later addressed by the Neoclassical brand of Realism. Here too, the issue at stake has been at the core of unmotivated disputes (Brecher, 1999), and the arguments exposed are sufficiently well known not to require further discussion here. Throughout the volume the issue is touched on in several chapters. To begin with, in Chapter 1 Cladi and Locatelli develop a deductive argument to trace the causal path that makes European cooperation a reasonable response to systemic pressures. While agreeing on the incentives provided by the system, Tom Dyson argues that layering in intervening variables such as executive autonomy and the national defence industry allows us to grasp a more nuanced explanation of the three major countries' attitudes towards the EU. While looking into domestic politics, Neoclassical Realism still considers the third level as key to understand states' foreign policy behaviour. In sharp contrast, the Liberal approach, as epitomised by two different chapters by Benjamin Pohl, Niels van Willigen, Cynthia M. C. van Vonno and Friederike Richter, claims that, in the absence of an external threat, the CSDP process is driven exclusively by domestic considerations. External factors are not completely ignored, but they are enmeshed with domestic politics. States do not necessarily respond to external pressures but they seek to shape their external environment, based on domestic factors. Hence, the issue regarding the lack of progress in CSDP and of a grand EU strategy can be explained with reference to domestic political considerations. Olivier Schmitt picks up this point, seeing CSDP as redundant, inherently flawed, and ontologically lacking any political strategy. In between the second and third levels of analysis stands Luis Simón, whose attention is focussed on the regional (i.e. European-wide) level.

Similarly to the first dimension, our conclusion is that methodological pluralism is a welcome addition to the study of EU foreign and defence policy integration. Each level of analysis grasps some aspects of the integration process, so there is no need to exclude a priori any of them.[1] The only cautionary note that should drive the researcher should be coherence in the research design. That said, as the previous chapters highlight, a multi-level analysis allows us to get a better grasp of the mechanisms at play: the effects of the current unipolar power distribution can be traced back to the incentive to bandwagon on the US (see Chapters 1 and 2). At the regional level, despite the lack of direct threats, power competition and different foreign policy priorities make EU states wary of the relative gains problem (see Chapter 8) which is inherent in defence integration. At the domestic level, party politics and the institutional setting help to explain why the national commitment to CSDP is often limited, hollowed out and varying (see Chapters 3, 4 and 7).

Finally, the third dimension (partially related to the second one) concerns the dichotomy between states as power and security seekers vs states as responsive to societal demands. Here the terms of the debate have been interpreted in different ways over the years. Probably, the dispute has been most heated (and proportionally less fruitful) when Offensive and Defensive Realists contended over the state's final goal – whether it is power, as Offensive Realists argue (see among many others Mearsheimer, 2001), or security, as postulated by Defensive Realists (see Snyder, 1991; Glaser, 1997). A second, long-lasting, dispute on a similar topic revolves around the absolute vs relative gains alternative (among many others, see Keohane, 1984; Grieco, 1988) – i.e. whether states are rational utility maximisers (as Keohane originally put it), or they are rather defensive positionalists.

However, the issue at stake here is different. Our purpose is to show how, in previous chapters, different authors have informed their analysis along two distinctive and incompatible assumptions: i.e. that states behave as unitary actors informed by realpolitik logic; and that states are something akin to a trans-mission belt, where their real need is to please and exploit societal demands. Throughout the volume, most contributors (see Chapters 1, 2, 7, 8, 9, 10 and 11) have adopted the former approach, whereas the Liberal, Constructivist and Transnational Governance scholars have focused more on societal demands (see Chapters 3, 4, 5 and 6). Opting for either vision has relevant analytical con-sequences: (over)stressing the need for power and security, for instance, led some Realists to explain European integration as balancing against the US – an hypothesis that all contributors to this volume would reject. In contrast, discard-ing power and/or security considerations (see in particular Chapter 4) would actually rip CSDP of its constitutive attributes and make it a public policy like any other (this conclusion is actually shared by Olivier Schmitt in Chapter 7). Intermediate positions are also possible: Tom Dyson recognises the govern-ment's need to please its constituency and interest groups, but concedes that this is ancillary to other *national* priorities.

The empirical section lends support to the idea that EU states can be assumed to be power and security seekers, even if governments have to negotiate among different interests: in particular, David Haglund contends that it is US power (or, better, how the US conceives of and uses its power) that drove the French rap-prochement with Washington. Likewise, Serena Giusti and Lorenzo Cladi high-light the European concern for power and security: as concerns the partnership with Russia, the shift from a *technical*, EU-inspired cooperation to a reactive (albeit erratic) stance came after security considerations, while, in the negoti-ations relating to the I–P conflict, EU states did not hesitate much to trade coher-ence with their own principles in exchange for more leverage at the negotiating table. However, this is just part of the story. As for the previous point of conten-tion, here too analytical eclecticism is required. Focussing on a single assump-tion (such as states as power or security seekers) risks driving the author to a conclusion which necessarily misses part of the story. However, when compar-ing the results of one analysis led under one assumption with the results reached by another analysis working with a different assumption, we can have a greater understanding of 'circumstantial differences' (Sterling-Folker, 2015, p. 40).

That a moment for analytical eclecticism in IR theory is due is perhaps unsur-prising, given the proliferation of theories that has taken place since the 1980s (Dunne *et al.*, 2013). Analytical eclecticism, however, should not be a substitute for a pick and mix approach to a particular phenomenon. Nor, we believe, should analytical eclecticism betray its scientific purpose. One should distinguish between research which uses theory to try to *make sense* of decision-makers' behaviour (Hayes and James, 2014) and research which uses theory deductively in order to *explain* decision-makers' behaviour. Our approach, which is evi-dently inspired by a mildly positivist view, holds that theories are nomological explanations, that is attempts to postulate causal relationships among phe-nomena. Admittedly, more often than not, theories turn into doctrines, and they come to shape or even reify the way political actors perceive the world. But, in our view, analytical eclecticism is more consistent with a vision of theory that keeps theories and observed phenomena as distinct. This is what we have tried to do in this volume.

What we would like to stress is that by adopting analytical eclecticism as a pick and mix approach there is the risk that theories get used in an opportunistic manner, so undermining the requirements for cumulativeness in scientific knowledge. In other words, this approach would echo the ad hoc adjustment lamented by Lakatos (1970). By doing so, we might end up in a situation in which no theory is given the necessary importance it deserves: if we only take what we need from each theory to reach an explanation, the analysis could end up being in fact much less theoretically informed than planned. Analytical eclecticism, as we understand it, is not just a celebration of diversity. It is a valuable approach that can allow scholars to engage in deeper theoretical understanding of substantial problems based on constructive inter-paradigmatic debate.

We are aware that, as CSDP is such a complex issue, this work should be considered as nothing more than a preliminary step in this direction: a comprehensive analysis might imply a structured comparison of many more different empirical observations than we could consider here – from actual EU policy outputs (like missions, institutional adjustments and capabilities enhancement initiatives) to small states' attitude towards defence cooperation. And the number of theories could be increased as well: in our effort we focussed almost exclusively on rationalist approaches, but, turning to the reflectivist camp, one might choose to adopt Critical Theory, Historical Materialism and the Paris School of Security Studies. Rather than an end-state, then, we hope our work will be just one of many future contributions to the theoretical analysis of European security cooperation.

Note

1 The reader may remember that this approach was suggested by Waltz himself in the closing pages of Waltz, 1959.

References

Brecher, M. (1999) International Studies in the Twentieth Century and Beyond: Flawed Dichotomies, Synthesis, Cumulation. *International Studies Quarterly*. 43 (2). pp. 213–64.

Dunne, T., Hansen, L. and Wight, C. (2013) The End of International Relations Theory. *European Journal of International Relations*. 19 (3). pp. 405–25.

Glaser, C. (1997) The Security Dilemma Revisited. *World Politics*. 50 (1). pp. 171–201.

Grieco, J. M. (1988) Anarchy and the Limits of Co-operation: a Realist Critique of the Newest Liberal Institutionalism. *International Organisation*. 42 (3). pp. 485–507.

Hayes, J. and James, P. (2014) Theory as Thought: Britain and German Unification. *Security Studies*. 23 (2). pp. 399–429.

Keohane, R. O. (1984) *After Hegemony: Cooperation and Discord in the World Political Economy*. Princeton, NJ: Princeton University Press.

Lakatos, I. (1970) Falsification and the Methodology of Scientific Research Programmes.

In Lakatos, I. and Musgrave, A. (eds) *Criticism and the Growth of Knowledge*. Cambridge: Cambridge University Press.

Mearsheimer, J. (2001) *The Tragedy of Great Power Politics.* New York: Norton.

Sil, R. and Katzenstein, P. J. (2010) Analytic Eclecticism in the Study of World Politics: Reconfiguring Problems and Mechanisms across Research Traditions. *Perspectives on Politics.* 8 (2). pp. 411–31.

Sil, R. and Katzenstein, P. J. (2010a) *Beyond Paradigms: Analytic Eclecticism in the Study of World Politics*. Basingstoke, UK: Palgrave Macmillan.

Sil, R. and Katzenstein, P. J. (2008) Eclectic Theorising in the Study and Practice of International Relations. In C. Reus-Smith and D. Snidal (eds) *The Oxford Handbook of International Relations*. Oxford: Oxford University Press.

Snyder, J. (1991) *Myth of Empire: Domestic Politics and International Ambitions*. Ithaca, NY: Cornell University Press.

Sterling-Folker, J. (2015) All Hail to the Chief: Liberal IR Theory in the New World Order. *International Studies Perspectives.* 16. pp. 40–9.

Waltz, K. (1979) *Theory of International Politics*. New York: McGraw Hill.

Waltz, K. (1959) *Man, the State and War. A Theoretical Analysis*. New York: Columbia University Press.

Index

Page numbers in *italics* denote tables.